LADY CHARLOTTE GUEST

To Heather and John with love

LADY CHARLOTTE GUEST

THE EXCEPTIONAL LIFE OF A FEMALE INDUSTRIALIST

VICTORIA OWENS

PEN & SWORD
HISTORY

AN IMPRINT OF PEN & SWORD BOOKS LTD.
YORKSHIRE – PHILADELPHIA

First published in Great Britain in 2020 by
PEN AND SWORD HISTORY
An imprint of
Pen & Sword Books Ltd
Yorkshire – Philadelphia

ISBN 978 1 52676 881 0

Typeset in Times New Roman 11.5/14 by
SJmagic DESIGN SERVICES, India.
Printed and bound in the UK by TJ Books Limited

Pen & Sword Books Limited incorporates the imprints of Atlas, Archaeology,
Aviation, Discovery, Family History, Fiction, History, Maritime, Military, Military
Classics, Politics, Select, Transport, True Crime, Air World, Frontline Publishing,
Leo Cooper, Remember When, Seaforth Publishing, The Praetorian Press,
Wharncliffe Local History, Wharncliffe Transport, Wharncliffe True Crime and
White Owl.

For a complete list of Pen & Sword titles please contact
PEN & SWORD BOOKS LIMITED
47 Church Street, Barnsley, South Yorkshire, S70 2AS, England
E-mail: enquiries@pen-and-sword.co.uk
Website: www.pen-and-sword.co.uk

Or
PEN AND SWORD BOOKS
1950 Lawrence Rd, Havertown, PA 19083, USA
E-mail: Uspen-and-sword@casematepublishers.com
Website: www.penandswordbooks.com

Contents

Acknowledgements   vi

Introduction   viii

Chapter One   The Marriage   1

Chapter Two   Unknown Country   14

Chapter Three   The Hot Blast   29

Chapter Four   A Fortune for the Babies   42

Chapter Five   Birth, Death, Inheritance and the
                   Electors of Glamorgan   58

Chapter Six   Reaching an Eminence: the *Mabinogion*   71

Chapter Seven   Lord Bute and the Dowlais Lease   87

Chapter Eight   Edward Hutchins   103

Chapter Nine   A Good Death   115

Chapter Ten   The Ironmaster   129

Chapter Eleven   '...the right on our side': The Strike of 1853   143

Chapter Twelve   Lady Charlotte Guest and Charles Schreiber   159

Appendix   172
Notes   174
Bibliography   202
Index   208

Acknowledgements

My thanks go to the Viscount Wimborne, for granting me permission to quote from Lady Charlotte's Manuscript Journals. I am also most grateful to Llyfrgell Genedlaethol Cymru / the National Library of Wales whose archives department now holds them, and the staff of the South Reading Room for their assistance and goodwill.

I am grateful also to Messrs Hodder & Stoughton, for allowing me to use of extracts from *Lady Charlotte Guest – Extracts from her Journal 1833–1852* and *Lady Charlotte Schreiber – Extracts from her Journal 1853–1891* ed. The Earl of Bessborough, (John Murray: London, 1950–52) and to Professor Sioned Davies of Cardiff University for allowing me to quote from her translation of the *Mabinogion*.

I would like to thank the following organisations and individuals for allowing me to reproduces images from their collections in this book: the National Library of Wales; Glamorgan Record Office; Cyfarthfa Castle and Merthyr Tydfil Leisure Trust; the Eliot family of Port Eliot, Cornwall; Cardiff University, with a word of special appreciation to Samantha Rees-Thomas and Su Ballantine; to Mr Steve Brewer of Merthyr Tydfil and his fellow trustees of the Alan George and John Owen Collections. I would like to thank Steve also for giving me a wonderful guided tour of Merthyr and Dowlais and pointing out the places which hold particular association with the Guests.

I must also express my warmest appreciation to Stephen K. Jones, for drawing my attention to Harriet Crewe's opinion of the young Charlotte Bertie and for providing some useful detail about the Dowlais Railway; to Stephen Rowson for showing me his collection of historical photographs of Lady Charlotte's family; to Monique Goodliffe and Erica Obey, for their generous and scholarly friendship; to Ted Rowlands, former MP for Merthyr and Rhymney, now the Baron Rowlands CBE, for telling me about his research into Sir John Guest's achievements; to Mary Owen of Merthyr Tydfil, both for drawing my attention to one of the famous stories about Lady Charlotte and for telling me about her research into the life of Enid Guest; to Mark Rathbone of Canford School, for showing me round the Guests' Dorset home; to Michael Freeman of Aberystwyth for directing me to John Ross Dix's description of an encounter with Lady Charlotte at Chepstow; to Mrs Catherine Smith, archivist of Charterhouse School, for confirming Edward Hutchins' attendance; to Claire, my editor at Pen and Sword History, for parrying my questions and to Antony Alderson for his good-natured and well-informed encouragement.

Special thanks to my husband David *sine quo nihil*….

Introduction

In February 1852, the *Bristol Times and Mirror* carried a story about the Dowlais Ironworks. Despite its 200 pubs and an almost equal number of chapels, the journalist who had written it made no attempt to hide his view that Dowlais was a bleak, ugly village, whose filth and stench shocked him to the core. But he was a conscientious man and having interviewed John Evans, who oversaw the day-by-day operation of Sir John Guest's commercial empire, he gave a full account of the iron making process.

The individual who really caught his curiosity was Guest's wife, Lady Charlotte. 'Though a fine, handsome and fashionable woman,' he wrote,

> her ladyship takes interest even in the minutiae of the works, and has so keen an eye to the mainpoint, that though she might possibly startle at the question 'what is the price of pigs?' [bars of pig iron] she knows what the price should be.

Local tradition maintained that on one occasion she had even rolled a bar of iron rail herself. Although her aristocratic mother, the Dowager Countess of Lindsey, apparently regarded Dowlais as a 'cinder-hole', Charlotte evinced no such disdain for the place and its people. On the contrary, the journalist confided, she set much greater store upon her marriage to the ironmaster in the Welsh hills, than she did upon her noble ancestry.

To illustrate the point, he told a tale of how the Guests had been giving a party at their grand house in London when a courier arrived from Wales with a tin box, to which Charlotte gave her immediate attention. When her fashionable visitors asked what the box contained, she explained that it held the Iron Company balance sheet.

Soon afterwards, they heard her murmur, as though speaking to herself, the freighted words –

'Three hundred thousand pounds – a very fair year.'

Not surprisingly, there was a gasp of amazement and a volley of questions.

'Three hundred thousand pounds profit? – what, you don't mean in one year?'

'In one year,' replied Charlotte to her friends' astonishment. The festivities resumed, but not before one elegant countess was heard to remark that she would be only too happy to live wedded to an ironmaster in a 'cinder-hole' if it meant a regular £300 thousand a year income.

The article proved piquant enough for the South Wales press to appropriate and recycle it. It would reappear over the spring of 1852 in both the *Cardiff and Merthyr Guardian* and the *Monmouthshire Merlin*. The balance sheet anecdote evidently lingered in folk memory and ten years later it resurfaced, albeit with minor variation, in John Randall's 1862 publication, *The Severn Valley*.

Even if it owed a certain amount to journalistic license, the story revealed much about Charlotte's standing as a female industrialist. Well-versed in her business and financially astute, she commanded affection and respect. Although she boasted that her blood was 'of the noblest and most princely in the Kingdom', she had indeed forsaken the aristocratic circles in which she had grown up to marry one of the country's rising entrepreneurs. At a time when trade – the production and sale of goods for profit – incurred the snobbish scorn of the landowning classes, she took a solid pride in being, as she triumphantly expressed it, 'in some sort a tradeswoman'. What was more, she took Wales, her husband's native country, and his home town of Merthyr Tydfil straight to her heart.

Over the years, Charlotte's story has received a fair amount of attention. In the 1980s her descendant Revel Guest collaborated with Professor Angela John to write *Lady Charlotte - A Biography of the Nineteenth Century* (Weidenfeld & Nicolson: London, 1989) an authoritative cradle-to-grave biography which has since been reissued as *Lady Charlotte Guest – An Extraordinary Life* (Tempus: Stroud, 2007). Early in the twentieth century, her son Montague brought out a two-volume chronicle detailing his mother's connoisseur-ship of fine china, an interest that she shared with her second husband Charles

Schreiber. Magniloquently entitled *Lady Charlotte Schreiber's journals: confidences of a collector of ceramics & antiques throughout Britain, France, Holland, Belgium, Spain, Portugal, Turkey, Austria & Germany from the year 1869 to 1885,* in order to compile it, Montague arranged for Charlotte's journals to be typed up in their entirety. Cherished by the Guest family, in the 1950s his typescript furnished the two 'crème de la crème' anthologies edited by Charlotte's grandson Vere Brabazon Ponsonby, 9th Earl of Bessborough:- *Lady Charlotte Guest – Extracts from her Journal 1833–1852* (John Murray: London, 1950) and *Lady Charlotte Schreiber – Extracts from her Journal, 1853–1891* (John Murray: London, 1952). Together, they provide a broad panorama of her activities.

But no publication, or indeed typescript, can convey the same charge as reading Lady Charlotte's handwriting. Impulsive and sloping, it fills page after page of her manuscript journals with the raw stuff of her day-to-day life. Housed in the National Library of Wales, these volumes have been the chief source of this book. As the anonymous nineteenth-century Bristol journalist realised, the experience of meeting her head-on in her own words is a revelation.

Victoria Owens, Bristol, 2019.

Chapter One

The Marriage

Lady Charlotte saw Dowlais for the first time on an August evening in 1833. Three weeks previously, she had married John Guest, ironmaster and member of parliament for Merthyr Tydfil. Greatly in love, the couple had spent a delightful honeymoon in Sussex, exploring the Downs and the coast. To set the seal on their affection, when they returned to London, they commissioned fashionable portraitist Alfred Edward Chalon to paint miniatures of them, each to be a keepsake for the other. The couple journeyed to South Wales by leisurely stages, pausing on their way at Reading, Bath, Bristol and Newport. It was when they stopped at Sully, near Cardiff, that John heard about the celebrations awaiting them in his home town. The people planned to greet the couple with illuminations, a firelight procession through the narrow streets and much drinking of toasts to their future happiness.

The news clearly appalled him. The previous year, it emerged, his election to parliament had been the excuse for a drunken rampage in which a child had been crushed to death. He could not risk anything like that happening again. That Charlotte should have taken his words to heart and agreed to forego the excitement of an exuberant Welsh welcome is a measure of her devotion. Bride and groom made a spur-of-the-moment decision to head at once to Dowlais, so that they should arrive a day earlier than expected, telling no one except the household servants about the change of date. They arrived under cover of darkness and Charlotte's first sight of the Dowlais Iron Works, its immense furnaces blazing beneath the night sky, would haunt her for the rest of her life. The spectacle was visionary, 'quite unlike' anything that she 'had ever before seen or even imagined', and for ever more she thought of industry – specifically iron manufacture – as the native element of the place, the source from which it drew all its life and vigour.[1]

*

1

Born on 19 May 1812, Lady Charlotte Bertie and her two younger brothers grew up at Uffington House, near Stamford in Lincolnshire. Their father died in September 1818, when Charlotte was 6 years old and her brothers, George Augustus Frederick Albemarle and Montague Peregrine, aged respectively 4 and 2. Since he had been a warm-hearted man, the death of Lieutenant General Albemarle Bertie, 9th Earl of Lindsey, soldier and nobleman, must have left a great void in the lives of his widow and children. Describing his 'animated, kind and humane ... disposition', and his capacity to form 'warm and unalterable' friendships, the 9th Earl's obituary in the *Gentleman's Magazine* struck a note of affection which went deeper than polite courtesy owing to the recently deceased.[2]

Three years after his death, his widow remarried, taking as her second husband her cousin, the Reverend Peter Pegus. For the Countess of Lindsey to wed an ordinary clergyman marked rather a sharp and swift loss of social standing. Pegus admittedly owned an estate which might have given him some claim to gentility, but since it was a slave plantation in the Windward Islands, at the height of the abolition movement, it proved rather a doubtful asset. Nevertheless, Lady Lindsey was clearly fond of her hard-drinking, hard-riding clerical relative and a daughter, Maria Antoinetta, known as Mary, was born the year after their marriage, with her sister Elizabeth following two years later.

To characterise the part that Pegus played in the lives of his stepchildren is not entirely easy. Charlotte's descendants unite in deploring his baleful presence. Monty Guest, presumably drawing upon his mother's reminiscence, considered that he was 'not by any means sympathetic' as a stepfather, and observed that 'He was an awful sinner.'[3] Her grandson the Earl of Bessborough credited him with a 'violent temper'.[4] Her great-granddaughter Revel Guest, writing in collaboration with Angela John, portrays him as capricious, prone to drunken benders and possessed of an 'unerring knack for breaking the charm' of any pleasant occasion.[5] Admittedly, Pegus ruffled the currents of family life with such outrages as sacking all the household servants at a stroke; downing a beaker of lamp oil which he had taken for beer, and building a grudge against his cousin and fellow clergyman Brownlow Layard who, much to his resentment, held the Uffington living.[6] At the same time, he had no difficulty in finding his feet among the hunting and shooting Kesteven squirearchy. In her journal, without any shade of dislike or resentment,

Charlotte mentions watching him school his brown mare in the Uffington paddocks, and riding through the Lincolnshire countryside with him to call on their neighbours, the Trollopes and the O'Briens. Perhaps his chief fault lay not so much in malice as in capriciousness, exacerbated by a want of self-command and control. A couple or so years after her marriage, mother to one infant and pregnant with another, Charlotte faced the possibility that she might die when giving birth. Setting out her plans for her adored 1-year-old daughter Maria, she admitted that she did not want her to be brought up by Lady Lindsey, because she foresaw what the little girl 'would have to suffer from Mr Pegus's temper'. Sometimes, he would 'be perfectly kind; he would <u>doat</u> on her –'. But she writes, her memory furnishing a shocking vignette of her stepfather's volatile temper,

> his wild, restless, fretful disposition, aggravated by ill health, cast a gloom over my Youth, which I should be very sorry that my little one should ever feel. His constant repining at trifles must have a blighting influence on any young mind that is in the habit of witnessing it.[7]

If Pegus worried his family, so did the older of Charlotte's two brothers, George Augustus Frederick Albemarle, the future 10th Earl of Lindsey. Too circumspect, even in the privacy of her journal, to discuss his afflictions openly, Charlotte often refers to Lindsey, as they called him, as her 'poor' or 'unfortunate' brother. Her son Monty, who was rather more outspoken, took the downright view that his uncle was 'a poor imbecile who had to be watched and treated like a baby.'[8] Lord Bessborough, a career diplomat, cautiously referred to the 10th Earl as being 'of weak intellect.'[9]

In 1827, Lindsey had gone to Eton. Early on, in what sounds like a piece of typical nineteenth-century public school bullying, he was forced early on to drink a nauseating mix of tobacco and water. Authority intervened, and he was sent home for a period of recuperation.[10] There may in fact have been more to the incident than meets the eye. Charlotte mentions in her journal that during February 1827, her brothers were 'ill at school with the Hooping Cough [*sic*]'.[11] Barbaric as it sounds, to induce vomiting was regarded as a cure for the disease, which perhaps accounts for the vile concoction that Lindsey was compelled to swallow.[12] After a year's convalescence at home, swayed by the views of well-meaning neighbours who maintained that to remove him from school permanently 'would not be giving him a fair chance', when Pegus escorted Bertie to Eton – he never gave the family much cause for concern – he took Lindsey at the same time.[13] Privately, Charlotte thought it 'scarce possible' for Lindsey to stay at a place where he had experienced such misery. He was, she wrote, 'too much alive to all unkindness', and his 'great depression of spirits and [...] settled melancholy' were all 'too evident' to ignore. Whether Lindsey had always been prone to dejection or whether it was the manifestation of some complication which had arisen from his illness is impossible to know. Pegus, as it turned out, shared something of his step-daughter's forebodings. On arrival at Eton, having said goodbye to Bertie, in an eleventh-hour change of mind, he took Lindsey back home with him to Uffington. There, the hapless boy resumed his education in the charge of a tutor, a young Cambridge graduate named Frederick Martin.

By the end of May 1828, Lindsey's state of mind alarmed his mother and stepfather so much that one 'Dr Willis' became a frequent visitor to Uffington House. The surname is suggestive. At some point in the eighteenth century, an earlier Dr Francis Willis (1718–1807) had treated King George III in his bouts of madness and established a private asylum for the treatment of psychiatric disorders in the remote Lincolnshire village of Greatford. Under the direction of his namesake and nephew, Dr Francis Willis (1792–1859), it later moved to Shillingthorpe Hall near Stamford, and it appears that this Dr Willis numbered Lindsey among his outpatients.[14] In his 1823 *Treatise on Mental Derangement*, the younger Willis emphasised the desirability of physicians making their home visits 'appear natural and un-designed', in order to conceal their true purpose 'from the knowledge of the patient.'[15] With the 10th Earl of Lindsey, he appears to have gone about his professional duties with great tact. 'I rode with Lindsey,' wrote Charlotte, in May 1830; 'we went [...] by the farm ... Near the wood Dr Willis came up to us and I conversed some time with him on Lindsey's going on.'[16] The forethought which, no doubt, went into planning this so-say chance encounter-cum-consultation says much both for Willis's discretion, and her own circumspect efficiency.

But Charlotte had no wish to become her brother's nurse, for she was avid to learn. Taking advantage of Mr Martin's scholarly presence in the household, she must have asked him to recommend books from the Uffington House Library for her to read. A scrap of paper inserted between the pages of her 1828–9 journal bears the instruction 'Read Knight; Man of Lawe; Wife of Bath's <u>Tale</u> (underlined); Friar; Clerk's; Squire.'[17] These stories, among the more decorous *Canterbury Tales*, tell of pure, virtuous love, as exemplified by sacrifice (the Knight); virtue betrayed by jealously and malice (the Man of Lawe); how a rash knight bound on a quest to find out what women most desire agrees to marry an ugly old woman in return for the answer – sovereignty; after he has heeded her lecture on the subject, she becomes young and beautiful (the Wife of Bath); a folk tale about the devil's bearing off a greedy bailiff (Friar); a wife who meekly bears the suffering inflicted by her callous husband (Clerk) and an incomplete narrative that refers to a ring which endows Princess Canace with the ability to understand the language of the birds.[18] If Mr Martin fastidiously chose to avoid the bawdier stories, his discretion was understandable; besides, Charlotte would later explore them for herself.[19] Her love of Chaucer lasted all her life; in her old age, although loss of vision made reading impossible, she could remember the General Prologue well enough to recite it in its entirety. She reckoned that it took her about thirty-five minutes.[20]

Joyriding on the scholarship of her brother's tutor, Charlotte's zeal for learning burned increasingly bright. With a ready command of Latin, she not only loved the works of 'dear, dear Virgil', but was quick to master Italian. On 9 July 1829, she mentions 'copying out one or two Italian sonnets from a book of Mr Martin's which he wanted to pack'. Upside down in pencil on the inside of the front cover of the manuscript journal appear the lines:

> *Colma non chieggio a miei pensier che donna*
> *Calma, e misa non anne; e gia veloce*
> *Nel non di mortal turbata e viana. Felicape*
> *onda va de' miei giorno a metter foce.*

> ['Do not crave to calm my thoughts, for the wretched have
> no calm; and already with speed in the sea of death, a dark
> wave swallows my days'][21]

For her to write the lines out suggests that she found them significant, and although it smacks of self-dramatising, it is easy to understand how she shrank from the notion of time, rising like a wave to engulf her, before she had achieved anything more than learning languages, reading poetry, making social calls and riding out with her stepfather. At the same time, the appeal of language learning was irresistible. As a small child, she had listened while her mother read her an English version of the Arabian Nights; aged 17, she set herself to learn Persian and Arabic and ordered Sir John Richardson's *Grammar of the Arabic Language* through Mortlock, the Stamford stationer. 'I received from Mr Mortlock's hands Richardson's Arabic Grammar,' she wrote on its arrival, and added, 'Had there been a heaven higher than the seventh, I should have been placed in it. My delight is extreme.'[22]

Yet for all her excitement, it is hard to say how far, among her Persian and Arabic grammar books, she was truly happy. By chance, in 1830 when Charlotte was 18 years old, a young woman named Henrietta Crewe visited Uffington House and, in a letter to her sister, described the home-life of the aristocratic Berties. 'Poor Lord Lindsey,' she wrote,

> what a misfortune it is to see a young man like him, the head of his family, in a state very, very little short of idiotcy [sic]... His sister Lady Charlotte has run away with all the intellect .... Whatever she does she succeeds in – she draws ... of course ... beautifully & etches -. She is musical, she is a Latin scholar; she is crazy after oriental languages, she rides twenty miles a day [and] goes out shooting.[23]

Despite these accomplishments, Miss Crewe did not find Charlotte entirely engaging. Not only did she look 'a vast deal older' than her years, but she had a 'rather too decided and hold-cheap a way with her, perhaps, to be perfectly pleasing.'[24] Admittedly, Miss Crewe allowed, 'in the course of a few years,' she might 'soften down into something very delightful', but the courtesy does not entirely draw the sting of her off-the-cuff observation. The young Charlotte Bertie was clever beyond doubt, but she was also opinionated, impatient and did not suffer fools gladly.

In all likelihood she was lonely and fretful. Her circle of acquaintance did not really extend beyond her family and the local gentry she met while out hunting or shooting with Pegus. Whatever Miss Crewe might suggest, Charlotte in fact had limited enthusiasm for field sports. One of the highlights of the Stamford year was St Brice's day – 13 November – on which there was an annual bull run. Since it followed fast upon Lindsey's birthday, 4 November, the family appear to have taken it as part and parcel of his celebration. A reluctant spectator, Charlotte would see the bull turned out in the town, between the Beast Market and St George's Square, and, unimpressed, watch as the scarlet-clad townsmen goaded it into displaying its 'agility and skill in tossing'. After a brief respite, they would take the bull into the water-meadows beside the River Welland for the crowd to taunt with their hats and handkerchiefs. 'Accidents always happen,' she observed drily, 'as it requires great quickness to avoid the bull with which he endeavours to retaliate [*sic*]. Sometimes baiting with dogs is [...] resorted to, & at 8 the poor creature is shot & immediately cut up by the multitude' avid to secure the best cuts of meat.[25]

Finding country life so often either tedious or distasteful, she turned for companionship to Mr Martin, the one member of the Uffington household who shared her intellectual and literary enthusiasms. Before long, their friendship deepened and intensified. One morning in March 1832, Rev. Brownlow Layard – another of Charlotte's mother's cousins and the vicar of Uffington – called and launched into an unprovoked 'volley of abuse against Mr Martin', the gist of which was that he had been showing Charlotte rather too much attention.[26] Whatever her excitable clergy relative might suppose, Charlotte probably was not in love with Martin. His kindness and fellow-feeling – one scholar to another in a rustically rumbustious household – counted for much with her, and she was genuinely fond of him, but she was too pragmatic about prospects – both his and her own – to lose her heart to him. Even so, her sense of justice was keen, and in her journal, she leapt to Martin's defence. 'I may be imprudent to write this,' she admitted,

> but I cannot, I will not stand his [Layard's] malignity towards the very best and kindest and most esteemed friend I ever had, [...] who has been tried and who has seen my cheek pale and my heart sick and all my influence and power at home gone, so that no interested motive could be assigned and who, throughout all, has never forsaken me, never for a moment wavered, never failed to give some kind consolation when my cause of distress was apparent, though

always having too much delicacy to let it appear as such,
or as advice; one, in fine, whose fairness and rectitude of
feeling have often given me strength and by example taught
me my duty when my heart has failed and I should have
wanted the courage to think and do aright. Such a friend,
perhaps the only sincere one I should else have I will never
give up.[27]

For all its surge, the writing is careful. It is not so much an out-pouring
of devotion as a fair-minded pledge of loyalty. Martin, she indicates, has
taken her part often enough; as a matter of justice, she will not allow
Layard's insults – 'volley of abuse' – to pass unchecked. So cryptic and
cautious has her journal become – Guest and John remark upon 'passages
erased by heavy black ink' – that identification of what precisely has
happened is all but impossible.

At the time of Miss Crewe's visit, Lindsey was 16 years old. As a
nobleman he was expected to marry and beget heirs; whether, to be
blunt, he had the mental capacity to contract marriage seems doubtful.
1811 had seen the enactment of an 'Act further to prevent the marriage
of lunatics' – a statute whose title spoke for itself. It was a dilemma
which all Dr Willis's conscientious care and vigilance was powerless
to resolve. When Lindsey was about 18 years old, the mischief-making
O'Brien neighbours contrived the jape of plying him with drink
and making him go through a pretend wedding with a Miss Posnett.
Fortuitously, Pegus interrupted the proceedings and somehow got
Lindsey home.[28] One consequence of the episode was that Lady
Lindsey became her eldest son's sole guardian; another was that Pegus
embarked on a series of intrigues with the intention of finding his noble
stepson a wealthy wife.

To witness her stepfather scheming on her brother's account caused
Charlotte much anger and distress. In London during May 1832, Pegus –
presumably with the wish of acclimatising his stepson to the man-
about-town role – contrived to introduce Lindsey to one of his female
acquaintances and arrange for the two of them to spend a fortnight
in Brighton together. Besides the moral objections, Charlotte found
the whole idea downright absurd. Lindsey was not yet 21; sometime
previously their mother had been appointed his sole guardian and Pegus's

nonsensical pretend seduction promised to make an ass of everyone connected with it, and the law to boot. In the event, Charlotte urged Pegus to make the pair wait for the dowager-countess's permission, with the result that he gave her predictably short shrift. He did not foresee that she would appeal to Lord Brougham the Lord Chancellor, whose intervention brought matters to a decisive halt. Lindsey did not go to Brighton and probably never saw the lady again, but Charlotte and her stepfather had an unpleasant journey from London to Uffington in one another's company – he resentful at finding his scheme thwarted, and she wretched at his tongue-lashing.[29]

The sour atmosphere lasted for weeks. On 10 June, in London once more and somewhat drunk after dinner, Pegus not only insulted Lindsey but also said something to Martin which reduced him to tears. 'The state in which I found him in the little room was terrible,' remembered Charlotte. Here was something more offensive than step-paternal exasperation; for Pegus to have caused the courteous and resourceful Mr Martin such extreme distress suggests that he may have been suspicious of the growing camaraderie between his stepdaughter and the tutor. With family tension running high, a month later, in July 1832, Pegus made another attempt to marry off Lindsey. This time, the chosen wife was a Miss Mellish, whom Charlotte described as 'a very rich heiress of about 4000000£.'[30] Miss Mellish's father declined to make the journey to Uffington, and took no steps to meet Lindsey, but nevertheless viewed the matrimonial prospect with enough enthusiasm to pledge that he would 'forward the business with his hapless daughter to the extent of his ability'. It was initially agreed that Lindsey, Mr Martin, Charlotte – who disliked the manoeuvring – and Pegus should at least meet him over dinner at 19 Eaton Place, Lady Lindsey's Belgravia residence. Lady Lindsey herself remained at Uffington. She thought the whole arrangement 'absurd', but did not countermand it.

Mellish arrived, without his daughter, and immediately took to Charlotte, expressing the hope that he and she would meet often in the future. After they had dined, Charlotte removed both Lindsey and herself from the discussion which, so far as she could judge, went ahead with ease. By the time they had finished the evening's negotiations, Pegus was 'very much pleased' with the outcome, and despatched a letter to Charlotte's mother by the night coach, while Charlotte went out onto the balcony and wept. Not only did she have acute misgivings about Pegus's latest matrimonial strategy for Lindsey, which she considered 'very unprincipled', but she also anticipated that her mother and stepfather 'would next amuse themselves with some horrible plan' for herself. That they should entertain any notion of allowing her to marry Martin was inconceivable.

The following morning, Mr Mellish called on Pegus and the Berties before breakfast in what must have been considerable embarrassment. He announced, that upon reflection, 'from Lindsey's appearance he could not recommend him to his daughter and begged to decline any further transaction'. In Charlotte's view, he had 'behaved well and honourably'; if his daughter was 'revolted at the idea of such a marriage de *convenance*', it was only to be expected. In view of the recent Brighton escapade, Pegus took the setback in remarkably good part, admittedly 'overthrown' by the news, but nevertheless calm. Taking Lindsey out in the carriage to call on a Mr Handley and Mr Tooke, he was, Charlotte reports, 'very kind to him'. She, meanwhile, was distraught. The 'silly affair' from which she had never imagined that any good would come had left her 'ill and unhappy', and full of 'apprehension of some dreadful misery' to herself, although she hardly knew what. 'Have I not reason to fear?' she lamented.[31] Sure enough, it would not be long before her mother tried to kindle her interest in a 67-year-old lawyer and novelist named Robert Plumer Ward, although Lady Lindsey must have seen from the outset that it was a lost cause.[32]

In May 1833, Charlotte and her family travelled up from Lincolnshire to stay in Lady Lindsey's house in Eaton Place for the London season. Flatteringly, the *Morning Post* recorded their presence under the heading FASHIONABLE ARRIVALS.[33] While they were there, they saw the sights, walked in Hyde Park and Kensington Gardens; purchased a monkey and some goldfish and, in what looks like a new foray towards husband-hunting, Lady Lindsey took Charlotte to Almack's fashionable assembly rooms.[34] On Sunday 19 May 1833, Charlotte's twenty-first birthday, it rained all day.[35] Besides going to church, the family watched a military 'Review', that is, a procession of troops in Hyde Park, which had been arranged in the honour of Ferdinand Philippe, the young Duke of Orleans.[36] Afterwards, they attended a reception and 'sumptuous *déjeuné*' at 1 Grosvenor Gate, home of Wyndham Lewis, sometime MP, and his beautiful gossipy wife, Mary Anne. It was conveniently close both to Hyde Park and Eaton Place and since Lewis was a sizeable shareholder in the Dowlais Iron Company, it was no surprise that Dowlais's managing partner, Josiah John Guest MP, should also be present. Except the enigmatic remark 'first meeting with Mr Guest', no word from Charlotte survives to set their meeting in any kind of context.[37]

Between early Autumn 1832 and the following summer, in place of daily entries, her journal shows only a long, frustrating gap. When her grandson, Lord Bessborough, compiled his anthology of extracts from her journal he surmised that, for reasons of her own, she destroyed the pages covering the period between September 1832 and May 1833.[38] Revel Guest and Angela John go further and insist that she 'burned' these missing pages because she thought they 'might cause pain to those who read them', in particular, to her husband.[39] Yet when Montague Guest – Monty – had his mother's handwritten journals typed up to facilitate compilation of his 1911 book about her interest in collecting fine china, his typists must have had access to certain pages which are no longer extant.[40] Monty, in other words, knew about the entries which Charlotte made during the months of May, June and July 1833, the period of John's and her swift courtship.[41] While he does not quote it at length, he nonetheless makes revealing use of the material.

At 1 Grosvenor Gate, in the heat of the moment, Charlotte gave all her attention to a young writer and aspirant politician, one Benjamin Disraeli. Not only had she enjoyed his novel *Contarini Fleming*, but her relative Austen Henry Layard had met him and been vastly impressed by his colourful waistcoats and velvet pantaloons. It was not long before she discovered that their literary tastes had much in common; Disraeli's 'admiration for Southey and Hallam,' thought Charlotte, 'would redeem a great many sins.' To crown her delight, fellow guest Lady Sykes invited her to join Disraeli and herself at the King's Theatre for a performance of Rossini's *Tancred*. At the opera, Charlotte found his conversation mesmerising. 'We ran on about poetry and Venice and Baghdad and Damascus and my eye lit up and my cheek burned and in the pause of the beautiful music [...] my words flowed almost as rapidly as his,' she remembered afterwards.[42] For him to befriend her was total enchantment.

If somewhat more calculating in his appraisal, Disraeli was not uninterested in Charlotte. 'By the bye,' he mused writing to his sister Sarah on 22 May 1833, 'would you like Lady Z – for a sister-in-law, very clever,

25,000L and domestic?' There was, he assured her, no question of its being a love match conceived on impulse. 'All my friends who married for love and beauty,' he insisted, 'either beat their wives or live apart from them. I may commit many follies in life, but I never intend to marry for "love", which I am sure is a guarantee of infelicity.'[43] Sarah Disraeli was unimpressed. 'Beware! Oh, beware of the 25,000L which belongs to a young lady who can spend the greatest part of it on herself & who will expect from you sooner or later three times that sum,' she replied, before asking caustically, 'Are you sure there is even that?'[44] Persuaded either by his sister's cynicism or his own, Disraeli, who was about to embark on an *affaire* with Henrietta Sykes, abandoned all thought of marrying Charlotte. By a remarkable turnabout, following Wyndham Lewis's death in 1839, he married the widow Mary Anne, and it proved a very happy union.

Between attending concerts and art galleries with Lady Sykes, and being shepherded to Almack's by her mother, as the days passed Charlotte joined Mary-Anne Lewis in carriage-outings, visits to the zoological gardens and dinners at 1 Grosvenor Gate, for which John Guest would be present. Even if Charlotte had not fallen in love with him precisely at first sight, their attachment nevertheless developed at great speed. Some outline of John's growing intimacy with Charlotte and her family emerges from the diary entries of Mary Pegus, who was 11 years old at the time. 'Mr Guest called after church here', noted Mary on 18 June; 'Mr Guest […] gave us a long history of his iron mines which amused me very much', she offered for 28 June, and on 10 July she recalled that 'Mr Guest had tea and spent the evening here.'[45] Mary-Anne Lewis, meanwhile, in a singularly racy and knowing disclosure, boasted that her friends were 'diverted' at her 'making Mr Guest marry whom [she] pleased.'[46] His wealth, which was considerable, made him a promising matrimonial catch, but finding a likely wife was a delicate business. Lady Charlotte Bertie had much in her favour. She was, to judge from her portraits, stylish; she was also energetic and intelligent. Her enjoyment of music and theatre spoke of taste; her skill in shooting and riding, not to mention her proficiency at billiards, showed stamina and competitive spirit. For the wife of a man of business, these qualities were distinct assets. Besides, Guest was childless; his first wife, Maria Ranken had died in 1818, before they had been married a year, her unborn infant perishing with her. In his middle age, with the iron-business fast expanding, he needed sons to continue his work and Charlotte, so much younger than he, had many child-bearing years ahead of her. Mary-Anne Lewis was quite hard-headed enough to appreciate the influence of these practical considerations.

If she also had some intuitive recognition that the couple would fall in love with one another, it was well-directed. Unlike the seasoned prosperity of the ancestral landowning classes, their meadows and copses garnered and stewarded over several generations, Guest's fortune had accrued swiftly and, to a large extent, through his own efforts. Although certain elements in Charlotte's background – her mother's marriage to Pegus, for instance, not to mention Lindsey's eccentricities – might have clouded her own marital prospects, for John the union with an earl's daughter could open seigneurial doors that usually remained closed to the rising class of rich manufacturers. If he was not precisely the son-in-law whom Lady Lindsey had envisaged when she paraded Charlotte at Almack's, he was not only rich, but also clever, sociable and extremely attractive, being tall and athletic with thick curly hair. As Mary had discovered, he was engaging in conversation and the gifts that he produced, a toy for her and a purse for Elizabeth, showed his generous side. Admittedly, at 48 years old he was considerably older than Charlotte, who had just turned 21, but he was still much younger than Plumer Ward, whose suit Lady Lindsey had not scrupled to encourage.

In later years, Charlotte veered between treating 12 and 13 July as the anniversary of John's proposal of marriage and, by way of explanation, Guest and John argue reasonably in their biography that he may have proposed on 12 July, for her to accept him the following day.[47] What is certain is that they became engaged after some seven weeks' acquaintance, and the wedding followed less than a month later. On 29 July 1833 in St George's, Hanover Square, the bishop of Gloucester pronounced Lady Charlotte Bertie 'sister to the Earl of Lindsey', and Josiah John Guest, Esq., M.P., of Dowlais House, Glamorganshire', man and wife.[48] John was tense and nervous throughout the ceremony and Lady Lindsey's face bore visible traces of tears, but Charlotte – her journal on a stable footing once more – remained 'collected' throughout, her voice 'steady, clear and perfectly audible' as she made her responses.[49] Three months previously, she had never seen John and barely knew of his existence, yet she had viewed their engagement as a time of 'unbroken peace' and 'unclouded happiness'. Fast in love with him, she gave him the private name of 'Merthyr', which is how she habitually refers to him in her journals. As his wife, she was faced the future with boundless optimism.

Chapter Two

Unknown Country

Merthyr Tydfil, John's constituency, was a hilly, thrusting place, which had expanded exponentially since its development in the mid-eighteenth century as a centre of iron production. To Benjamin Malkin, who travelled through the area at the start of the nineteenth century, it was a town 'that never had a premeditated plan [...] but grew up by accident', around the first furnaces and forges.[1] In response to a growing need for labour, dwellings went up, initially in what Malkin terms 'scattered confusion', the available land between them being developed over time so as to form 'irregular streets' of cottages.[2] Since they lacked adequate sanitation and drainage, cholera epidemics were a frequent occurrence and levels of infant mortality were high. Industry permeated the entire place in a literal sense; not only did stacks and furnaces dominate the landscape but, as T.E. Clarke, author of an 1848 Merthyr Tydfil guidebook remarked, 'heaps of cinders' spread over the entire area. Formed from the dross of the mines and the molten slag of the furnaces, they could attain a great height, smouldering for years as they continued their inexorable encroach.[3] The Morlais Brook, which ran a little way to the north, burst its banks at intervals, being swamped by cinders dumped in it.[4]

Yet Charlotte loved the place, and took straight away to Dowlais House, John's solid, unpretentious home right at the edge of the ironworks. Large enough to accommodate numerous servants, a total of ten children and frequent visitors, it lent itself to hospitality on a lavish scale. One of the ground-floor rooms, for instance, was sufficiently sizeable to accommodate a dinner for some thirty-two iron-works staff and agents.[5] The library, which was furnished not only for reading and writing, but also housed a billiards table, seems to have been one of her favourite rooms and probably served her as a study.[6] The Guests also had a choice of marital bedrooms. In 1838 John, who tended to catch cold easily, insisted that they relinquish the bedroom they had used for the previous five years, and in which their children Ivor, Katharine and Merthyr *bach* were born, 'for the Brown one', which may have been warmer.[7]

Since John's forebears contributed greatly to shaping Merthyr's development as an iron town, the history of the place had entwined itself inextricably with the history of his family. His grandfather, also named John Guest, had moved from the Shropshire town of Broseley in the 1750s to set up a furnace to smelt iron on land near Merthyr Tydfil. After all, with large reserves of iron ore and coal nearby, together with limestone to serve as a flux in the smelting process, it was an ideal location. Together with Isaac Wilkinson, father of John 'iron-mad' Wilkinson, he leased the site from the Earl of Plymouth. The venture was not entirely successful and in 1765, Wilkinson and he transferred it to Anthony Bacon. While Wilkinson moved out of the district, Guest drew upon his experience to secure the post of manager of an ironworks at nearby Dowlais. Established in 1759, the Dowlais concern came into being when nine commercially-minded gentlemen signed 'Articles of Co-Partnership in Merthir [*sic*] Furnace' by way of setting up a business devoted to iron manufacture. Having invested a total sum of £4,000 in the venture, they acquired leases of land near Merthyr Tydfil which authorised them to build a furnace, extract ore and coal, harness the nearby river for power and put up one of Isaac Wilkinson's patent blowing engines. There were sixteen shares in the business, and each partner held either one, two or three sixteenths' interest, according to his contribution to the capital investment.[8]

Guest proved an adept manager under whose supervision the nascent company prospered. Pleased, the partners renewed his contract in 1780, and two years later, he bought out one of their number – Thomas Harris – acquiring his shareholding for £2,600.[9] In time, Guest's son Thomas succeeded him in his managerial post and inherited his interest in the business; on 2 February 1785 Josiah John, Charlotte's future husband, was born to Thomas and his wife Jemima Revel at Pwll yr Whiad, a small settlement on the hillside above Merthyr Tydfil. The place itself no longer survives; largely engulfed by Dowlais Great Tip in the nineteenth century, the more recent Ffos y Fran land reclamation project has obliterated all remaining trace of it. Before long, there would be two more children: a son, Thomas Revel, and a daughter, Sarah. Jemima died in 1791, and the task of raising the Guest infants fell to a woman known as Mari Aberteifi – Mary from Cardigan – whose career as a turkey farmer suggests that she had strong business instincts.[10] For their formal education, the boys were despatched to their Shropshire relatives and attended Bridgnorth Grammar School. Years later, John took Charlotte to see it, and intrigued, she described how they 'found his initials, J.J.G. cut out with a pen-knife [...] on one of the old oaken desks.'[11]

Thomas Guest, meanwhile, managed the iron works in collaboration with William Taitt, the astute, if sharp-tongued, gentleman who had married his sister Sarah. Taitt's surviving correspondence suggests that he was apt to seize the upper hand. A letter to Guest of May 1799 gives the flavour of his managerial style. 'I do not wish to interfere with the taking or discharging men,' he wrote,

> but if you will Act so injudiciously to discharge the Principal men of any department, without having previously Secured another equally good, I shall always be constrained to interfere however unpleasant to myself...[12]

Meanwhile, the closing years of the eighteenth century saw successive buy-outs among the original Merthir Furnace partners. In consequence, by 1801 interest in what had become a highly profitable business lay in the hands of three individuals: onsite managing partner Thomas Guest with two shares; a semi-sleeping partner named William Lewis who held six shares, and Taitt with eight.[13] Thomas Guest died in 1807, leaving his sons Josiah John and Thomas Revel one share each. Having no children of his own, Taitt, planned to divide his share-holding between his wife's nephew, Josiah John Guest, whose abilities clearly impressed him, and his blood nephew, Alexander Kirkwood. In a severe, if sparsely punctuated, note to Josiah John of January 1809 he set out the full gravity of their future responsibilities. 'Alexander and you have had enough Dancing at this time,' he asserted; 'you must now Stick to business–.'[14] Taitt could not, of course, foresee Kirkwood's death from consumption in 1814, but he ended up leaving his entire interest in the company to Josiah John Guest.

Added to the one share that he had already inherited from his father, the bequest gave a massive boost both to Josiah John's power within the organisation and to his standing among the other Merthyr ironmasters. They were a formidable set of entrepreneurs. William Crawshay II (1788–1867), the 'iron king' of Cyfarthfa, made it for a time the largest ironworks in the world. Anthony Hill (1784–1862), whose forbears had taken over the Plymouth Works from the Bacon family, had a reputation for being the most scientific ironmaster of the district. By way of initiating improvements in transportation, in 1802 Samuel Homfray (d.1822) of Penydarren encouraged a Cornishman named Richard Trevithick to build a steam locomotive which proved capable of hauling ten tons of iron and seventy men over a distance of nine miles.[15] Unfortunately, because it also destroyed the track over which it ran, its career came to a premature end, and it was converted for use as a stationary steam engine, but the episode at least secured Merthyr Tydfil's place within railway history.

Under John Guest's management – he seems, around this time, to have dropped the name 'Josiah' – the Dowlais Ironworks flourished, expanding to outstrip even Cyfarthfa. With an eye to the needs of a new generation, John set up a school for the children of his workforce. His strong sense of public duty led him to offer himself as a parliamentary candidate, and in 1826, the Devon town of Honiton returned him as its MP.[16] But then his progress faltered. His commitment to the cause of parliamentary reform lost him the Honiton seat in the 1831 election and around the same time, demand for iron slumped. It boded ill for Merthyr Tydfil, which was already simmering with discontent at the failure of Whig Prime Minister Charles Grey's Reform Bill to which John had given his fervent support. In the face of widespread unemployment, the existence of the local 'Court of Requests', whose bailiffs having the power to seize and distrain the property, of debtors was one particular source of grievance to the impoverished townsmen. Another was the existence of the Corn Laws, which – by way of supporting the agricultural and landowning interest – kept the price of bread artificially high.

In May 1831, William Crawshay II of Cyfarthfa reduced his workers' wages, which precipitated a drastic turn of events. Unemployed ironworkers and miners formed themselves into armed bands, to the terror of the district. Rioters ransacked the Court of Requests, looting the distrained goods and destroying the accounts books; the much loathed truck shops came under attack and threats were made upon the lives of company managers and agents. Early in June, John Guest and the other ironmasters – being the chief employers of the place, they had an interest in maintaining the peace – met the magistrates and the High Sherriff of Glamorgan at the Castle Inn to discuss appropriate measures to take in the crisis. At some point, the terrified stipendiary magistrate John Bruce Pryce appealed for help, with the result that eighty Argyll and Sutherland Highlanders were despatched from Brecon garrison to Merthyr.[17]

The arrival of the troops was the ultimate provocation. While the Highlanders surrounded the Castle Inn, a crowd of aggrieved townsmen marched up under a banner dipped in calves' blood – in other words, a red flag – to demand higher wages and cheaper bread. At one point, John Guest had faced them from an upstairs window and promised that when things had calmed down, he would be willing to see what he might do towards meeting their requests. Unfortunately, far from calming the crowd his words only exacerbated their hostility and the troops opened fire. Four days' rioting followed before the authorities reasserted themselves. Reprisals, when they came, were harsh. Lewis Lewis, known in Welsh as Lewsyn yr Heliwr, and supposedly the mastermind of what became known as the Merthyr Rising, received a death sentence, although it was later commuted to transportation for life; many of his associates faced either imprisonment or transportation. A young man named Dic Penderyn was less fortunate. Charged with the fatal stabbing of one of the Scots troops, he was found guilty and hanged, despite the widespread and lasting belief in his innocence. It made him a martyr.[18]

But the Rising left a lasting impression upon John Guest, who gave up his truck shop soon afterwards and rallied large numbers of the town's workmen behind a petition for free trade.[19] In 1832, when Merthyr Tydfil became an enfranchised borough under the new Reform Act, he stood successfully for election as its first MP. The stance that he had taken in the Rising clearly appealed to Charlotte's imagination, although when John showed her the landmark places of the Rising, she remarked only that the Merthyr riots, 'serious as they were, were not nearly so amusing and caused not nearly so much alarm as our mock one of Nov 1830.' Her allusion to the Uffington gentry's arming themselves with pistols and walking sticks to ward off rick-burners at the time of the agricultural 'Swing Riots' betrays a certain lack of understanding.[20] It would take time for her apprehension of her husband's commitment to the town he so ardently served to deepen and mature.

*

There were other aspects of John's life which she would have to learn to accommodate. On their first full day in Wales together, the newly married Guests had walked by the ruins of Cardiff's ancient Castle.[21] 'We scrambled among the old ruins –' Charlotte recalled in her Journal before adding, with disquieting directness, 'I think Merthyr said this was the site of his first walk with Maria after their engagement.'[22]

In the early months of her marriage, her thoughts turned often to John's first wife Maria Elizabeth Ranken (1794–1818). John and Maria had married in April 1817; she was one of the eleven children of Charles Ranken (c.1750–1802) and his wife Mary Grant.[23] Ranken who, among other occupations, had been a partner in Cunningham's Bank, Belfast, fled from Ireland with his wife and family during the 1798 Rebellion and settled in South Wales.[24] Before Maria's birth, two older Ranken daughters – Mary (1792–94) and Elizabeth (1793–94) – had perished in their infancy, and Maria inherited her dead sisters' frailty as well as their Christian names. She died of tuberculosis in her twenty-fourth year, within twelve months of her wedding and John commemorated her short life with a tablet in Llandaff Cathedral. According to Charles Wilkins, nineteenth-century historian of Merthyr Tydfil, in the course of her brief marriage, her one contribution to John's business had been to try to persuade him to allow the labourers of the Dowlais Ironworks to have Sunday as a day off. She protested, apparently, that she could not bring herself to accompany him to church while his workforce broke the Sabbath. Since ironmaking 'campaigns' tend to last for months, even years at a time, throughout which the furnaces need a continuous supply of fuel and ore, cessation of all labour for one day in the week was rather a steep, not to say impracticable, demand. Nevertheless Maria got her way. At her behest, Sunday working at Dowlais apparently ceased, except for what – in a useful phrase – was deemed to be 'absolutely necessary'.[25]

Whatever the truth of the story, Charlotte's marriage placed her among the people and places whom Maria had known. The day after their Cardiff Castle ramble, John took her south to the coastal village of Sully, on the way pointing out King's Castle farm to which Maria had been sent for her health, and where she had died.[26] Sully Manor was the home of Evan Thomas, the chairman of the Glamorgan Magistrates and his wife Alicia, Maria's sister. When the Guests arrived, besides meeting and greeting the Thomases, Charlotte found herself introduced in succession to Alicia; to the third Ranken sister Sarah Anne; to Sarah Anne's husband William Daniel Conybeare, Rector of Sully, and to old Mrs Ranken, now a widow who lived near her surviving daughters and their respective husbands. Her journal account of the meeting gives the sense that she did not find it entirely easy. 'Mr Thomas,' she relates,

> is one of those stately, pale, elegant personages whom once seen you can never forget. Mr Conybeare is an original – wild and clever – his daughter very pretty and lively – by far the most fascinating and loveable of all the strangers I was presented to that morning.[27]

That of all the company present, it should have been 16-year-old Mary Elizabeth Conybeare who made the warmest impression upon her 'by far' is a telling observation. After Evan Thomas's death, John purchased his Sully estate; Charlotte, always unsettled by the memories of Maria which surrounded the place, never entirely liked it.[28] In time she warmed towards Conybeare, a future Dean of Llandaff and clearly a loveable man who, according to his obituary, lived 'much in the broad sunshine of life'.[29] A distinguished palaeontologist as well as a clergyman, he sometimes joined the Guest children for fossilling expeditions along the Sully shoreline and helped Charlotte to design and establish the Sully village school.

During Charlotte's first Christmas at Dowlais, in a maladroit if well-intentioned gesture, John gave her all the letters he had ever received from Maria. Quite what she made of this gift is uncertain, but unsurprisingly she preferred not to read them in his presence. Either by chance or design, on 26 December he took his nieces, Sarah-Anne and Eliza Hutchins, to visit the neighbours, thereby giving Charlotte a clear opening in which to pursue her predecessor's correspondence in private.

The early letters intrigued her. She marked both Maria's affection for John, and observed that 'she connected with him much', and appalled, traced her gradual decline as tuberculosis tightened its grip, leaving the hapless invalid to light on 'any slight improvement in health which might occasionally have gleamed upon her hopeless but deceitful malady'.[30] The exchange of confidences which followed the first Mrs Guest's marriage, she pronounced 'perfectly beautiful, perfectly expressive of the most devoted and engrossing attachment'. The observation probably owes more to tact than pleasure. Whatever John's thinking had been when he gave Charlotte his gift, it is rather disquieting to suppose that he assumed she might actually relish reading the reflections of a dying woman and witnessing the themes of love and death play themselves out so close to her new home. Charlotte's account of the experience in her journal is self-conscious, as though she anticipated that John might be curious enough to read her reflections. She claimed that she could, 'read for ever' the letters which Maria despatched from Clifton, 'where she was sent as a last hope in the continuance of her short [...] life and happiness'. With what feels like a special effort, she muses on the 'joy' with which Maria anticipated,

> the Saturday on which 'her adored husband, her beloved Josiah' was to return to her, and the pleasure with which she looks forward to his taking her back to her 'own dear house at Dowlais' are hardly so melancholy to peruse as the little trifles which her [*sic*] sometimes mentions, the little arrangements for her reception, and for her or her dear husband's comforts, which she expresses the wish to have made, even in those hours of pain.

The slip over the pronoun points to her efforts in trying to strike a fitting tone and convey her condolences for his loss of the love of the wife whom she had so recently succeeded. When John returned from his outing, she confessed to being 'not quite in the highest spirits'.[31]

To claim that Maria haunted Charlotte's thinking from beyond the grave would be excessively fanciful, but John's memories of his dead wife were always a sensitive area and Charlotte could not help making unforeseeable slips. When the Guests were on their way to Uffington in 1836, they broke their journey at Newnham on Severn in Gloucestershire. In the village, Charlotte could find nowhere for them to stay but 'a wretched public house'. She ordered the 'best dinner' that it could provide, but decided that it would be wisest for them to travel on to Gloucester before nightfall. When John, who had been visiting his Forest of Dean coalmines, caught up with her, he explained that the miserable inn had been a splendid place in the past, and it was where he and Maria had spent their wedding night.[32] 'This quite overset me' admitted Charlotte, before launching into bitter self-reproach and recrimination. 'What a lovely couple they must have been,' she wrote, 'from all accounts dear Merthyr must have been remarkably handsome then, and the ardour of his first love must have been blessed indeed.' Acutely conscious of the hurt she had unintentionally caused her husband and in agonies of regret, she dwelt silently upon 'poor Maria and her sad fate' for the remainder of the evening.

If she tried to avoid thinking about Maria, Charlotte soon came to hold Wales – its language, its people and its traditions – in the deepest affection. John, she observed, could discuss matters raised by his workmen 'all in Welsh', and with her zest for languages, she arranged to take Welsh lessons from the Rector of Dowlais, Evan Jenkins.[33] It is not clear how fast she progressed, but by the end of September 1833, she was 'construing' part of St Mark's Gospel 'from Welsh to English'.[34] Sociably, John introduced her to his friends and neighbours, among them – Merthyr schoolmaster Taliesin Williams, the son of the poet Iolo Morganwwg, the Vivians of Swansea, and Augusta Hall, Lady Llanover and her husband Benjamin, MP for Monmouth and First Commissioner of Works. Hall oversaw the rebuilding of the Houses of Parliament after a disastrous fire in 1834 and known as 'Big Ben', his nickname transferred itself to the bell whose installation he supervised.

By way of diversion, early in their first autumn together, John took Charlotte to explore something of the beauty of the Welsh landscape, specifically the waterfalls of the Vale of Neath. As a romantic adventure, it proved less than successful and in her journal Charlotte gives a graphic account of the various mishaps lying in wait for unwary nineteenth-century sightseers. No sooner had the Guests set off on their hired horses with their guide, than Charlotte's side-saddle slipped round her pony's belly. Since the mishap, which was more humiliating than injurious, occurred when they were ambling along an 'English-looking' lane, she was well-placed to dismount so that one of the gentlemen could adjust her side-saddle and tighten the girth.[35] Just as they climbed a steep slope, the saddle slipped again and, deciding that it did not fit the fat pony well, the Guests decided to change horses; it was a time-consuming procedure, since it also meant changing saddles. At length, they remounted and rode along a high ridge above the river Hepste, and to reach the first waterfall, led the horses down a precipitous path. 'I scrambled down very well,' Charlotte recalled 'and we were repaid by the sight of a very fine cascade.' To cross the river and continue on their way, John lifted her onto the pony which she rode 'a la Turque', presumably sitting astride the cross saddle, while he and the guide waded across, leading the horse. Having once more exchanged mounts, the next part of the tour took them along the top of a precipice. Perilously, Charlotte's side-saddle slipped for the third time, her frightened horse jibbed, leaving her semi-suspended over a vast drop and absorbed in talk, John and the aged guide 'unconsciously' continued on their way, unaware of the drama behind them. Only when Charlotte called out did they return to hold the horse while she 'disentangled' herself.

At the next waterfall, she and John shared a reviving oatcake, sitting on a convenient rock by the stream. Not long after they had remounted, and ridden on, Charlotte realised that she had left her spectacles somewhere near their picnic place. John and the guide went back to look for them, while she took refuge in a nearby cottage. By the time the gentlemen had found her glasses, it was about four in the afternoon. With a two-and-a-half-hour journey back to Dowlais ahead of them, the Guests decided to head for home. Unimpressed, the old guide told them that they should have ridden to the waterfalls 'on the small mountain poneys which were accustomed to the scramble', instead of the 'large animals' which they had hired.

Purposeful travel, Charlotte soon realised, made more appeal to her than aesthetic raptures. At the end of October 1833 John had the happy idea of taking her to meet fellow manufacturers in the industrial midlands and north-west. In Birmingham, their first port of call, they visited the Church Street Manufactory of Sir Edward Thomason, a silversmith and maker of ornamental castings, who took them over his works and showed them all the gifts he had received from the various monarchs for whom he had cast medals. In her journal, Charlotte conscientiously, if without any especial enthusiasm, described Sir Edward's mosaic (a gift from the Pope); the Order of the Lion and Sun (from the Shah of Persia), and an exquisite diamond-studded green and pink filigree snuffbox, a present from the Sultan of Turkey.[36] Since John had never seen Charlotte's former home, they detoured to spend a week Uffington House where Lady Lindsey gave them an ecstatic welcome and, in a moment of private maternal anxiety, made a point of warning her daughter never to travel on the new railways 'lest some accident should befall'.[37]

Their next destination was to be Manchester, where John had arranged to meet Thomas Houldsworth, MP and mill owner. Charlotte enjoyed

Manchester rather more than Birmingham and thrilled to the vitality of the place. In Houldsworth's mill, she watched the process of mercerisation or 'gassing the thread' – passing it through a flame or gas light so as to remove stray fibres – at close quarters and studied an embroidery machine as it stitched a motif upon a piece of velvet. On the same day, they called at the Atlas Foundry, Messrs Sharp, Roberts and Company's locomotive works on Manchester's Great Bridgewater Street, where she and John saw a 'steam coach' under construction and marked the manufacture of iron billiards tables, which were evidently one of Sharp Roberts' side-lines.[38] Besides the products of the factory, its contrivances – 'gizmos' in modern parlance – caught Charlotte's imagination. Most striking was the 'moveable platform' which not only conveyed the Sharp Roberts workmen from one storey of the building to another, removing the need for stairs, but also served as a lift for a waggon, which it conveyed from the loading area, high up in the building, to the courtyard at ground level.

John needed to go to Liverpool to settle the terms of an outstanding contract. Tired after the day's business, rather than go by road he headed to the Manchester and Liverpool Railway's Castlefield station where the Guests boarded the next Liverpool-bound train and arranged for their carriage to be lashed on a flat-bed truck behind it. Entranced, Charlotte, who was already something of a covert rail enthusiast, dismissed her mother's forebodings without a qualm. By train, she observed in a burst of up-to-the minute travel-savvy, 'the 36 miles took exactly an hour and a half'; with post horses, it would have taken four hours.[39] Remarking that she had never experienced 'a pleasanter expedition', she added revealingly that the engine went 'twice as fast and many times more easy than [her] little Locomotive'.

It begs some intriguing question both about the extent of her knowledge of the Dowlais Ironworks' motive power and, specifically, about the locomotive to which she laid possession. Admittedly, by 1833 the Neath Abbey Iron Company, from which at this time the ironworks obtained its locomotives, had provided them with four: – *Success* (built 1831–2); *Perseverance* (1832); *Mountaineer* (1833) and an unnamed engine known only as No 4.[40] It is certainly possible, if no more than conjecture, that Charlotte unofficially laid claim to one of them. At the same time, and deepening the mystery, of an order dating from 1853, the year after John's death when she had taken over management of the works she would write:

Menelaus [that is, engineer William Menelaus, one of Dowlais' key personnel] to take old locomotive *Lady Charlotte* and attach a temporary saw upon the bank to finish off a stack of some three hundred rails remaining unsawn & to cut in future all saw-bars to their proper length. This is to cost about £20 and can be done at once.[41]

While there would be a certain logic in supposing that this *Lady Charlotte* was 'her' locomotive, it is fair to add that the official records make no mention of the engine under this name. At the same time, it is clear that the experience of joining John on a business expedition had the effect of awakening what, for Charlotte, was to be a deep-seated interest in both the industrial life of the nation and the transport systems that served it.

But at home in South Wales once more, her stamina soon waned. Although she set herself a course of study in Welsh language and literature, with Ariosto and Chaucer 'for […] relaxation,' before long she felt too ill even to go to church, and forsook Welsh grammar for the novels of Sir Walter Scott.[42] Towards the end of November, she mustered enough spirit for a day's shooting, and three days later travelled with John to London, but while he attended the House of Commons, she stayed in bed, sickly and weak. She rallied at the chance to watch *The Butterfly's Ball* at the Adelphi Theatre, billed excitingly as an 'Operatic Extravaganza', but it proved disappointing. 'Dull, with a horrid, bloody interlude', was her damning verdict.[43]

Tacit recognition that she was pregnant encouraged her to agree to see in the New Year at Uffington, before John and she returned to London for the next parliamentary session. She found her family at odds both with one another and with their neighbours. 'Poor Bertie … not going on well; the Rectory at variance […] the O'Briens in disgrace,' she observed, summarising the various grievances.[44] In a strained atmosphere, it took little to upset the domestic apple cart. When the Guests, with Lady Lindsey's concurrence, accepted an invitation to dine with Brownlow Layard, Pegus took umbrage and said that if the Guests ate at the Rectory, he did not want them to sleep at Uffington House. Refusing to be drawn into the clergy dispute, John told Pegus that he had no business to issue threats, at which Pegus turned bellicose and replied that if John 'chose to call him out he would meet him'.[45]

The confrontation has its comic side, but Charlotte could find no amusement in the spectacle of her stepfather, his festering grudge against Brownlow Layard blown out of all proportion, challenging her cool-headed husband to a duel. Instead, her reluctance, on her mother's account, to quarrel with Pegus vied with her sense that putting off the visit to the Rectory would assuredly injure Layard. Weeping, she confided her worries to John who announced next morning that he had just received letters summoning him immediately to London on urgent business. It was a lie, but Charlotte had little conscience where Pegus was concerned and her husband's tactics caused her no qualms. In retrospect, John may have been less than sanguine about his behaviour. Both Charlotte and he had some idea that Pegus saw through the fiction and it may be no coincidence that in their future dealings with one another, the Tory clergyman seldom made any attempt to hide his dislike of the Whig industrialist. On one occasion, in Charlotte's presence, Pegus damned John's political allies as 'Blackguards, [...], scamps and merchants', which gives a powerful sense of his style of debate.[46] Having cut short their stay at Uffington, the Guests headed at once to London, only to find their leased house in Grosvenor Square cold and forlorn, with no servants on hand and nothing ready for their arrival. John, showing great forbearance in trying circumstances, remarked that 'better is a morsel of bread and peace withal than a stalled ox and strife'.[47] In the circumstances, it may have been fortunate that Wyndham Lewis and kind hospitable Mary Anne lived nearby at Grosvenor Gate.

In the middle of March, Charlotte describes how John impulsively kissed her 'in the middle of Regent Street, in broad daylight'.[48] Although for the most part she avoids drawing attention in her journals to her pregnancies, it is possible that she had just told him that he was going to be a father; apparently, that evening, he thoughtfully returned from the House at the unusually early hour of nine o'clock. From her throwaway allusion to 'little Ivor', Charlotte appears to have been certain that the baby was a boy.[49]

Despite having limited enthusiasm for dinners and parties, she continued gamely to accompany John through the social whirl, gracious at his side. She realised, but did not care to admit, that her marriage stood against her. As the wife of an ironmaster, the social element in which she had moved with relative ease as the daughter of one Earl of Lindsey and sister of another, was no longer so welcoming. On 8

May 1834, the Guests dined at the home of William Thompson. Owner of the Penydarren Ironworks and MP for London, Thompson shared enough common ground with John Guest for congenial conversation, but Charlotte, pregnant, tired and utterly out of sorts complained about the 'hot, stupid dinner' before venting her discomfiture in a piece of snide snobbery. 'Conceive the horror,' she confides, 'of seeing a fat woman sit opposite to one in a yellow gown, and an amber cap with red flowers, and the still greater horror of that fat lady claiming to be an acquaintance. She proved to be Mrs Hudson.'[50] George Hudson of York, sometime draper grown rich through railway speculation was a political adventurer in the Tory interest. His reputation for dispensing bribes among the York voters widely, if unfairly, said to give their support to 'anyone they can get anything by', was never going to endear him to a reform-minded parliamentarian like John Guest.[51] But Charlotte's spiteful remarks about his wife probably owed more to her resentment of Elizabeth Hudson's presuming to claim her friendship, than any wish to dissociate herself from the Hudsons' politics.

The episode shows her at a loss, caught in the cross-currents of London society and lashing out at the nearest target. But she enjoyed talking to Sir Gore Ouseley, orientalist and sometime British ambassador to Persia, who shared her taste for languages, and Mary Boyle, the aged Countess of Cork, who had known Dr Johnson, Lord Byron and Scott.[52] By way of making her own entrée into London's smarter circles, Charlotte agreed, albeit with misgivings, to host a concert. Learning that Mary Anne Lewis was to give a party on the date she first chose, she very nearly abandoned the whole idea, complaining that it caused more trouble than it was worth. But once John and the Lewises had persuaded her to choose another date, she engaged the rather distinguished singers Giulia Grisi, Giovanni Battista Rubini, Antonio Tamburini, and Theodore Victor Giubilei, whose performances, together with a 'very pretty' supper, ensured that the evening went ahead in fine style.[53] There was even a flattering paragraph about it in the *Morning Post*.[54]

She longed for her son to be born in Wales and when London physician Dr Lococke told her – in Lady Lindsey's presence – that it would not be safe for her to travel to Dowlais to give birth, Charlotte was desolate. But the advice was good. Over the summer of 1834, Merthyr Tydfil, which was always a stormy place, experienced repeated raids by mobs of disaffected workmen who called themselves the 'Scotch Cattle'.[55] Opposing local employers' usage of labourers from outside the immediate area as strike-breakers, the Scotch Cattle had a mission to prevent strangers from learning the specific craft associated with skilled work in the mines and ironworks, and ransacked the homes of employers who employed incomers. In June, the *Cardiff and Merthyr Guardian* reported attacks on homes of Mr Johnson of the Bute Works and his clerk David Peregrine; furniture and windows smashed at the homes of miners Richard Jones and Richard Jenkins, and three houses gutted near the Argoed Collieries in Monmouthshire.[56] All, apparently, bore the Scotch Cattle's mark – a daub of a bull's head left in the wake of the destruction. As though to confirm the wisdom of Dr Lococke's counsel, only the day after his visit, an aggrieved anonymous letter arrived, telling John that Dowlais House would be sacked 'unless all the Irish were discharged from the Works'.[57] Defiantly insisting that there was no real danger, Charlotte nevertheless resigned herself to giving birth in London. Much relieved by the decision, her mother moved in to the Grosvenor Square house to await developments.

At about midday on 3 July, after a morning spent in writing letters, Charlotte was 'taken ill' – a phrase that became her accustomed euphemism for going into labour. Her 'dear child', a girl, was born at two in the afternoon. When John returned from the Commons an hour later and Lady Lindsey told him that he had a daughter, all thought of sons and heirs vanished from his mind. Overwhelmed with pleasure, he rushed to Charlotte's room to kiss her and the adorable baby. The child would, of course, be given the first name Charlotte after her mother. But her second name, the name by which she was always known, was Maria.

Chapter Three

The Hot Blast

Charlotte brought her baby home in the second week of August 1834 and soon afterwards, her mother, stepfather, brothers and half-sisters made the long journey from Lincolnshire to Dowlais to meet and greet her. As matters turned out, no sooner had they paid their respects to 'MISS CHARLOTTE MARIA GUEST' as 12-year-old Mary hailed her new niece than they found themselves borne off 'by train waggon', to view a nearby lime quarry.[1] Mary and Elizabeth 'very much' enjoyed this outing, but their parents took a different view.[2] Pegus suspected an imminent ambush and insisted upon bringing a loaded gun with him, while rail-averse Lady Lindsey travelled in dread lest they 'slip off the plates'.[3] That she ever agreed to board the train says much both for her courage and, in all probability, for John Guest's power of persuasion. Even when they stopped, she was no happier. The blasting in the quarry terrified her; the works put her in mind of a 'den of thieves'; and, in her opinion, the rugged hills to the north of Merthyr Tydfil looked 'wild enough for *banditti'*.[4]

Nothing daunted, John took great trouble to ensure that his wife's relatives enjoyed themselves. He escorted them round the school that he had established and showed them iron-making in progress at the works. To please Pegus, he initiated a shooting party, which ended prematurely when Lindsey shot a dog; John gave him a stern lecture afterwards about managing his gun.[5] Mary did not know quite what to make of Dowlais and thought it 'a very odd looking village', but she loved helping Charlotte and nursemaid Susan look after the baby. With her sister Elizabeth, she had a long, thrilling ride in the hills – 'Elizabeth rode the little chestnut and I rode the black poney [*sic*]', she remembered.[6] On 20 August, the whole party – Guests, Lindseys, Pegusses – went to stay at Thomas Guest's house in Cardiff to experience something of Welsh culture at the Eisteddfod. It gave Charlotte the chance to show off the wealth of local learning. Augusta Hall, who won a prize for her essay 'The Advantages Resulting from the Preservation of the Welsh Language, and National Costumes of Wales' was the Guests' near neighbour, and local schoolmaster Taliesin Williams, awarded the medal for the best ode in Welsh on the subject of the British Druids, was their friend. Charlotte had the distinction of being invited to join Lady Bute and her party on the judges' platform.[7] Mary, to her delight, danced no fewer than '8 times' at the Ball which closed the festivities.[8] If nothing else, the visit gave the Uffington party a generous taste of Welsh society and culture.

Autumn advanced; Charlotte's relatives went home, and much to her disappointment John Russell, the Dowlais Ironworks' surgeon who doubled as the Guests' family doctor, decided that Maria was not thriving and needed a wet-nurse. Charlotte protested; 'I could never bear,' she wrote, 'to see my child derive its nourishment from the bosom of a hireling.'[9] But it was vain. Russell was obdurate; John took his side and before long, a young woman was recruited to nurse the baby. It became something of a pattern. Charlotte clearly had difficulty in feeding her infants and found herself compelled, albeit reluctantly, to engage wet nurses for baby after baby as her family grew.

Outside the nursery, November 1834 witnessed a political upheaval. When Viscount Althorp, Leader of the House of Commons and Chancellor of the Exchequer, succeeded his father to become the 3rd Earl Spencer, his elevation to the House of Lords had some unexpected consequences. Whig prime minister Lord Melbourne had always valued Althorp's staunch support, and in the face of agitation from the more radical MPs, doubted whether his ministry could survive without the backing of his old ally. Having outlined the situation to King William IV, Melbourne offered to resign and at the same time made Lord John Russell, leading spirit behind the Great Reform Act, leader of the Whigs in the Commons. The king, who liked neither Russell nor his reforms, promptly accepted Melbourne's resignation and having installed the Duke of Wellington as a stop-gap prime minister, invited the Tory Robert Peel to form a new government. 'The Tories chuckle,' observed Charlotte, who was in Uffington when the developments became known and therefore saw her stepfather's reactions at first hand, 'the Whigs despair – but the Liberals say "Any government but a weak one."' 'This does not,' she added caustically, 'look like the Revolution some people predict.'[10] Initially reluctant to take up the king's invitation, Peel accepted at the second time of asking and prepared to call a general election.[11] Once the Guests were back in Wales, John, as Merthyr Tydfil's sitting MP, sought to gauge the level of his support.

While Charlotte waited eagerly to see what part she might play in his campaign, John's nephew Edward Hutchins called to speak to her. Edward's position within the Dowlais Iron Company at this time was hard to define, but being the nephew of the managing partner lent him considerable status. The eldest child and only son of John's sister, Sarah, and her Bristolian husband, also named Edward Hutchins, his father died in 1817 and his mother a year later, at which point, the Guest brothers, John and Thomas, had stepped in.[12] Not only did they arrange for Edward, now aged about 10, to be educated at Charterhouse School, but between them, and with the help of Thomas's wife Anne, they also brought up his sisters Sarah-Anne and Eliza.[13] Over the years, the widowed John appears to have treated Edward almost as a son and it is hardly accidental that on the evening of Charlotte's stealthy arrival at Dowlais, he should have been on hand to welcome her.[14]

John's regard may have given Edward a certain sense of entitlement in iron-related matters, for the purpose of his visit was to ask a substantial favour. He had recently obtained a copy of a treatise touching on British iron production. Entitled *Sur l'emploi de l'air chaud dans les usines a fer de l'Ecosse et de l'Angleterre* – 'On the use of hot air in the ironworks of Scotland and England' – it had appeared in the French journal, the *Annales des Mines,* and was the work of French inspector of mines, the distinguished mineralogist and, perhaps, industrial spy, Ours-Pierre Armand Petit-Dufrénoy (1792–1857).[15] In view of its subject matter and provenance, its potential interest to the British iron industry was immense, but few ironmasters had sufficient command of French to be able to read it. Knowing something of Charlotte's facility with languages, Edward judged that she was just the person to translate it into English.

Linguistic provenance aside, its specialist content presupposed a fair degree of scientific and metallurgical know-how. It concerned the Hot Blast, an innovation which promised to have far-reaching consequence for iron manufacture, which had come about through a series of experiments which James Beaumont Neilson, engineer of the Glasgow gas works, undertook in the 1820s. With the co-operation of a number of Scots ironmasters, Neilson had developed a system for pre-heating

31

air before it entered a blast-furnace by passing it through a hot 'vessel or receptacle', in the expectation that it would save fuel and reduce costs.[16] So confident were Neilson and his syndicate of supporters of its success that in 1828 they patented the process. It would prove to be rather a contentious move, since the understanding at the time was that patents were granted for inventions, which were not the same as the application of scientific principles. In future years, Neilson's patent would be repeatedly challenged in the courts.[17] But the spirit of the age tended to admire heroic industrial innovators and champion their right to reap rewards from their work, and when Neilson charged various companies with infringing his patent, the courts unanimously gave judgement in his favour.[18]

Litigation aside, Neilson's work implicitly challenged settled opinion about the best way of making quality iron. Among early nineteenth-century ironmasters, there was a widespread consensus that pig iron produced in warm weather was harder – and therefore more difficult to work – than iron produced in frosty conditions. The usual explanation for what they termed 'the summer effect' was that the summer air was 'debased'. The metallurgist David Mushet (1772–1847), for instance, believed that in winter the air was drier and 'better suited for combustion' because it retained more oxygen.[19] It was not unknown for manufacturers to take such measures as painting the pipes white – a 'cool' colour – or setting them either in cold water or over ice so as to preserve a cold blast in their furnaces.[20] In 1833, just when Dufrénoy was in Britain to conduct his comprehensive analysis of the economic and metallurgical consequences of the hot blast's application, commercial curiosity concerning the merits of Neilson's innovation was keen, with British ironmasters weighing up the question of whether it was worth paying the shilling per ton royalty for the right to use it. Indeed, Dufrénoy's survey had even wider scope than its title suggested. Besides the ironworks of Scotland and England – '*les usines a fer de l'Ecosse et de l'Angleterre*' – its coverage extended to those of Wales. It also recounted trials of the hot air system made at Fourchambault, Vienne, La Voulte and Rieupéroux in France, and at Wurttemberg in Germany. For each site that he visited, Dufrénoy compiled tables to show the amounts of fuel required and the respective cost for producing a ton of pig iron before and after the hot blast's adoption, and provided detailed illustrations of the heating apparatus he found in use. Recognising the value of Dufrénoy's treatise to the entire British iron trade, it is no surprise that Edward should have scented an opportunity in the making.

Although she agreed to translate the work, Charlotte found it neither easy nor congenial. The French text, she complained, was 'full of technicalities', and she foresaw that producing an English version would take a long time.[21] Nevertheless, she persevered and by the end of her second day, she reckoned that she had completed about a sixth of it. But distraction in the shape of some worrying letters from Lindsey's old tutor Frederick Martin, now a curate in the remote Norfolk parish of Brandon Parva, soon got in the way.[22] Besides some embarrassing effusions about her 'blessed little girl', he engaged in some barefaced begging and asked for the sum of 'about £200', to be 'lodged for him at a banker's'.[23] It was distressing, not least because she had been genuinely fond of Martin in the past, and did not care to see him either indigent, or making a fool of himself. With John's backing, she wrote a 'firm' response instructing him to write no more begging letters, while promising that she and John would be 'willing to render him any service' that lay within their means.[24] It evidently had the desired effect, for Martin somehow recovered himself. In 1840, he secured the post of chaplain to Connop Thirlwall, the newly appointed Bishop of David's, and later became Rector of the Lincolnshire parish of South Somercotes and a prebendary of Lincoln Cathedral.[25]

Flattered to find himself invited to stand as parliamentary candidate respectively for Breconshire and for his old Devon seat of Honiton, John nevertheless declined on the ground that he wished to continue to serve as member of parliament for Merthyr Tydfil.[26] The Marquess of Bute meanwhile, a Scots aristocrat with vast land-holdings in South Wales, was avid to find a local Tory to contest the seat. Being both the largest landowner of the area and, although it was a well-concealed secret, owner of the *Cardiff and Merthyr Guardian*, Bute's influence was considerable. His first candidate of choice was ironmaster Anthony Hill of the Plymouth Works, but Hill's political enthusiasm was lukewarm. While he dithered, in a development which Charlotte thought 'absurd', local solicitor William Meyrick, legal adviser to William Crawshay of Cyfarthfa, stepped in to fill the vacancy.[27] Meyrick was less than popular and it was not long before the local Tory interest began to urge the Merthyr electorate not to be too hasty in pledging their votes; their handbills promised that an unnamed

'Gentleman of Independent Principles' was already waiting to announce his candidature. 'I doubt,' scoffed Charlotte, 'if they will offer anyone more independent than Merthyr.'[28] With Martin out of the way, she put Dufrénoy aside so as to follow her husband's progress with the local voters. 'Elections,' she remarked, 'are very amusing from the individual character they exhibit & bring into play.'[29] It was her first experience of canvassing and she welcomed the chance to gain some purchase upon the priorities of the Merthyr electors.

She accompanied her husband when he rode round the hamlet of Troedyrhiw to solicit promises of support from its inhabitants and collaborated with Edward in writing a 'squib' for one of John's election placards.[30] The 'squib' appears to have given him mixed feelings about the wisdom of permitting her continued involvement in his campaign, particularly since her occasional lapses of discretion worried him. One of Charlotte's Welsh lessons with the Rector somehow turned into a discussion about the recent canvass of nearby Aberdare, and when John learnt about the conversation he took her roundly to task for expressing her opinions too openly upon subjects about which, in his view, she should have kept quiet. It left her 'very unhappy', and in a rather confused journal entry she attempted, if not to exonerate herself, then at least to suggest that there were mitigating circumstances on her side.[31] Women, she allowed, 'have nothing to do with politicks'; further, she did not want John to think that she 'interfered' in matters on which she was, perforce, ignorant. At the same time, in a *volte face* she argued that,

> perhaps a wife might be sometimes excused, if in the course
> of the conversation she is present at, she is led away to
> express some feeling and interest in what so nearly concerns
> her husband.[32]

What emerges most powerfully from this vexed passage is her longing to talk through the local political issues of the day. But John had, to all purposes, silenced her and indicated that her views upon such questions as Meyrick's candidature and 'jobbery' by the other ironmasters who were all Tories counted for nothing. Besides, he was hardly ever at home. Once, she used to 'be half the day with him', now he spent all his time canvassing with Hutchins. To be sure, he had left her early in the morning 'in anger and without *one* kiss', and for the rest of the day she had had 'no one to speak to but Baby'.[33]

Although she found it 'uninteresting', she persevered with rendering Dufrénoy's erudite monograph into fluent, serviceable English for John to 'correct'.[34] Since she was probably more proficient in French than he, it is likely his corrections touched more upon references to the specific operations that Dufrénoy had observed than issues of syntax, grammar and general vocabulary. Examination of her treatment of Dufrénoy's description of Neilson's method of heating air gives some sense of the proficiency of the finished work. 'Dans la première experience,' writes Dufrénoy,

> l'air fut chauffé dans une espèce de coffer rectangulaire en tôle de 10 pieds de long, sur 4 pieds de haut et 3 de large, semblable aux chaudières des machines à vapeur. L'air provenant de la machine soufflante était introduit dans cette capacité, où il s'échauffait avant de se rendre dans le haut-fourneau. Malgré l'imperfection de ce procédé, qui ne permit d'élever la temperature de l'air qu'a 200° Fahrenheit (93.3 cent), on pouvait déja pressentir que l'idée de M. Nielson était destinée à produire une révolution dans le travail du fer.[35]

Despite her comments about the sheer difficulty of rendering the arcane technical language into English, Charlotte provides a clear, unambiguous account of the process in language which is neither self-conscious nor clumsy. 'In the first experiment,' it runs,

> the air was heated in a kind of rectangular box of sheet iron, ten feet long, four high and three wide, similar to the boilers of steam engines. The air proceeding from the blowing machine was introduced into this space, where it was heated, previous to being conveyed into the blast furnace. Notwithstanding the imperfection of this process, which did not admit of the air being heated above 200° Fahr, it became immediately apparent that Mr Neilson's idea was destined to produce a revolution in the manufacture of iron.[36]

If terms such as *tôle* (sheet metal) and *chaudières* (boilers) sent her to the dictionary, her rendition of the phrase *on pouvait déja pressentir*, (literally, 'one could already foresee') as: 'it became immediately apparent…', shows her ease with the idiomatic sentence structure, while at the same time, keeping faith within her English to the thrust of Dufrénoy's French. It is an extremely efficient translation which reveals just how much flair Charlotte brought to a task which she professed to find unrewarding.

Around this time, she read 'Two books illustrative of female industry', loaned by an unknown acquaintance.[37] From her rather vague reference to 'Mrs Inchbald's Life and that of Olympia Mocata [*sic*]', it seems likely that the respective works may have been James Boaden's two-volume *Memoirs of Mrs Inchbald*, published in 1833, and Caroline Bowles Southey's *Olympia Morata: her times, life and writings*, published in 1834.[38] Since both concerned the lives and works of women translators it is easy to imagine why the lender of the books supposed that Charlotte would appreciate them. Morata was a prodigy of the Italian Renaissance who translated Homer 'with great strength and sweetness', while the Suffolk-born actress Elizabeth Inchbald had a gift for rendering French and German plays into slick, performable English drama.[39]

It seems inconceivable that the books did not play some part in bolstering Charlotte's commitment to the work on which she was currently engaged, and if they served to spur her tenacity, the encouragement was timely. Although he was a conscientious MP, John disliked having to solicit votes. When his opponent William Meyrick bragged that he had the support not only of the ironmasters Crawshay, Thompson and Hill, but also of Lord Bute and the landowner Robert Clive, Charlotte riposted, 'Let us see whether Merthyr cannot beat them all', but John lacked her buoyant outlook.[40] What was more, the pressures of campaigning while seeking to maintain reasonable relations with his fellow ironmasters taxed his forbearance to the limit. The tetchiness which showed itself in 'The frequent rebuke […] harsh words and a harsher tone' became a recurrent theme of Charlotte's journal, and it is clear that the uncertainty of the election's outcome put him increasingly on edge.[41]

Broadly speaking, John thought of himself as a Liberal, insofar as the term existed, and regarded his opponents as Tories, but party boundaries at this time were not entirely clear-cut. Where voters' principles were flexible, their loyalties could easily slip. Aberdare man Rowland Fothergill, for instance, fended off John's request for the promise of his vote with the misty assertion that he was 'undecided, his political feelings leading him one way and his personal obligations another.'[42] Crawshay initially fudged matters by claiming that he would wage 'open warfare' upon Guest 'if a proper man came forward as his opponent, but that he would not support a factious opposition got up for the purpose of putting him to expense', which looks like a snub for Meyrick.[43] Later, Crawshay rather unscrupulously offered to 'withdraw Meyrick' – prevent him from standing – in return for John's agreement to retire at the next election so as to make way for William Thompson.[44] Thompson, meanwhile, preferred to stand for Sunderland; he continued to serve as its MP until 1841, when he was elected to represent his native county of Westmoreland.[45] John's supporters assured him one evening that he could be 'certain of a large majority', only for '20 promises' of votes to 'turn round' – that is, turn against him – overnight, such was the fickle mood of the electorate. He accused Charlotte of wasting his time, which she thought unreasonable. 'I only remember to have occupied his time during part of two evenings since my return to Dowlais,' she riposted, 'and then he was employed with me on what was his business rather than my pleasure, the trans. of the system of making iron by hot air–.'[46] She had recently guessed, rightly as it turned out, that she was once more pregnant. 'I am far from being in a fit state to enter upon nine months of illness which I believe I may expect', she observed with unusual frankness.[47]

The canvass of votes proceeded with scant scruple on either side. William Crawshay plied one of his acquaintances with seven glasses of gin in rapid succession 'in order to betray him into a promise to give his vote against his promise.'[48] John Guest, meanwhile, had secured the promise of votes from the tenants of Hon. Robert Henry Clive, Tory member of parliament for Ludlow, owner of much property around Merthyr Tydfil, and the 'Mr Clive' of whose support Meyrick had been so confident. It defied the accepted thinking of the time, which maintained that tenant-electors should vote as their landlord directed them, but although Clive did not share John's political convictions, he took the view that having made their promises to Guest, his tenants were conscience-bound to keep them.[49] Since so many of the Merthyr Tydfil voters were apt to be evasive and blow hot and cold over their support for Guest, it began to look as though Clive's tenants' votes would play a pivotal part in determining the election's outcome. Seeing how the numbers stood, Meyrick's henchmen rode round Clive's Merthyr properties threatening to take vengeance upon the tenants if they did not vote for the Tory candidate. Votes at the time were given by a show of hands, which meant that if an elector should renege upon his pre-election promise of support, his back-sliding was plain to see and could pave the way for ugly reprisals. Taking matters into his own hands, Edward made a short-notice call upon Clive in Ludlow to seek reassurance that he would keep to his agreement. If it was a blatant and pushy piece of advantage-seeking, as a strategy it proved effective. Obligingly, Clive wrote to reiterate his view that a promise, once made, was 'inviolable as an oath', which effectively gave his tenants leave to support Guest at the poll without fear of eviction.[50]

As December advanced, Charlotte devoted more time both to the small Maria and to Dufrénoy. 'Wrote my trans: two hours', she noted on one especially rewarding day, and added that she had 'played a few moments to my baby some beautiful Welsh tunes'.[51] Maria was an alert, responsive infant and Charlotte adored her. 'It is a lovely morning', she observed after one of John's snubs; 'I shall be content if the bright sun smile upon my darling Maria, and shall feel something of reflected pleasures in looking on her happy face.'[52] Shortly before Christmas 1834 she ordered herself an Election waistcoat made of Welsh flannel in John's political colours, purple and yellow.[53] Elections at this time were not held everywhere on the same day, but local returning officers were free to set a polling day of their choosing within a given period. At Merthyr, the day chosen for the 1835 poll was 8 January, and as the New Year approached, excitement mounted. Then, in the last hours of the canvass on 7 January 1835, Meyrick pulled out of the contest, professing that 'instead of gaining, he was hourly losing, voters', and admitting himself beaten.[54] John Guest was returned uncontested as Merthyr Tydfil's MP.

On 9 January, his supporters held a celebratory dinner at the Bush Inn, where he proposed the toast 'Prosperity to the Iron Trade', amid applause, cheering and cries of 'We'll send you again and again.'[55] Fresh from his recent Eisteddfod triumph, Taliesin Williams responded with a toast to Lady Charlotte to which, generous in his success, John returned thanks, cheerfully informing everyone present that although she had been 'brought up a member of the aristocracy', she was 'the only one of her family who was not a Tory'. Later in the month, William Crawshay, gracious to a commercial competitor and political rival, hosted a ball at the Castle Inn in Merthyr, 'as a mark of respect to the Member of the Borough'. On 20 January, the Guests themselves gave a Ball in the granaries above the Dowlais stabling, for which Charlotte designed transparencies bearing such mottoes as 'W.R.' [William Rex] and EGLWYS Y BRENEN [church and king] to be hung in the windows, and arranged for the company clerks to chalk John's coat of arms on the floor. Wax lights lit the rooms, their walls bedecked with evergreen, the band of the Cardiff militia provided music and – whether or not they supported John's Radical politics – the local gentry came in numbers. Travellers from further afield hit a set-back. Snow, thick on the roads, delayed the London mail coach. The local press had considerable fun at the expense of a party of the Guests' smart friends who arrived too late for the fashionable quadrilles, but had to make do with country dances like 'Sir Roger de Coverley' and 'Boulanger'.[56]

A few weeks later, an outbreak of cholera dampened the festive mood. At first, the Guests sent baby Maria to stay with the family of John Russell, whose home promised to be a safe refuge from the disease. Marking its rapid spread, they soon decided that their wisest course was to take refuge with Lady Lindsey and Pegus at Uffington. Having re-accustomed herself to the patterns of life in rural Lincolnshire, Charlotte resumed her work on Dufrénoy's treatise. 'Wet Day', she wrote in the middle of February; 'Merthyr [...] corrected iron hot air [*sic*] for me.'[57]

Although Charlotte makes little of completing her translation, in mid-April 1835, still at Uffington, she turned her attention to etching. It was one of the accomplishments she had acquired before her marriage, and she found it useful in copying Dufrénoy's detailed illustrations. It is not impossible that John and Edward wished to refer to them in their attempts to find a way of using the hot blast technique without having to pay royalties to Neilson. During the previous winter, Charlotte had observed the men at Dowlais Ironworks 'trying to heat one of the furnaces with hot air', although at the time they succeeded only in 'burning their pipes'.[58] In time, their handling of the heating apparatus became more assured. On 12 March 1836 an injunction was issued against Guest and partners restraining them from infringement of Neilson's patent, which indicates that a species of hot blast was in use and effective at Dowlais by that date. Caught, as it were, red-handed, John was quick to settle with Neilson and his fellow patentees, and pay the shilling-per-ton royalty on iron produced by their method.[59] It is possible that Charlotte's etched copies of Dufrénoy's schematic plans, furnished with English captions and labels, contributed to the ease with which he had sought, if not precisely, to adopt Neilson's method, then at least to draw upon aspects of its utility.

Seeking publication of Charlotte's translation, at some time during the summer of 1835, the Guests approached the firm of John Murray to undertake the work. Rather more than a year later, advertisements for *On the use of hot air in the Ironworks of England and Scotland* [...] – a modest octavo, priced at 5s 6d began to appear in the London newspapers. To all appearances, the English text was anonymous, the title page stating only that the work was 'Translated from a report made to the director-general of mines in France, by M. Dufrénoy in 1834 [*sic*]' but not naming the translator. The entries in John Murray's ledgers were equally uninformative about the origin of the English version, referring to the work only as 'Hot Air (On the use of)', with a caret mark adding the scribbled note, 'By M. Dufrénoy'. The illustrations, however, carry clear marks of Lady Charlotte's involvement, recycling the engravings that had appeared in Dufrénoy's *Rapport*, which appear in mirror-image form with the initials 'C.E.G.' – Charlotte Elizabeth Guest – and the date when she made the etching beside each picture. The completed work included a number of observations – each designated 'Note by the Translator' – which, from their detailed knowledge of the ironworks and coal deposits of South Wales, were clearly the work of an industry insider. The remark, for instance, that before they introduced the hot blast, both Guest at Dowlais and Samuel Homfray of the Penydarren Ironworks, were using raw coal rather than coke to fuel their furnaces evinces considerable local knowledge.[60] Edgar Jones, incidentally, twentieth-century chronicler of the Dowlais Iron Company's successors Guest, Keen and Nettlefold, suggests that one of the reasons why the introduction of the hot blast technique may have been relatively slow in South Wales was that the availability of 'rich bituminous coals ... discouraged innovations designed to reduce fuel costs'.[61] Certainly the concluding 'Note by the Translator' not only gives a complete overview of the hot blast apparatus in use respectively at Dundivan in Scotland and Pentwyn, Clydach and Dowlais in Wales, but also appraises the efficiency of the system and the quality of the iron produced in each place. Dufrénoy includes no corresponding commentary and this state-of-the-art survey of British iron-manufacture offers an authoritative epilogue to the English version of his treatise.

Charlotte's role within the work did not for long remain a secret to the iron manufacturing *cognoscenti* among whom the book sparked considerable interest. On 1 October 1836, when it had been out for less than a month, John Wilson, co-proprietor of the Clyde Ironworks and member of the syndicate which held the patent rights to the Hot Blast process, came looking for her at Dowlais to request a copy. He was apparently 'anxious to see [it], as he did not understand French.'[62] Two months later, the *Cardiff and Merthyr Guardian* publicly and jubilantly identified her as the translator of *On the Use of Hot Air*, praising her disregard of all 'temptations to indolence' and 'frivolities of fashion', and applauding her ready devotion of 'time and talents to useful […] works by which mankind may be benefitted, and the interests of Science advanced.'[63]

If it yielded little financial return, the engagement with Dufrénoy's survey of British iron manufacture nevertheless had a significant outcome. It gave Charlotte a sense of vocation and helped to set the course of her future. Despite chafing about the demanding French and the amount of time taken up in translating it, she actually revelled in her new-found knowledge of iron smelting; furnaces, the apparatus used to heat the blast, not to mention that respective hot and cold 'make' produced at different British ironworks. Having gained some specialist knowledge of the subject she sought to learn more about it. John, who had been so dismissive of her curiosity about his political fortunes, marked her growing interest in the iron trade with pleasure and encouraged it. Happy and exhilarated, Charlotte related that she had 'undertaken the office of Merthyr's secretary, to write all his letters and keep them copied and arranged'.[64] It was, she decided, a 'beginning in earnest'.

Chapter Four

A Fortune for the Babies

At the end of May 1835 the Guests left Lincolnshire – their refuge from the South Wales cholera epidemic – for London and rented a house in smart Upper Grosvenor Street which was well-placed was for John's parliamentary business. The idea that she ought to make her mark upon London Society still carried much weight with Charlotte. For advice on the sensitive subject of how she and John might gain some footing in smart London circles, she approached her distant but well-connected relative, Lord Stuart de Rothesay. Rather than advise her himself, Lord Stuart de Rothesay promised to consult his wife.[1] It was not the response that Charlotte, who thought Lady Stuart de Rothesay 'cold', wished to hear. Nevertheless when she called in early in June, she found Lady Stuart de Rothesay unexpectedly gracious and ready to listen. She recommended that Charlotte apply for tickets to Almack's Assembly Rooms and that the Guests host a ball.[2]

Both diversions were a world away from translating Dufrénoy's learned discourse on Neilson's Hot Blast. Trying earnestly to follow Lady Stuart de Rothesay's counsel, Charlotte's inexperience showed. Had she been more familiar with the London calendar, she would have realised at once that since the season ended around mid-summer, June was rather late to start planning a Ball. In the event, Lady Stuart de Rothesay recognised her own mistake and advised the Guests to postpone it until later in the year.[3] For her Almack's tickets Charlotte applied to another relative, Lady Willoughby de Eresby, who was one of the patronesses charged with deciding who might be granted admission to the Assembly Rooms. Lady Willoughby de Eresby apparently gave her one ticket only and that, Charlotte complained, was 'for Ascot night when [...] nobody cares to be there'.[4] It is possible that, despite having attended Almack's Balls under her mother's chaperonage before her marriage, Charlotte failed to appreciate the full complexity of the arcane admission system, and confused tickets with vouchers. Possession of a voucher meant that the holder had satisfied one of the patronesses – they served, in effect, as dragons-in-the-gateway – of his or her credentials and could therefore purchase a Ball ticket. If it meant paying twice over, first for the voucher, and then for tickets, since attendance at an Almack's Ball even on an unfashionable evening promised a certain entrée into London Society at its most refined, people generally considered the money well spent. But Charlotte interpreted her single admission document as a straight snub to John. So, indeed, did the *Morning Post* which, reporting Charlotte's presence at Almack's, embarrassingly gave her name as 'Lady C Bertie'.[5]

Having offered Charlotte her help, Lady Stuart de Rothesay clearly had second thoughts. She called at Upper Grosvenor Street on 16 June and deftly extricated herself from every undertaking that she had previously made. Too 'delicate' to introduce Charlotte to her acquaintance, at a stroke she discouraged her from harbouring any thought of attending 'the good parties'; reneged on her previous pledge to introduce her to 'foreign Ambassadors', and declined any future invitation to dine with the Guests on the ground that she rarely went out, 'except to balls with her daughter'.[6] A mistress of the elegant put-down, all she would do on Charlotte's behalf was to distribute some of her calling cards 'to young men'. At the time, Charlotte, who had warmed to Lord Stuart de Rothesay, felt the barbs of this exchange with his wife too keenly to laugh them off. Years later, she came to recognise the shilly-shallying for what it was, namely a snide inference that by marrying an ironmaster, a 'tradesman', she had compromised her position within the social order. 'Though my husband,' she wrote in fury, 'is peculiarly formed to shine and rise, and is infinitely more eloquent than half the lordlings that I meet, and though my own rank is high enough to assist me, the consciousness frequently obtrudes itself that in this aristocratic nation the word Trade conveys a taint.' To her mind, it was arrant, mischievous nonsense. 'The children,' she vowed, 'shall never feel that there live any on earth who dare look down upon them.'[7]

But bad luck which owed nothing to Lady Stuart de Rothesay's snobbery would bedevil Charlotte's late June dinner party. Not only did the presence of her husband's enemy Lord Bute among the company make her 'very nervous', but at almost eight months pregnant, the warmth of the evening left her so unwell and uncomfortable that she had to abandon her visitors to recover herself in the garden. Pacing back and forth in the open air restored her spirits and she rejoined the ladies of the party just as the meal ended and they were settling into conversation in the drawing room. No sooner had she arrived than Mary-Anne Lewis launched into a story so risqué and malapropos that it silenced the gathering at a stroke. 'All the Mammas,' Charlotte remembered, 'looked grave & the young ladies blushed.'[8] Seeing her friends so discomfited, she felt herself redden with shame.

Fortunately escape was at hand. Although London physician Dr Lococke forbade her to take what he damningly described 'unnecessary journeys for [...] amusement only', she and John were prepared to take a flexible view of what constituted necessity. In the middle of July, they left London for Wales. It was their home after all and Charlotte wanted her second baby to be born there. When her mother and brothers tried to frighten her with the thought that she might be 'taken ill' – her euphemism for going into labour – on the way, she affected not to notice.[9]

Once more in Dowlais, far from resting or nesting, she determined to build upon all that she had learned from Dufrénoy to deepen her understanding of John's business. For a long-term project, she hit upon the idea of writing a history of the iron trade; more immediately, she decided to find out all that she could about steam engines. After all, since the works relied on steam for its power, it behoved her to understand something of its use and application. Her first instinct, predictably, was to consult likely books on the subject, but reading the fine detail of steam engineering theory left her so perplexed that she had to lie down on the sofa. John, when she told him about her efforts, offered to give her a tutorial. It was not entirely successful, probably because they did not begin until after ten o'clock in the evening, by which time both pupil and teacher were tired.[10] Reasoning that for an instructor, she really needed someone who had daily dealings with steam engines and understood their workings from a practical point of view, the following day she approached a Dowlais man named Josiah Rickards calling at his office in the works. 'I want him to try to explain to me the steam engine,' she reasoned, smarting from the recollection of John's late night lecture, 'which will, I fear, be almost too long a task for Merthyr's patience.'[11]

Mr Rickards may not have known what to make of her request, for he protested initially that he was either 'too busy' or 'too ill' to teach her anything.[12] But besides being the wife of the managing partner, by reason both of her habitual courtesy and her persistence, Charlotte was not an easy person to disregard. Eventually, having produced a plan of a cylinder and a piston, he gave her a lesson on the operation of steam power. Realising that it would benefit from practical illustration, he also showed her the motion of what she called 'the little punching engine' – presumably, the engine that embossed finished iron products with the maker's details – and analysed its workings. She described Mr Rickards's lecture as 'satisfactory', but the word hardly rings with enthusiasm.[13] Indeed, her interest in stationary steam engines, as opposed to locomotives, appears quickly to have waned. Later in the year, John gave her a copy of Charles Partington's *Historical and Descriptive Account of the Steam Engine* which she read on a carriage journey across the Midlands. Unimpressed, both by Partington's text and her husband's commentary upon its key points, in her journal she passed judgement with the single terse statement: 'It is not a book for which I have much respect.'[14]

Despite her family's forebodings, by late summer, Charlotte had still not given birth. Her trusted nurse Mrs Driscoll had to leave on 29 August and her replacement, Mrs Sackler, looked 'terrible […] as if she drank and swore'.[15] To Charlotte's chagrin, no sooner had Mrs Driscoll departed than the spasms of labour began.[16] John had a meeting to attend in Neath, but he never got there. His son and heir Ivor was born before eleven o'clock in the morning. Named after Welsh hero Ifor Bach ap Meurig of Morlais Castle, he was a quiet, easily contented baby whom Charlotte unconditionally adored.

John, at this time, was extremely busy. A conscientious MP, the day after Ivor's birth he had hastened to London for a crucial vote on the Municipal Corporation Bill. Meanwhile his acumen, aptitude for making useful contacts and flair for recruiting energetic, knowledgeable company agents made his works, trading either as the Dowlais Iron Company or Guest, Lewis & Co, supplier of choice to new railway companies both in Britain and overseas. By the mid-1830s, he was about to embark on a major infrastructure project of his own.

In common with the other Merthyr ironworks, historically Dowlais had relied on the Glamorganshire Canal for carriage of essential goods between Merthyr and the port of Cardiff. Promoted by Richard Crawshay of Cyfarthfa at the end of the eighteenth century, at the time of its planning, the canal promised to offer more efficient bulk transport than either the turnpike road, or the horse-drawn Merthyr Tramway. Over the 1790s it opened to traffic by stages to connect Merthyr Tydfil with the docks at Cardiff, by way of Abercynon, Pontypridd, Taff's Well, Tongwynlais and Llandaff. But it never entirely fulfilled its early promise, being much prone to leaks and stoppages. 'The breach in the canal has put out of our power to send you either the Potatoes or the blacking dust, unless it is by land,' wrote Thomas Vaughan of Pentyrch to Robert Thompson in 1794, 'and I cannot find any degree of certainty when it will be navigable again [....]'[17] 'I hear your canal has given way', observed ship-owner William Hood in a scathing letter to the Dowlais Works of 1817. 'This will be a great disappointment to us, as the cargo you have shipped per the *Diana* is so ill an assortment as to do us very little good.'[18] Often, it was short of water. In 1825, for instance, John received a tart rebuke from Thomas Reece, clerk to the Navigation Company, for sanctioning the despatch of many heavily laden vessels in high summer. 'I have observed several of your Boats aground,' Reece complained, adding that, 'when others pass they are very much injured [...] and some of our Sills are considerably damaged from the blows received by the overladen Boats.'[19] Yet despite its congestion, over-crowding and inadequate water, for years the Merthyr iron companies viewed the canal as an essential artery.

To compound its failings, the location of its Merthyr terminus, which was near Cyfarthfa, had never suited Dowlais. Plans to build a branch canal to the Dowlais works, which would have been a considerable challenge, proved short-lived, since Richard Crawshay apparently used his influence within the Canal Company to ensure that a scheme potentially beneficial to his chief competitor be abandoned at an early stage.[20] Seeing the nation's rail network expand, Dowlais, Penydarren and Plymouth, their collective patience with the Glamorganshire Canal Navigation Company wearing thin, mooted the possibility of building a railway between Merthyr and Cardiff. In October 1834 Anthony Hill, probably in association with John Guest, commissioned a preliminary survey from Isambard Kingdom

Brunel.[21] At the time, Brunel's association with the Great Western Railway was only just beginning; his shipbuilding career lay in the future, and work on his suspension bridge at Clifton had come to a halt following riots in Bristol surrounding the 1831 Reform Bill. Tellingly, Charlotte refers to him as 'Mr Brunel of the Thames Tunnel' – the venture in which he had collaborated with his father Marc. For the cost of proposed line's construction, he gave an initial estimate of £190,649, a figure which he soon revised upwards to £286,031, to allow for moderating the gradients, besides building mineral branches and shipping staithes.[22]

The birth of Ivor may well have spurred John's zeal for the project. On 12 October 1835, he chaired a meeting of coal owners and ironmasters in Merthyr Tydfil's Castle Inn. Having agreed that the Glamorganshire Canal was not fit for purpose, the attendees resolved to form a company to 'establish a communication' between Merthyr and the port of Cardiff by means of what was to be known as the 'Taff Vale Railway', and to petition parliament for its enabling legislation.[23] Anthony and Richard Hill of the Plymouth works, and William Thompson and William Forman of Penydarren joined John and Thomas Revel Guest and Edward Hutchins on the Committee, but William Crawshay of Cyfarthfa, prime shareholder in the canal, was conspicuously absent. Despite the Canal Company's fierce opposition, the Taff Vale Railway received its Act of Parliament on 21 June 1836, and construction began soon after.

For a remote line that did not connect with the fast-expanding national rail network, building the railway promised to be a sizeable undertaking. Over its 24¼ mile length, the mainline would cross the Taff near Quakers' Yard on a six-arch viaduct at Goitre Coed and the River Rhondda on a fine skewed arch stone bridge at Pontypridd. In its original form, it included tunnels near Quakers' Yard and at Ynyscoi, and an incline just north of Abercynon, to negotiate a gradient that was too steep for locomotives. The intention was that branches should connect the various ironworks and collieries with the main line.[24] Although the committee appointed Brunel as engineer in chief to the venture, he tended to leave decision making to his onsite deputies as he became busier with other schemes. Nevertheless, he recognised the constraint of building in the narrow and twisting Welsh valleys and made what, for him, was the unique decision to build the line to Stephenson gauge of

4ft 8½in, rather than the 7ft broad gauge which he generally preferred. John would chair the committee and Edward Hutchins served as its treasurer.

Perhaps John pushed his nephew into accepting the post with the idea of steadying him, for Edward's thinking at this time turned on several matters which had nothing to do with the Taff Vale Railway. He had, for instance, recently persuaded John to lend him £5,000 with which to purchase a share in the Blaina Ironworks.[25] He had also met 'a very wealthy heiress' named Anne Ross to whom, Charlotte observed, he had 'given his heart […] & perhaps a tiny bit of it to her fortune.'[26] To judge from the Blaina Iron Company's rather elegant cast iron viaduct in Exeter, they were an able firm who worked to high standards. Nevertheless, Charlotte considered Edward's association with the Blaina business ill-judged because, in her view, he lacked the necessary 'firmness and forethought' to wield any constructive influence with the other partners. At the same time, although it seems counter-intuitive, she reasoned that were he to be placed in a position of responsibility, the experience might well 'improve his character'.[27]

Miss Ross, meanwhile, who had 'not a relation or friend in the world', had asked Charlotte to present her at court. Touched after the rebuffs she had endured at the hands of Lady Stuart de Rothesay, Charlotte quickly befriended her, although she thought Miss Ross 'rather a spoilt child' who was prone to such 'indecorous' behaviour as asking Edward 'to walk with her' and 'receiving young men's visits'.[28] Ignorance of etiquette notwithstanding, Miss Ross's fortune was certainly eye-catching. At the end of February 1836, in a mildly bizarre development, Mr Pegus announced that he wished to meet Miss Ross on the grounds that 'she might suit Lindsey for a wife', and persuaded Charlotte to make the necessary introductions. Charlotte exculpated herself from actually brokering nuptials, with the terse observation that Anne was 'quite old enough to know her own mind'. In the event, Pegus opted to pursue 'far more splendid … matrimonial schemes' for Lindsey, in which Charlotte privately doubted that he would achieve anything approaching success, but her assessment of Anne's capacity for clear-thinking proved well-founded. Before long, Anne told Edward straight out that she could never love him.[29]

Soon afterwards, the Guests seem to have decided that it might be just as well to see her safely married and John's friend Edward Divett, Exeter MP and free-trade enthusiast, struck them as an ideal husband. Just as Mary-Anne Lewis had played match-maker between John and herself, so Charlotte invited Anne and Divett to dine and orchestrated opportunities for *conversazioni* so that they might discover how much they enjoyed one another's company. Her strategy worked surprisingly well. After a courtship almost as brief as the Guests' Edward Divett married Anne Ross in June 1836.

It was a cheering diversion in what, for Charlotte, was a bleak year. In the spring, John who hankered, perhaps more than she appreciated, after the life of a country gentleman, purchased Sully Manor which had become vacant on the death of Evan Thomas.[30] Her liking for the place was lukewarm at best, and she did not share his enthusiasm for treating it as a rural retreat-cum-shooting lodge. The Guests, with 20-month-old Maria and baby Ivor, spent Easter at Uffington where Charlotte gave way to overwhelming melancholy. Guest and John surmise that she may have suffered a recent miscarriage, which would certainly account for her depression.[31] Walking by herself through the parkland, Charlotte saw a clump of white violets which, in her imagination, 'seemed to rise up in judgement […] and rebuke.'[32] The flowers stirred some painful memory of Lindsey's hapless tutor who had once been so kind to her and she picked them, 'almost fearing to see poor Martin's shade'. Then, abrupt in her journal, she unaccountably addresses John straight out:-

> Merthyr! – You may destroy them if you are displeased at a burst of feeling – a state rarely experienced for one whom I know that I have deeply wronged.

What lies behind this cry from the heart is not clear, although Charlotte's loss of restraint and composure is so out of character as to be downright shocking. Then – 'Why do I write this?' she muses, as though seeking by sheer effort of will to recover her poise.

> I should not give way were I not very weak – I am Iron now, and my life is altered into one of action, not of sentiment –.

> Ambition is not my idol – but my plaything. I am ambitious because I have lived the last three years in excitement and require it still as a dream. I have youth and riches and rank and beauty – yes, even beauty. [...] I say it not in vanity, for I can laugh at the idea of it –. [...] I who was as <u>nothing</u>, and worse than nothing once, have now all these advantages – and is it not enough to make me ambitious? I have a restless, active mind and can I wonder that (when I have health withal) I am tempted to apply its powers to the acquisition of any object I may have in view.[33]

In this extraordinary passage she takes herself to task with a vengeance. Compared with the energy of her self-assertion, some the objectives that she proceeds to list for herself seem relatively small-scale. Predictably, they include 'Society', although her level of dedication to the pursuit of social success was prone to fluctuate. Then there is 'Getting Lindsey to go with the Whigs' - a mission which, in the light of Pegus's robust Tory views, she must have known to be doomed. But then, in a burst of magniloquence, she mentions '<u>amassing</u> such a fortune for the babies as to make them very well off hereafter'. Her fierce underlining reflects her fierce mood. 'Business,' she asserts, 'is everything – even pleasure is but a business, for balls and parties are only pleasant to me as contributing to one of my objects.[34]

The degree to which her tone and purpose are at odds with the submissiveness expected of women on the cusp of the Victorian era is apparent from an exchange that took place one evening at Dowlais when John's brother Thomas joined the Guests for dinner and the conversation turned into a debate about the merit of investing money in land. To reinforce one of her points, Charlotte turned to Thomas for support and, amused, he remarked that it 'was a subject on which <u>he</u> should never think of asking his wife's opinion.'[35] At the time, Charlotte laughed good-naturedly and professed to share his view that the subject was one on which 'no woman could be a competent judge'. Only in her journal did she admit that the male banter cut her to the quick, and a line of verse by Shakespeare's near contemporaries Francis Beaumont and John Fletcher, 'Since I can do no good because a woman', surfaced in her memory to torment her.[36] It is a statement which, by chance, George Eliot quotes in the opening chapter of

Middlemarch (1872) by way of introducing Dorothea Brooke, another (albeit fictional) Victorian woman who found her gender at odds with her aspirations. 'How deeply I have felt this inferiority of sex!' reflected Charlotte,

> And how I am humiliated when it is recalled to my mind in allusion to myself! Knowing that most wives are but looked upon as nurses and housekeepers (and very justly too) I have striven hard to place myself on a higher level – and dear Merthyr […] has always aided and encouraged me. I have given myself almost a man's education from the age of twelve when I first began to follow my own devices – and since I married I have taken up such pursuits as in this country of business & Iron making would render me conversant with what occupied the male part of the population. Sometimes I think I have succeeded pretty well, but every now and then I am painfully reminded that, toil as I may, I can never succeed beyond a certain point, and by a very large portion of the community my acquirements and judgements must always be looked down upon with contempt, as though of a mere woman.[37]

The sheer injustice of the circumstances – her circumstances, despite having a husband who knows her thinking, respects it and even allows 'that some women are rational beings' – beats hard upon her pulses. It is perhaps the time at which she comes closest to advancing a doctrine of feminism. But she stops short of questioning how far her bafflement and frustration is shared by women generally, and for all the resonance of her allusion to 'this inferiority of sex', she does not so much advocate any extension of female rights as voice her own private grievance. The tenacity of her focus on her own experience, implicit in her reiteration of the pronoun 'I' muddies the waters of her argument. It is unclear whether her prime purpose is to deplore the thinking which maintains that femininity is inconsistent with any form of worthwhile achievement, or whether it is to secure recognition of her own 'acquirements and judgements'.

Yet if Charlotte's business instincts were out of kilter with the climate of her own time, they chimed well with the spirit of the age in which John had grown up. It would be surprising if, in the course of their marriage, she did not absorb and espouse some of his opinions. In her bold talk about amassing a fortune for her babies, she envisages a role for herself which is not unlike that of an able, ambitious eighteenth-century woman, married to a man of commerce. In his 1726 publication *The Complete English Tradesman*, Daniel Defoe argued that a tradesman should 'let his wife into an acquaintance with his business, if she desires it and is fit for it', in order that she might learn 'such and so much' of his trade as 'may make her assisting and helpful to him'.[38] As he was quick to explain, this arrangement had the solid, practical advantage of equipping the wife 'to keep up the business for herself and children, if her husband should be taken away'. While it is doubtful that either Guest had ever read *Defoe's Complete English Tradesman*, John was, by birth, an eighteenth-century man with expectations to match. It was his good fortune that Charlotte, loving and clever, was happy to keep the books, write the letters and maintain the 'works journal' for his business. Since it played to her organisational strengths, the work suited her well. It also made her privy to John's commercial thinking, which served to heighten her own determination to provide lavishly for her children's future.

But Charlotte did not always find business so congenial. Early in the Autumn of 1836, John took her to Cornwall. It should have been a delight, since she yearned to see the legendary birthplace of King Arthur, to which, at the time of their wedding, he had promised to take her. He seems optimistically to have thought that this trip, during which he intended to do some intensive research into mine pumping engines, fulfilled his side of the agreement.

The Guests set out on 9 September. On their way to the Swansea Ferry, they called briefly at the Neath Abbey Ironworks, which rather suggests that John wished to ask Joseph Tregelles Price, the managing director, for directions to the Cornish mines which used pumping engines built at Neath Abbey. Even before their departure from Dowlais, Charlotte had complained about not feeling 'strong enough for the undertaking', adding fretfully that John was always ill when he travelled alone and that if she did not go with him, he would have no one 'to prevent his over-fatiguing himself'.[39]

Having stayed overnight at Swansea, they caught the 5am ferry. Charlotte thought sea-crossing vile – 'the very worst part of the journey' – and to compound her wretchedness, Ilfracombe, where they disembarked, turned out to be 'not such a pretty place' as she had anticipated.[40] Exhausted after the early start, she went to sleep in the carriage that took them from Barnstaple to Bideford and missed all sight of the Devon countryside. The Bideford inn where they had planned to break their journey looked so uninviting that they went on all the way to Holsworthy. The steep wooded banks of the river Torridge put her briefly in mind of Welsh river valleys, but while John got out to examine the inclined planes by which wheeled tub-boats negotiated the different levels of the Bude Canal, she felt 'too tired' to join him.[41]

Having made their way south west towards Truro, they called at the 'Consolidated Copper Mine', – probably Great Consols at Gwennap near Carharrack – where John made straight for the pumping engine. Trying to be cheerful, Charlotte reported that it was 'beautifully finished and kept in a bright state'.[42] It was also economical, using no more than three tons of coal a day, which John took to be a very modest amount. From Carharrack, they drove through Cornwall's mining hinterland to Redruth, where Charlotte, who was again 'very tired,' thought they should have stayed. In fact, the next day they travelled on to Falmouth to admire Pendennis Castle before returning to Truro to attend a Ball. Exhausted, she made no secret of her disappointment at not having visited Tintagel – 'Except St Michael's [Mount] it was the only place in Cornwall I cared about' she wrote – while resigning herself to a bleak drive though the lead- and iron-mining district around Perranzabuloe. John had an appointment with Redruth engineer William Sims – sometime associate of Richard Trevithick – who showed the Guests the engines in use at the Charlestown tin mines near St Austell and Charlotte once again noted their economical fuel consumption, and described the lagging of the boilers and cylinders.[43]

For John, the Cornish visit was highly satisfactory. Not only had he taken the opportunity to view some state-of-the-art steam engines at work at close range, but he also managed to recruit a skilled engine man, Samuel Truran of Chacewater, to join his staff. Truran moved to Dowlais with his family in 1837, and in time became the Dowlais Iron Company's chief mechanical engineer.[44]

If Charlotte found it less rewarding, once she was at home again, her old energy flooded back. She resumed her study of the Welsh language and by early November, had begun to translate *Hanes Cymru* – literally, Welsh History – by which she probably means Rev. Thomas Price's compendious *Hanes Cymru a Chenedl y Cymry O'r Cynoesoedd hyd at Farwolaeth Llywelyn ap Gruffydd* [*Welsh History and the Ancient Welsh Nation up to the Death of Llywelyn ap Gruffydd*].[45] She also took advantage of her role of 'confidential secretary' to her husband to appraise his competitors. 'Mr Anthony Hill,' she decided,

> is a gentleman. Mr Bailey has a low-born purse-proud cunning. Mr Thompson is the Alderman in every sense and has not the uprightness which I should have been inclined to give most city merchants credit for. The Harfords are Quakers of rather an American stamp. Mr Crawshay is beyond all rule and description and quite one of those meteoric beings whom it is impossible to account for.[46]

Anthony Hill, whose family had managed the Plymouth Works over many generations, was held in high respect throughout the district.[47] The reputation for guile that she ascribes to Crawshay Bailey of Nant-y-glo may have owed something to his purchasing large areas of land in the Rhondda Valley and surrounding areas at its relatively low agricultural value, ready to exploit the valuable coal which lay below its surface.[48] William Thompson who acquired the Penydarren Works through his marriage to Amelia Homfray, served as an Alderman of the City of London from 1821 until his death in 1854.[49] The Harford family, of Ebbw Vale and Sirhowy, came originally from Bristol. They were indeed Quakers, although it is not clear quite what Charlotte means by her reference to their 'American stamp'.[50] In the eighteenth century, Yorkshireman Richard Crawshay had, stage by stage, assumed control of the Cyfarthfa Iron Works. By 1836, it was under the control of his grandson, William Crawshay II – the Crawshay whose actions had helped precipitate the Merthyr Rising, which may account for Charlotte's description of him. He built not only the grandiose Cyfarthfa Castle, but also a fine house at Caversham Park near Reading.[51]

*

At Dowlais House, the Guests by contrast lived on the very margin of the Works, which was at times altogether too close for comfort. Dressing on a November morning in 1836, Charlotte felt the house tremble. Puzzled – it reminded her of what she had read about earthquakes – as she continued dressing, she thought that 'something – not perhaps very awful – must have happened at the works'.[52] Hearing the windows rattle, she supposed that Ivor, by now, over a year old, was deliberately shaking the bars. Then there was a vast explosion and the sound of escaping steam; at once she realised that a boiler had burst. Running from the room as the house shook she heard the sound of falling masonry. John, who had come to look for her, was in the passage outside and appalled, they realised that neither of them knew what had happened to toddler Maria. Charlotte thought she had been downstairs eating breakfast with John while, in the stress of the moment, he could not remember what he had done with her, or whether she had been with him at all. After a moment of numb shock, they found Maria safe with the housekeeper, neither hurt nor unduly frightened.

Outside, a crowd surged across the Guests' garden. Everyone who had relatives at the works was anxious for their safety. John, who had planned to go Blaina on some mission of Edward's, stayed to survey the damage, establish the accident's cause, reckon up the losses, and, above all, comfort the survivors. Charlotte, meanwhile, reflecting how much more worried she would have been if the explosion had occurred when he was at the works rather than at home, tried to compose herself and to work out what had happened. She identified the boiler which had exploded as 'the centre one of the New Forge Engine', which was situated 'very close to the House'. Caught in the blast, the boiler stack crashed down from its 120ft height, breaking all the Guests' windows, and killing a man and a boy as it fell. Inside, the house was 'strewn with bricks, cinders and broken glass'. To her surprise and consternation, Charlotte later found a brick in her bed and a piece of iron 'weighing several pounds' embedded in an internal wall. Apparently it had passed straight between two servants who had been talking in the first-floor corridor.

The *Cardiff and Merthyr Guardian* published an account of the disaster, complete with a full description of the boiler. A new installation, it was apparently 42ft long and 6ft in diameter. Despite its weighing 18 tons and being set in solid masonry, the sheer violence of the blast had blown it clean off its foundation. It came to rest some ten yards away, at right-angles to its original position. The explosion also destroyed the stack; observers marked how it rose from its base, seemed to pause, 'as if poised' in the air before crashing across the Guests' lawn.[53] A large piece of masonry hit a house nearby, home to seven people. Somehow the man who had been sleeping in the room on which it fell escaped injury but the other inhabitants were less fortunate. John Howe the fireman and the boys, David Thomas and John Jones, all lost their lives, while 'the wife of Daniel James, founder', was badly hurt. As for the buildings, besides the broken windows of Dowlais House, the New Forge was blown to smithereens – 'damage' which the *Merthyr Guardian* estimated at not less than £1,000, 'without taking into account the loss occasioned by the suspension of the works'.

At the inquest, the jury returned a verdict of accidental death upon the deceased, and the coroner explicitly ruled out any question of culpability on the part of John Watt, the Dowlais Company's chief engineer. Watt linked the cause of the explosion to the rupture of a boiler-plate immediately over the fire. The Dowlais Company's decision in 1838 to name a new plateway locomotive 'John Watt' may well reflect the esteem in which John Guest held his colleague.[54] Another outcome of the explosion was the invention by Dowlais man Adrian Stephens, with John's encouragement, of a steam whistle designed to sound as an alarm when the water in a boiler dropped below a safe level.[55]

The Guests spent Christmas of 1836 at Uffington. For much of Christmas Day Charlotte lay on the sofa, her head against John's fond shoulder, although she rallied when her Layard cousins called in the afternoon. It should have been the start of a double celebration, both of the season and of Bertie's twenty-first birthday which fell on 26 December, but events did not go according to plan. Dressing for dinner, Lindsey inadvertently set his shirt on fire which put paid to the festivities at a stroke. 'It was,' wrote Charlotte, 'the most dreadful shrieks I ever heard.'[56] Pegus, in an act of true heroism, defied all danger to put out the flames with his bare hands and saved his stepson's life.

As the turn of the year approached, Charlotte grew thoughtful. She had every reason to face the future with optimism. The new year,

1837, would bring her twenty-fifth birthday. She had given birth to two children, including an heir, and a third was imminent. *On the Use of Hot Air* had attained some success in ironmaking circles, which was, by any reckoning, an achievement. Above all, over their three happy years of marriage, John and she had developed an intuitive understanding of one another which deepened their mutual love.

Chapter Five

Birth, Death, Inheritance and the Electors of Glamorgan

Having shown such courage on Christmas Day, as soon as the New Year got under way, Pegus turned disagreeable. Charlotte did not go into detail about his behaviour, except to say that he was 'uncivil' to her and that she 'dreaded the idea of being confined at Uffington'.[1] Since iron business called John back to Dowlais, although it meant leaving her mother just when Lady Lindsey's care might have been welcome, she decided to return with him to Wales, taking the children with her. They had a trying journey, with snow on the ground as far as Leicester. Then John fell ill and as soon as they reached Birmingham, they had to find a doctor for him. Worried, Charlotte slept little throughout the four days of travel.

On reaching home, the previous two months' ironworks correspondence awaited her, needing to be copied and filed. Soon, bitter mid-winter cold gave way to rain, which brought illness in its wake. The servants caught diseases; John fretted with a heavy cold and, adding to the gloom, his brother Thomas, who was away in Dublin helping friends whose business had failed, wrote to say that he had contracted influenza.[2] On 27 January, in a burst of vim, Charlotte went out for a short, cold walk before persevering with her translation of Price's historical *magnum opus*. All too soon, her energy left her; the following day she felt 'unwell' and guessed that she was about to go into labour; sure enough, Katharine, 'a nice fat baby', was born in the middle of the afternoon.[3] Wanting her to have a distinctively Welsh second name, her parents tossed a coin to decide between Gwladys and Tydfil. It fell to Gwladys, which Charlotte considered 'one of the prettiest Welsh appellations'.[4] In practice, the child came to be known as Cattws.

Thomas's correspondence from Ireland suggested that he had resigned himself to a prolonged bout of ill-health, until, in a change of tone, he wrote begging his wife and sister-in-law to come out to Dublin without delay. Although they set off the day after his letter had reached them, Charlotte, absorbed by her new baby and trying to write birthday verses for John, failed to recognise the urgency of the situation. News of Thomas's death reached the Guests, shockingly, on 2 February 1837, John's birthday. 'He had hardly been ill a week', wrote Charlotte, stricken. 'For my own part, I can only say that, except my husband, I feel that I have lost my only friend.'[5]

Her warmth towards Thomas Revel Guest is both striking and surprising, since he had a reputation for being a killjoy whose presence 'was sufficient to stifle any and every frivolity'.[6] But Thomas was a man of mystery. To all appearance, he was an active, versatile businessman. Employed as the Dowlais Iron Company's agent in Ireland, in 1820 he married Anne, the daughter of Thomas 'Governor' Biggs, who owned a textile mill in Bandon, and the couple settled in the city of Cork.[7] Five years later, in 1825, Thomas announced that he had 'retired from the Iron Trade' and expressed his thanks to his Irish friends.[8] Although it may have sounded like a farewell, he was still in Cork in 1827, selling 'Newfoundland Cod Fish and Prime Scotch Herrings' from premises in Half-Moon Street.[9] A year later, his stock-in-trade had expanded to include 'Scotch Crown Window Glass and Bottles'.[10] By the early 1830s, he was back in Wales, active within the Wesleyan Methodist Society, and campaigning for the introduction of gas lighting throughout Merthyr Tydfil, both in the streets of the town and in its Works.[11] Possessed of a keen sense of public duty, besides being a director of the Taff Vale Railway, Thomas was a trustee of the Glamorgan Infirmary; a Cardiff alderman and, to crown a civic life of distinction, in 1836 he became the town's first elected mayor. To attain such honorifics suggests that Thomas, for all his earnestness, did not lack the ability to make himself agreeable and Charlotte clearly recognised his more amiable aspect.

But Thomas's will revealed that, behind his business dealings and service to the community, his life had taken some hidden twists. Although he left the bulk of his property to his childless wife Anne, he also made provision for a 'reputed' son and daughter, known variously as Thomas and Sarah Guest or Thomas and Sarah Johnson. For the boy's support, he put aside the large sum of £200,000 to be invested and the interest applied for his maintenance and training as a surgeon and apothecary. Provided that young Thomas qualified to practice, he was to receive the

capital on attaining the age of 24; if he failed to qualify or refused to
enter the surgical profession, he would be entitled only to the modest
sum of £1,000.[12] Thomas Revel Johnson (c.1817–63) for the record,
played his alleged father at his own guileful game. Having qualified as a
surgeon and apothecary at Dublin University, he promptly sailed out to
Australia where he not only became a highly successful journalist, but
in time, and presumably with the benefit of his inheritance, established
a popular New South Wales newspaper – *Bell's Life in Sydney and
Sporting Reviewer*.[13] It suggests that journalism had probably been his
career of choice all along. For Sarah, Thomas imposed fewer conditions;
she would receive the capital sum of £2,000 on reaching the age of
24, unless by that time she were married, in which case he directed his
trustees to settle upon her and her children both the interest and principal
of her legacy, giving her husband a life interest in the money, if they saw
fit. Being his brother's trustee and executor, John must have registered
the Johnson siblings' existence. Actuated both by loyalty to his dead
brother and concern not to undermine Charlotte's regard for him, he may
have preferred to tell her nothing whatever about them.

Thomas's death had another strange sequel. Wishing to preserve
some 'bond of connection' with Thomas's widow Anne, Charlotte asked
her to 'stand sponsor' to baby Cattws at her christening, only for Anne
to decline flat. Her ostensibly pious reasoning was that since she was
going to move back to Bandon in Co. Cork, she would not be able to
fulfil the sponsor's obligation of ensuring that the child be brought up to
lead a Christian life. But these scruples bordered on bigotry. If Thomas's
widow genuinely wished to sever all contact with the Guests, it raises
uncomfortable questions about her marriage. None of Cattws's other
sponsors – Bertie, Mary Pegus and Charlotte's friend and namesake
Lady Carbery, born Catherine Charlotte Evans-Freke – lived nearby and
none of them attended the baptism. It took place in the course of a bleak,
sad service with solemn hymns, a 'funeral sermon on poor Thomas'
and all the congregation dressed in mourning. Distressed at the sight of
Maria and Ivor in their diminutive black garb, Charlotte somehow held
back her tears. The men observed no such restraint; John openly wept
while Edward Hutchins 'sobbed violently'.[14]

Edward inherited one half of Thomas's sixteenth-part share in the Dowlais
Works. The implications for his future within the business caused

Charlotte some anxiety. Although she thought him 'good-hearted', she observed that he was prone to 'careless thoughtlessness', which sounds like habitually slipshod working practice combined with an inability to foresee difficulties before they arose.[15] Unchecked, it could be a source of much future trouble for John, as managing partner. Knowing that if he were to become a partner in the Dowlais Iron Company it would preclude him from retaining an interest in 'any other Iron Work in South Wales', Edward was already taking steps to extricate himself from Blaina. 'He would never have done any good there', mused Charlotte, trying to take a pragmatic view of his conduct, although she could not help adding that his departure would be 'a great blow' to Blaina proprietor Thomas Brown.[16]

She was not the only person to view his increased involvement in the Dowlais works – specifically, the possibility of his actually becoming a partner – with misgivings. Towards the end of April, Wyndham Lewis and his brother William called on John to debate the matter in frank terms. The key issue was how the existing partners were to interpret Edward's new status in the light of Thomas's bequest. Charlotte was probably not party to their discussion, but discussed it with John afterwards. 'Although Edward has half the residue of his uncle's property,' she noted, 'it is in doubt whether he could have one of his shares and thus become a partner.' Although the existing partners could not dictate what Edward was to do with his property, the Lewises, at any rate, had considerable objection to making any concession which would increase his importance in the business. Thinking the matter over, Charlotte sought to take the long view. 'As long as my darling Merthyr continues to manage,' she wrote,

> all would go well (though the influence of Edward's carelessness would in some degree be pernicious to the agents, etc) but when the time comes that Merthyr is no longer at the helm, I fear exceedingly all the evil that his [Edward's] rashness and inexperience may entail – and to my babies it may be a very serious matter.[17]

For the time being, the question of his future hung, unresolved, in the balance, but it weighed so heavily with the partners that eventually Wyndham Lewis, who wanted an intermediary, asked Charlotte to broach the subject with Edward directly.[18]

At the time of their meeting, Edward said he was 'very low' and apparently his doctors had advised him to take a sea voyage for his health; he planned to visit America, albeit without much enthusiasm. Perhaps he angled rather too obviously for Charlotte's sympathies for, mindful of Lewis, she told him that before he left the country it was crucial to establish precisely what his future position was to be within the Iron Company. Her journal at this point is neither easy to read nor to understand. She writes,

> The result of what I gathered from him [i.e., Edward] was, that he had no claim to be a partner as long as Merthyr lived and managed everything, and he might still be consulted after that period if he liked his Exc. [Executors?] but if not, he should endeavour to gain admittance to the concern.

Her gist appears to be that Edward, floundering in the face of her demand, professed no wish to be a partner while John was alive, but might reconsider his view if the circumstances changed.[19] Privately, Charlotte considered that in the event of her husband's demise, Edward's 'admittance to the concern' would be fatal, but she bracingly assured him that the chance of any misfortune's befalling John was so remote that it did not bear thinking about.[20] Gloomily, Edward informed her that if any disaster were to befall him at sea, she should be aware that he had named John as his sole executor.

In the early hours of 20 June 1837, King William IV died at Windsor. The next day, the Guests hastened to St James Street near Buckingham Palace for a glimpse of the new monarch, Queen Victoria.[21] Her accession, incidentally, would require John to make a wholesale amendment of his Dowlais Market Bill which – having recently passed through the House of Lords – had now to have all reference to the late king expunged and, more particularly, all the regal-personal pronouns altered.[22] Drastic document revisions aside, the Guests prepared to return to Wales in short order. Death of the monarch meant dispatch of sovereignty and the royal prerogative down the line of succession. At the time, it resulted in the dissolution of parliament and the need to hold a general election.[23] Not surprisingly, Wyndham Lewis encouraged John to 'go and see his constituents.'[24]

For reasons which are not wholly clear, in 1837 John allowed himself to be persuaded to stand both for re-election in Merthyr Tydfil, and as a prospective parliamentary candidate for the County of Glamorgan. He made his agreement conditional upon the understanding that, should he be returned as Glamorganshire's MP, another candidate would be found for the borough.[25]

After the 1832 Reforms, Glamorganshire had returned two members. One of them, Christopher Rice Mansel Talbot, was a local landowner who intended to stand for re-election; the other, Swansea based porcelain manufacturer Lewis Weston Dillwyn, preferred to stand down. It suggests that John's decision to contest the county seat may have sprung from a wish to ensure that the county's growing industrial interest should have parliamentary representation. His rival for the seat that Dillwyn was about to vacate, was the resplendently named Edwin Richard Windham Wyndham-Quin, better known by his Irish title of Viscount Adare. A member of organisations as diverse as the Royal Geographical Society, the Royal Archaeological Society and the Society for the Preservation of the Melodies of Ireland, although clearly a man of wide interests, Adare was assuredly no industrialist.[26] Born at Dunraven Castle on the Glamorgan coast, he had spent a certain amount of his adult life in Dublin, both as an undergraduate at Trinity College and later, to study astronomy at the Dublin Observatory under Sir William Rowan-Hamilton. If he lacked John's experience, his title and background nonetheless appealed to the county landowners.

For John to contest the county seat with Lord Adare was a considerable step for him to take. Admittedly in political terms, Adare was a relative novice, a point on which the Whig press made much, decrying him as the 'Tory pet' and seizing on his 'frightful [...] ignorance on political matters.'[27] At the same time, the electorate of rural Glamorganshire had radically different concerns and priorities from the voters of industrial Merthyr Tydfil. The *Cardiff and Merthyr Guardian*, always apt to take a cynical view of John's politics, could hardly believe it. In mocking incredulity it reported that the Mayor of Swansea had actually invited 'Mr Guest, *risum teneatis* [can you contain your laughter?] to stand for the cinder tips – we beg pardon – the county.'[28] Making fun of her husband and disparaging his hard-working town was exactly the sort of snobbery guaranteed to catch Charlotte on the raw. Whether she specifically asked John to take her canvassing with him, or whether he judged that her presence would lend a piquant, memorable note to his campaign is unclear, but she was certainly there at his side. After all, her aristocratic credentials were at least as venerable as Lord Adare's, and she had a keen eye and a ready memory, both of which could be useful.

Electioneering in the county, as the Guests soon learned, differed vastly from campaigning in Merthyr. Despite the thrust of the 1832 Reform Act, in rural Glamorganshire, landowners still held sway. When John and Charlotte went to meet the voters of Caerphilly they arrived in time for the annual Fair. It soon emerged that John had misjudged his date. While the *Cardiff and Merthyr Guardian* reported 'a very successful canvass by Lord Adare', on the subject of his Liberal rival, it was scathing; 'Mr Guest also canvassed,' it announced, 'but he had neither the smiles of the fair nor fair promises.' Not only was a parliamentarian who favoured repeal of the Corn Laws – protectionist legislation designed to subsidise the rural economy and keep out cheap, imported foreign wheat – unlikely to receive a warm reception at a farmers' annual junket, but John's failure to oppose the New Poor Law also stood against him. 'Will you support those who would do away with the Corn Laws, and so bring you to poverty?' demanded a correspondent to the paper. 'Will you be persuaded to give your votes to those who are for dividing the husband from the wife, the parents from their children? [...] Will you be smuggled out of your senses by the hacknied word Reform?'[29]

The letter writer touched a popular nerve. John would soon become a butt for teasing throughout the agricultural part of the county. 'What business has Guest, so obtrusive and rude,' ran one verse,

> Among the staunch friends of Adare to intrude?
> Send him back to his furnace, or else he will find
> A furnace here heated not quite to his mind.[30]

'Glamorgan's welcome dost thou boast?' quipped another,

> We'll put it to the test.
> Thou reckonest without thy host,
> Thou most unwelcome Guest.'[31]

*

Although the 'unwelcome Guest' gibe became a recurring motif of the campaign, Charlotte remained stalwartly confident of her husband's success. Tuesday 18 July found them in Bridgend, at the heart of Adare territory. 'We had, considering all things, a great many promises and there was a good deal of enthusiasm in our favour', she recalled. Apparently, the townspeople wanted to unhitch the Guests' horses and draw their carriage through the streets – a flattering tribute which John forbade.[32] But not everyone remembered the Guests' reception as being quite as enthusiastic as she made out. 'The canvassing party,' reported one correspondent to the *Cardiff and Merthyr Guardian*, 'consisted of the *would-be* new county member and the Lady Charlotte', together with a few clergy, one of them 'under ecclesiastical censure'; a 'radical lawyer' and 'about 20 ragged urchins'. The candidate's solicitation of Bridgend's votes apparently met 'with an audible but unequivocal negative'. To add insult to injury, on the same day that it printed this disparaging letter, the *Cardiff and Merthyr Guardian* also gave a list of 'Lord Adare's supporters', which ran to rather more than a column of close-set type.[33] In Neath, where John canvassed on Wednesday 19 July, the same paper described him as being surrounded not by eager adherents, but 'men … anxious to obtain drink', who disappeared as soon as they realised that none was forthcoming. By chance, Lord Adare was in Dowlais on the same day. If Charlotte is to be believed, no sooner did he hear cries of 'Guest forever!' than he panicked and made the local constables escort him to safety without having secured the promise of a single vote.[34]

The profound tension between protectionist landowners on the one hand and the free-trade manufacturers on the other characterised the entire campaign. One aggrieved letter-writer in the *Cardiff and Merthyr Guardian* took exception to John's statement, made apparently at a meeting in Cardiff, that the South Walians were 'a manufacturing and not an agricultural people'.[35] Professing himself to be 'a Whig of the Old School', the correspondent remarked, in gleeful horror, that John wished to open the universities to 'Dissenters, Papists, Jews, Turks, Infidels and Mahommetans'; maintained that the revenue of the church was 'public property' which could usefully go towards paying off the National Debt; favoured the expulsion of the bishops from the House of Lords and, a piece of great effrontery in the year of the new queen's accession, eagerly anticipated Britain's becoming a republic 'like […] America'.

Wild as they were, these allegations probably held some truth. John's approach to religion was heterodox insofar as he attended both church and chapel, and included both Anglican clergy like Evan Jenkins, and spiritual mavericks like neo-Druid, future Chartist and pioneer of the Co-operative movement, William Price of Llantrisant among his friends.[36] Perhaps he was ahead of his time in recognising the wisdom of abolishing the requirement that holders of public office and members of the universities subscribe to the thirty-nine articles of the Church of England. At the same time, he took good care to ensure that his own sons should be brought up as Anglicans and therefore eligible to matriculate within the University of Cambridge. Nevertheless, his opposition to the Corn Laws was implacable. When Sir John Tyrell, MP for the agricultural constituency of North Essex, protested in 1836 that the landed interest was not sufficiently protected by tariffs in the region of 25–50 per cent, John gave him a scathing answer. 'The price of iron,' he said,

> was at this time about 9l. per ton, and as the duty on importation was 1l. 10s., the protection was about, fifteen per cent., with which he begged to contrast the duty upon a few articles of agricultural produce. The duty on hops imported was 8l. 11s. per cwt. equal to 200 per cent. at least; on the importation of potatoes (one of the great necessaries of life,) 2s. per cwt. or about 100 per cent.; on the article of bacon 28s. per cwt., or about sixty per cent; and, in addition, the important articles of beef, mutton, and pork, were entirely prohibited. He further begged to assure the hon. Member, that if he would consent to fix a fair and equitable duty on the importation of corn, for himself he would say, and he thought that he spoke the sentiments of a large portion of the iron-trade, that they wanted only free trade without any protecting duty whatever on the importation of iron.[37]

His gist was that the iron trade would readily give up the limited protection which it enjoyed, if only Tyrrell and his farmer friends would loosen their grip upon the legislation which privileged them at the expense of the poor.

It was a stance which the Glamorgan landowners utterly reviled. John came third in the county, trailing behind both Adare and Talbot.

Charlotte, who made herself a nosegay of oak and laurel leaves to wear on the day of the poll, had to endure the embarrassment of discovering that the Tory Talbot had adopted the same leaves as his victory emblem. Overcome, she ripped her posy apart, vowing that she would never 'wear colours again'.[38] At least in Merthyr Tydfil, her husband had been unopposed – a detail which led the *Merthyr Guardian* to complain that 'if this wretched borough is not disfranchised, its continuance will be fraud upon the Reform Bill'.[39]

Having made herself accommodating throughout John's canvass, in mid-August, Charlotte undertook one of the ceremonial tasks which often fell to the wives of railway company chairmen, namely to lay the first stone of the Taff Vale line. Directors, overseers, workmen and interested public gathered at the site of the Rhondda Bridge in Pontypridd to watch the festivities. Presented with a minute, ornamental trowel, Charlotte made the best possible fist of things by making graceful play of laying the mortar. But given a diminutive hammer with which to set the stone in place, she 'rebelled outright' at the rank absurdity of the thing. Seizing a labourer's mallet, she swung it against the block with all her strength to hit it home.[40] Reporting the incident, the *Merthyr Guardian*, treated it as a great joke and remarked that she had carried out her duties in a 'very work*man*like manner'.[41] But jokes often mask emotions which arise at inappropriate moments. In the light of her remarks about the patronising 'contempt' which so often greeted 'women's acquirements and judgements', it is tempting to think that Charlotte's private frustration held its own eloquence.

The Guests' friend Charles Babbage, mentor of mathematician Ada Lovelace, inventor of the 'Difference Engine' – a precursor of the computer – was keen to encourage women to attend the lectures of the British Association for the Advancement of Science. A few weeks after the stone-laying ceremony, Charlotte accompanied John to Liverpool for their 1837 Meeting. Mindful that Guest, Lewis & Co had supplied the Grand Junction Railway Company with an immense amount of iron rail, Charlotte was careful to note and appraise the quality of travel that the new route from Birmingham to Liverpool offered. She made a somewhat guarded reference to the rough track, but admired its sheer scope and speed of construction.[42] In the course of the conference John attended a lecture 'On the Difference between the Composition of Cast

Iron produced by the cold and hot blast' given by Thomas Thomson, Glasgow University Professor of Chemistry, and gave it his keenest attention.[43] Feeling the demands of the railway builders upon his pulses, at the end, he raised some vigorous questions which show just how far the merits respectively of the hot and cold blast continued to preoccupy him. He wished, for instance, to know what attempts there had been to ascertain the amount of iron lost by weight in the course of converting respectively hot and cold pigs to bars. Probed by Michael Faraday who chaired this part of the conference, he disclosed that at Dowlais he was 'in the habit of smelting three hundred tons a week of hot blast iron [and] he had nine furnaces at work with cold blasts'. In the course of production, he had observed that a rather greater proportion of hot blast iron was lost in the process of converting it into malleable form – that is to say, into bars – than of cold blast iron. He had the strong sense that 'the character' of the hot blast iron was inferior to that of the cold, the increased temperature giving rise to 'silver and alumination [*sic*] which was prejudicial to the iron.' In answer to Faraday's questions he also revealed that he had discovered that rapid cooling 'produced white iron of as good a quality as possible'.[44]

Charlotte, meanwhile, attended a lecture-cum-demonstration by the engineer William Fairbairn (1789–1874) which broadly addressed the same subject – namely the differences in strength of iron made respectively by the hot and cold blast method.[45] It promised to play straight to her interest in the subject, which the experience of translating *Sur L'emploi de L'Air Chaud* had so recently nurtured. Fairbairn described a series of experiments on thirty-nine different samples of British cast iron. They had initially involved suspending a weight from the middle point of a square inch bar of each type of iron which rested horizontally on supports four feet and six inches apart. The weight was gradually increased until the bar broke. Fairbairn noted the bar's 'deflection and elasticity [...] at the different stages of loading', examining first, whether any 'appreciable weakening' of the metal occurred if the loading was continued over a prolonged period and second, whether changes of temperature made any difference to the strength of the iron.[46] In practice, despite blandly describing the lecture as 'interesting', Charlotte appears to have found it less than stimulating. It disappointed her to discover that although Fairbairn discussed the properties of iron produced in Scotland and Yorkshire at some length, he barely mentioned South Wales. A habitual hoarder of useful information, she recorded his conclusion that 'Hot Blast iron made in Scotland' – perhaps she means from Scottish ore – 'seemed generally to be the strongest', while 'in England … the result was just the reverse', but added that the lecture had elicited 'nothing very new or striking'.[47]

Yet her curiosity concerning the history of iron manufacture remained keen. The following November, she accompanied John to another talk on the subject, presented this time by Arthur Aikin (1753–1854) at the Royal Society of Arts.[48] A chemist, botanist, metallurgist and founding member of the Geological Society, the fact that Aikin had travelled extensively in Wales and published an account of his visit made it unlikely that he should fall into Fairbairn's error of side-lining the Welsh contribution to the iron industry.[49] To Charlotte's surprise – and perhaps that of his RSA audience – he chose in his discussion to focus upon 'antiquarian researches among Hebrew, Greek, etc.', in other words, iron usage in the ancient world. Her chief concern, when the lecture ended, was that her projected history of iron manufacture would add nothing to Aikin's research. Besides, practical matters claimed much of her attention. Only a few days before the RSA event, she recorded that Dowlais agent Mr Davis had just accepted an order for '1000 Tons of Rails for America T pattern, mixed iron @ £10 17s 6d', to be delivered to Liverpool in four months' time.[50] At the same time, the likeliest explanation of why her projected 'History of the Iron Trade' fell by the wayside was its eclipse by the *Mabinogion* upon which she would begin working early in 1838. But Harry Scrivenor, ironmaster of Blaenavon, covered the ground which she had relinquished and his *Comprehensive History of the Iron Trade throughout the World from the earliest records to the present period* appeared in 1841.[51]

Mindful of his brother's early and sudden death, John could not help but reflect upon his own mortality. With the election resolved, he began to think about 'weaning himself […] from Dowlais'.[52] He was now 52 years old and in ten years' time, the works' lease would expire. Meanwhile, vast number of competing firms had grown up in the vicinity of Merthyr Tydfil and were, in Charlotte's words, 'creeping fast' upon Dowlais's footsteps. Not surprisingly, he began to think of moving to 'some country place' and cutting himself loose from business. Although she was less than convinced of the plan's wisdom, Charlotte let him have his way. In fact, John soon changed his mind about retiring, but in November 1837 he took the practical step of making a will. It provided that, in the event of his death, Charlotte was to be his sole executor, his sole trustee and the children's guardian.[53] If he were to die when Ivor was still a minor, she was hold the interest in the Iron Company on trust until he came of age. It was a significant pledge of confidence in her abilities.

While recognising John's trust in her, she could not, of course, foresee what part this bequest would play later in her life. At the time, she asked Mr Jones the lawyer to insert into the will a clause to the effect that if John should die before her and she were to marry for a second time – 'to be such a fool [...] as to form a second connection', as she expressed it – her rights as sole trustee should cease. The precaution probably sprang from her resentment of Pegus's recent manoeuvrings to persuade Lindsey to break the entail on the Uffington estate, in other words, to do away with the deed that restricted its sale. Thinking Pegus's scheme both objectionable and wrongheaded, she also reasoned that if John and she were to collude in it, they would implicitly admit Lindsey's competency, and disempower themselves from intervening 'in the event of his making a bad marriage, or any other such casualty occurring'.[54] Having initially left the matter in the hands of family solicitor Charles Ranken, Charlotte soon found herself embroiled in dispute both with her stepfather and his lawyer, Benjamin Austen. Pegus remained obdurate in his resolve to break the entail and, despite both John and her relative Lord Willoughby sharing her distaste for the scheme, there was little that she could do about it.[55] The whole episode shook her considerably and when John drew up his will, the sense of having 'suffered so much from a step-father', loomed large in Charlotte's thinking. Better by far, she reasoned, that under the terms of John's will she should forfeit her favoured position – 'become an outcast from him, from his house and from my own poor children' is her rather melodramatic interpretation – than there should any possible threat to his children's inheritance.

She made her inclinations known with every confidence that the circumstances they were intended to address would never arise. John, she surmised, was likely to outlive her. 'My only wish,' she wrote, 'is to do my duty and to relieve my husband in his avocation as far as I am able.' As for the notion that she might remarry, it was surely 'too absurd to contemplate'.[56]

Chapter Six

Reaching an Eminence: The *Mabinogion*

'Whatever I undertake,' Charlotte once wrote, 'I must reach an eminence in.'[1] Besides her association with the Dowlais Iron Company, it is upon her translation of the mediaeval Welsh stories known collectively as the *Mabinogion* that her fame or 'eminence' rests. What is remarkable is that her defining accomplishment seems to have reached her pretty well by chance through the happy accident of her involvement in assertive Cymric circles at a propitious time.

The Guests were firm supporters of the *Cymdeithas Cymreigyddion y Fenni* [the Abergavenny Welsh Society] and regularly attended its meetings. Founded in 1833, the Society owed its origin to a burst of curiosity about Welsh history and literature which arose at the end of the eighteenth century and had owed much to the zeal of lexicographer William Owen Pughe and London-based antiquary and skinner Owen Jones, otherwise known as Owain Myfyr. Pughe founded and edited the *Cambrian Register,* a short-lived, irregular journal devoted to Welsh antiquarianism, and Jones brought out a three-volume assemblage of poetry, law and music drawn from his collection of mediaeval manuscripts which he entitled the *Myvyrian Archaiology of Wales*.[2]

Among his other literary activities, Pughe was a pioneering translator of the *Mabinogion* and his achievement in bringing the stories into the public eye merits some attention. His edited translation of part of 'Pwyll, Lord of Dyfed' appeared in the 1795–6 volumes of the *Cambrian Register*.[3] By way of introduction, he explained that he had found a Welsh version of the tale in 'the *Red Book* of Jesus College, Oxford', that is, the manuscript now known 'The Red Book of Hergest,' or in Welsh *Llyfr Coch o Hergest*.[4] Setting out his rather stately English rendition of the story on one side of the bi-columnar page with the Welsh adjacent, Pughe thoughtfully made it accessible in both languages. As though to whet his readers' appetites for more mediaeval stories, he commented that Welsh language was remarkably rich in narrative. 'Several romantic tales' survived, he asserted, some 'in old manuscripts' like the *Llyfr Coch*, and others 'recited from memory by the common people'. 'Pwyll' was one of a number of stories 'variously denominated *Mabinogion* or juvenile amusements'.[5] Pughe's notion that the stories of the *Llyfr Coch* addressed youth probably stemmed from his bringing some creative etymology to bear upon the sentence which appears, refrain-like, at the close, of the four inter-related stories – 'Pwyll', 'Branwen', 'Manawyddan' and 'Math': *Ac felly y terfyna'r gainc hon o'r Mabinogi* ['So ends this branch of the Mabinogi'.] Since the Welsh word *mab* denotes a boy or son, *Mabinogion*, which loosely resembled a Welsh plural noun, may well have suggested itself as a collective name for stories which, Pughe reasoned, touched in some way upon youth, or were intended for the young. Yet it is doubtful how far (if at all) the language sustains this interpretation. Guest and John explain that, strictly speaking, in Welsh, *mabinogion* is 'a non-word'; admittedly it appears in the *Llyfr Coch* manuscript at the close of 'Pwyll,' but only through scribal error.[6]

The *Cambrian Register* extract of 'Pwyll' finished at the moment when the eponymous hero is fruitlessly spurring his horse in pursuit of Rhiannon's ambling steed, who mysteriously outstrips him.[7] Unfortunately, at just this critical point in the story, Pughe's circumstances changed, and his interest in the tales of the *Llyfr Coch* faltered. Not only did he inherit an estate in Denbighshire, management of which demanded much of his time, but also, in a somewhat bizarre development, he engrossed himself in interpretation of the writings of self-proclaimed prophetess Joanna Southcott.[8] In 1826 he advertised his intention 'to publish by subscription *Y Mabinogion or, the Ancient Romances of Wales*, with a literal version in English', but being so distraction-prone, he was not a reliable author on whom to stake subscription money and the project seems to have withered on the vine, much to the disappointment of his admirers.[9] Just enough of the material was available to tantalise them and in February 1829, a correspondent to the *Chester Chronicle* enquired whether Dr Pughe had 'made any progress towards the publication of his *Mabinogion*', adding that it was anticipated 'with anxious solicitude by the literati of Wales.'[10]

In the short term, the literati of Wales had no option but to wait. Then, in October 1836, the *Hereford Times*, an English paper with roots close enough to the border to take Welsh matters seriously, announced that plans were under way for establishing a society 'with the object of publishing Welsh manuscripts'. Urging that 'no time ... be lost in appointing a committee of superintendence and issuing a prospectus', the Herefordshire journalist invited his 'contemporaries throughout the Principality to put their shoulders to the wheel'.[11] In January 1837, the *Cardiff and Merthyr Guardian* carried an enthusiastic article on the likelihood of the Welsh Manuscripts Society's formation.[12] Not to be out-done, the *Monmouthshire Merlin* rallied to the cause with some counter-intuitive Latin quatrains, which opened with the stern exhortation *Somnos inertes excute, Cambria* [Shake off your lazy slumbers, Wales...][13] But by June so little had happened that the *Merthyr Guardian* doubted whether the proposed society remained alive at all, and enquired sarcastically if it had actually 'perished during the late inclement season?'[14]

By October 1837, plans to promote the publication of mediaeval Welsh literature remained so nebulous that one of the visiting speakers at the autumn meeting of the *Cymdeithas Cymreigyddion Y Fenni* suggested 'formation of a society for the publication of Welsh Manuscripts', as though he was the first person to think of the idea.[15] Rev. Arthur Jones, meanwhile, one of the clergy present, execrated the sheer 'apathy' shown by the Welsh over 'publishing their manuscripts', and Charlotte's historian acquaintance Rev. Thomas Price, better known by his Bardic name of Carnhuanawc, publicly agreed with him.[16] Yet somehow amid the general frustration, it looks as though a plan began to take shape. It is no more than surmise, but Carnhuanawc and his friend Rev. John Jones otherwise known as Tegid, appear to have suggested to Charlotte that she might care to bring out an edition of the *Mabinogion*. All three of them must have known that it would be well-received; not only did Charlotte have sufficient linguistic facility to make a success of the work, but she also had the means to finance its publication on a lavish scale.[17] If the clergy hatched the venture, they had every reason to be confident that Charlotte would fall in with it. Impressed by her abilities, *Cymdeithas* supporter Judge John Bosanquet of Dingestow sent word that he was willing to lend her his transcription of the *Llyfr Coch o Hergest*. Charlotte was completely won over. 'By God's blessing,' she wrote, 'I hope I may accomplish the undertaking.'[18]

Ironically, no sooner had she taken up the idea than the members of one of the fledgling, provisional Welsh Manuscript Societies voiced their resentment at her appropriation of the work and expressed a wish 'to take the *Mabinogion* into their own hands.'[19] But it was too late. With the support of her clergy colleagues Charlotte, who had by now taken the project to her heart, held fast to her objective. She would translate and annotate the Welsh texts herself and publish them at her own expense.

She began to work on 'Iarlles y ffynawn' on New Year's Day 1838. Departing from the literal sense of the Welsh word *ffynawn*, which denotes a well, she preferred, with some aesthetic flourish, to call her English version of the story 'The Lady of the Fountain'. As a choice for the opening tale of the collection, it may have been Tegid's idea, and to judge from Charlotte's comments, it owed nothing to ease of translation. She found the language of the story 'rather difficult' to grasp, let alone turn into English, and complained about its being 'cramped' and archaic.[20] By this time she had decided on what was, in broad terms, to be her method of working. Either she or Tegid would transcribe 'one story at a time' from Judge Bosanquet's version of the *Llyfr Coch* 'in a fit manner to go to the Press (viz. in modern orthography, which will be more general useful)'. At first, she was not at ease with the handwriting of the scribes who had compiled Bosanquet's manuscript, but trusted Tegid, who evidently had a proven command of palaeography, to produce fair copies from which she could translate.[21] Later, she would make her own transcriptions. Once she had drafted an English version of each story, she despatched it to Carnhuanawc for comment. He was a keen critic, as his frank appraisal of her treatment of 'Lludd ac Llefelys' shows.

'I am quite disappointed in your treatment of the *Tair Gormes* [three oppressions]' he informed her. 'The story,' he continues,

> is one of the most important of all the collection [...] by your way of telling it, you deprive it of much of the interest which it would possess if given as a literal translation.[22]

Having voiced his general dissatisfaction, rather than suggest improvements, he pointed out the elements in the tale which, in his opinion, required annotation. He also drew Charlotte's attention to a version of the story which related that the currency of the invading Coraniaid was Elf money which, 'when kept in the pocket or coffer turned into withered leaves and bits of fungus.'[23] In her finished text, Charlotte condensed his gist into a conscientious note.[24]

She liked background information and, keen to set the stories within the fullest possible historical, literary and topographical context, her textual commentary provided extensive background gloss. It is no accident that her off-the-cuff response to reading Judge Bosanquet's English version of 'Culhwch and Olwen' was to observe that it offered 'a great field for annotation'.[25] She viewed her notes as an opportunity to enjoy herself. Arthur's dog Cavall – more particularly, the stone bearing his alleged pawprint – caught her attention; so did his mare Llamrei, after whom John Guest's mare was named. 'Her name implies bounding or curvetting', Charlotte explained.[26] Discussing Branwen, she not only cited an article about the apparent discovery of her tomb at Ynys Bronwen on Anglesey, but also arranged for the inclusion of a sketch of Branwen's burial urn.[27] In a note on Cardiff, location of a joust in 'Geraint', she supplied what amounts to a miniature essay on the town's mediaeval history.[28] Reference in the same story to a 'woman's saddle' prompted her to observe approvingly that there could be no question of the women of the *Mabinogion's* adopting so 'unbecoming a practice' as to ride astride.[29] Erica Obey remarks tellingly upon the 'magpie-like nature of the notes', which are in her view, 'a true *wunderkammer*, a collector's cabinet, jammed with curiosities.'[30]

But Charlotte did not lack scholarly purpose and her intention was to advance the case that through its narrative tradition, Wales, 'the Cymric nation' had 'strong claims to be considered the cradle of European Romance.'[31] To bolster the assertion, she appended versions of the stories from other European cultures to her translations. For 'Iarlles y ffynawn', 'Peredur', and 'Geraint', for example, together with the Welsh text 'in modern orthography' and her English translation, she also supplied facsimiles of the sources of variant versions of each tale. It meant commissioning handwriting expert and lithographer Joseph Netherclift (1792–1863) in a drastic change from his stock-in-trade business of testifying as an expert witness in forgery trials, to make copies of the relevant manuscripts. The identity of the woodcut illustrator is more elusive, although a number of the pictures bear the attribution 'B. Williams' in minute script. To print the finished work she chose William Rees of Llandovery. By mid-December 1837, before Charlotte had even started on the work, Rees had heard of her intention to publish the *Mabinogion* and, recognising the likely prestige of the project, wrote to ask Taliesin Williams to recommend him for the work.[32] Since printing in the mid-nineteenth century was an art form, and Rees one of its most distinguished practitioners, his engagement with the venture served to heighten its prestige.

Her ease with mediaeval Welsh grew with familiarity and by the summer of 1838, travelling from Penarth to Dowlais, even though she had forgotten her dictionary, she found that she could read 'Geraint ab Erbin' with ease.[33] Her commitment to the Welsh stories was evident from her continuing to work on them throughout the European tour that John and she made in the late summer of 1838 to celebrate John's being made a baronet in Queen Victoria's Coronation Honours. Viewing it from the heights of the peerage, Charlotte had thought such a 'paltry distinction' unworthy of him, but John relished the notion of his eldest son's becoming 'Sir Ivor Guest' when he came of age. He also appreciated the tremendous reception that he received in Dowlais, with the townsmen riding out to meet Charlotte and himself and unhitching the carriage horses to haul them into the town, which was lit up especially in his honour.[34] But the Guests had been keen to go abroad and early in August, Edward and Anne Divett installed themselves at Dowlais to oversee matters in John's absence, while Charlotte and he sailed out to Antwerp.

Their holiday travel would take in, among other places, Liege, Aix Le Chapelle, Cologne, Bonn, Coblentz, Mainz, Frankfurt, Heidelberg, Baden, Furstenburg, Zurich, Lucerne, Lausanne, Geneva, Chillon, Lake Maggiore, Florence, Rome, Paris and thence back to London. A high-point of their tour, incidentally, was a visit to the Zurich works of Swiss cotton manufacturer and machine-wright Hans Caspar Escher (1775–1859) where to her high satisfaction, Charlotte discovered a number of iron bars stamped with letters 'GL', signifying

Guest, Lewis & Co. Other delights of the trip included an enchanted drive along the banks of the Rhine; sight of a spectacular shooting star at Carlsruhe and a visit to the Vatican Library, although she was disappointed not to allowed access to its Welsh manuscripts. At Lausanne, the day after a thunderstorm, she made a working copy of the Welsh text of 'Geraint ab Erbin' and began, at intervals, to translate it. Despite some worry over the question of whether the printed copies of 'The Lady of the Fountain' would be ready in time for the October *Cymreigyddion* and fretting over John's health – 'he feels the cold much' she lamented – she read 'Breuddwyd Rhonabwy' and 'Lludd ac Llefelys'.[35]

Hearing nothing from the publishers, her anxiety about the 'Lady of the Fountain' grew. 'I have been very much annoyed at still hearing nothing of the 1st no. of my Book', she wrote, travelling through Italy in the early autumn of 1838.[36] At the time, she was continuing both to work 'very hard' and to sit for Florentine sculptor Lorenzo Bartolini who was making portrait busts of John and herself.[37] Her fears for her publication were groundless for, unknown to her, the South Wales newspapers already carried announcements to the effect that 'On Wednesday the 10th inst will be published in Royal 8vo THE MABINOGION OR ANCIENT ROMANCES OF WALES […] Part one containing THE LADY OF THE FOUNTAIN, with an English Translation and Notes by Lady Charlotte Guest.'[38].

As the Guests continued on their way, something happened to bring home to them all the associations of Wales. They had stopped at a place which Charlotte calls 'Fassard' (possibly St Maurice sur Fessard in north-eastern France). John happened to ask the hotel ostler a question in what was perhaps rather hesitant French, and to his and Charlotte's surprise, the man replied in English. The Guests enquired eagerly about his home and background, and when it emerged that the ostler was 'a Welshman who after serving in the battle of Waterloo had settled in France', John switched language to Welsh, and received an enthusiastic Welsh response. Charlotte surmised that many years must have passed since last the man had heard the sound of his own language, and she was entranced to hear the two of them in conversation.[39]

Far away in America, meanwhile, Edward had recovered from any heartbreak that he had suffered over Anne Ross. News reached John and Charlotte announcing that he had married Isabella, the daughter of Juan Baptista de Bernabeu, sometime Spanish Consul in Baltimore, and his English wife Bathsheba. The experience of raising their family had brought Juan and Bathsheba much grief. Four of their ten children – Josepha, Maria, and two little girls both named Isabella – died in infancy; a son, Alonzo, died at sea. Of the remaining five, John Joseph and Maria Louisa both married, the one to Ellen Moale, the other to Dr Richard Sprigg Steuart; Carlos remained single, as did Clara, the youngest of the family.[40] Edward married the surviving Isabella de Bernabeu – half-English; half-Spanish; securely American and staunchly Catholic – far from home and amid her Catholic relatives. In all probability, the news took the Guests, happily absorbed in their European travel, completely by surprise. Nevertheless, someone – probably John at long range – arranged to place an announcement of the marriage in the *Cardiff and Merthyr Guardian,* so that Mrs Hutchins's arrival in Wales did not take Edward's old friends entirely by surprise.[41] Although Charlotte was apt to look askance at Isabella's religion – she could not abide anything that smacked of what she dismissively called 'Popery' – her journal entries of the 1840s make frequent mention of 'Mrs Hutchins', which suggests that, by and large, the two women were on companionable terms. Before long, the Hutchinses with Isabella's sister Clara settled at Llansantffraed House, just above the Usk between Abergavenny and Brecon.

On returning to London, Charlotte hastened to Longmans to acquire a copy of the newly issued 'Lady of the Fountain'. The sheer quality of the production, which owed much to Rees's design skills, impressed her immensely and gave her every possible encouragement to complete the next number without delay. Her mentors soon caught up with her. Tegid, with the connivance of a friendly Fellow of Jesus College, managed to extract the actual *Llyfr Coch* from the College library so as to give her the chance of seeing and handling the fifteenth-century volume for herself when she paused in Oxford on her way from London to South Wales.[42] A fortnight before Christmas, Carnhuanawc came to Dowlais House to discuss his correction of Charlotte's translation of 'Geraint ab Erbin' – she had sent it to him from Italy – and to help her plan the accompanying notes. A few days later, he introduced her to Théodore Claude Henri, Vicomte Hersart de la Villemarqué (1815–95), a fellow specialist in Celtic narrative. At the time, Villemarqué was working on his collection of Breton folklore, *Barzaz-Breiz – Chants Populaires de la Bretagne*.[43] He let it be known that the Parisian *Ecole de Chartes* had mandated him to attend the Abergavenny *Cymreigyddion* and write a report 'On Welsh Literature'.[44] Since the early Breton language had a close relationship with Welsh, and the folk songs, ballads and stories touched upon some the same figures as the *Mabinogion* tales, Carnhuanawc no doubt thought there were sound scholarly reasons for Villemarqué and Charlotte to make one another's acquaintance. Literary specialisms aside, Charlotte at first found the Breton count entrancing company and described him as 'a clever and agreeable young man.'[45]

But Villemarqué's charm hid a rather unprincipled approach to textual research. Before long, Charlotte began to think that he was taking advantage of her kindness.[46] Not only did he demand substantial payment for making a copy of the French romance *Le Chevalier au Lion* which turned out to be illegible, but he also tried to forestall her publication of 'Peredur' by bringing out a French edition of the story before it appeared in her *Mabinogion* sequence, having had the temerity to ask Tegid to transcribe the Welsh text for him.[47] Unamused, Charlotte abandoned her work-in-progress on 'Geraint ab Erbin' to give all her energy to completing the wandering and rather episodic story of Sir Peredur, the Welsh Perceval or Parsifal, before Villemarqué's version was published. By dint of sheer hard work, she finished her transcription of the Welsh text on 27 March 1839, and began to translate the next day. At three o'clock in the morning of 29 March, she gave birth to Montague John, her fifth child and third son. 'Thank God my dear child looks very large and strong,' she observed.[48]

The infant Monty was not only vigorous, but also unusually well-behaved and undemanding upon his mother's time. She may, for once, have been glad to employ a wet-nurse. Determined to trounce her rival, before the middle of April she had set Netherclift, the lithographer, and Williams, the wood-cut engraver, to work on the 'Peredur' pictures and facsimiles.[49] At the same time, she persuaded an anonymous but sympathetic acquaintance to visit the British Museum Reading Room on her behalf, and look out illuminating sections of the Arthurian stories *Sangreal* and *Percival de Galles* for citation in her notes. Treating travel as a chance to translate, she made some useful progress with 'Peredur' while crossing the Bristol Channel on the Penarth ferry.[50] By mid-May, it was ready to go to press. Relieved, Charlotte reflected that within seven weeks she had 'transcribed it, translated it, written the notes, provided the decorations and brought it almost out of the printer's hands'[51] If the experience had been punishing, stealing a march on Villemarqué was ample compensation, and with 'Peredur' finished, she resumed her work on 'Geraint ab Erbin'.

August 1839 brought some diversion for Brunel's viaduct at Goitre Coed, by which the Taff Vale Railway was to cross the Taff, was close to completion and John and Charlotte decided to inspect it for themselves. Although it was a showery day, they rashly abandoned their closed carriage, preferring to ride out along the tram-road to the site. Impressed by the height and grace of the arches, Charlotte thought its setting within the steep valley gave it 'a very fine effect'.[52] Exhilarated, she and John had their horses taken round to the far side of the river, while they crossed the bridge by the scaffolding and visited the tunnel that was under construction on the opposite bank. Having remounted, they went on to Abercynon to see how the inclined plane had progressed. But the light rain of the morning gave way to an afternoon's deluge and Charlotte realised that she had mistakenly instructed the carriage driver to meet them at Pontypridd, 4½ miles away. John was not pleased. In October, they revisited the viaduct, this time in the company of Edward and Anne Divett. 'It was rather fine but very cold', wrote Charlotte, recalling a day of brimming excitement. 'When the carriages had reached that point of the turnpike road nearest to the viaduct,' she continued,

> we got out and walked to it. There was more scrambling
> to get there than some of the ladies liked – We crossed by
> the scaffolding as I had done before & all the party went
> back over it in the same way except Merthyr and myself
> and we went over the bridge itself, scrambling over the
> rough masonry – Three of the six arches were not closed
> and in these places we had planks thrown down across
> for us & I believe I was the first female that ever crossed
> this bridge.[53]

By chance, a rare description of Charlotte survives from about this time. It appears in an anonymous publication, *Pen and Ink Sketches by a Cosmopolitan*, the work of American writer John Ross Dix. Dix claimed that, having attended the British Association for the Advancement of Science's meeting in Bristol, he went on to Chepstow to look at the castle and while he was there, observed 'a tall loosely dressed lady [...] carrying a large folio under her arm'. Continuing, he relates that,

> Two sweet little girls were with her. I felt curious to know who she was and enquired of the old woman who kept the gate. She informed me that it was Lady Charlotte Guest [...] wife of Sir John Guest, the great Welsh Iron Master.[54]

There is some puzzle here, for the British Association for the Advancement of Science's Bristol meeting took place in 1836, before Cattws was born, so perhaps one of 'sweet little girls' was actually Ivor in his baby-skirts. The description of Charlotte as 'tall' is consistent with her appearance in the Buckner portrait and if she was pregnant at the time, it would explain the loose dress. The folio under her arm may have been a sketch book, which she might easily have taken with her, when escorting her infants to Chepstow for an outing.

At risk of digressing further, in the context of examining Charlotte's work as an editor and translator, it is worth reflecting that, in addition to her taste for history and mediaeval poetry, she also had a thorough-going enjoyment of fiction. Besides Scott, her long-term favourite novelist, she devoured the works of Dickens and pursued *Martin Chuzzlewit* as it appeared by monthly instalments over 1842–44. She objected to the 'coarseness' of Charlotte Bronte's *Jane Eyre* and commented that she was glad that it was not the work of any of her daughters, but allowed that it was 'striking'. Surprisingly perhaps, she did not explore the novels of Jane Austen until the 1870s, some sixty years after they had first appeared. They did not entirely appeal to her, *Pride and Prejudice* least of all, and she questioned cagily whether she was fully 'alive to their very great merit'.[55] If her reading matter tended to veer towards the more literary end of the market, it is refreshing to find that in 1835 she mentions finding 'a silly book, *Village Belles*' in the works office (of all places) which she appears to have relished.[56]

On 12 August 1840, a couple of months or so before the publication of 'Geraint ab Erbin', Charlotte gave birth to her sixth child and fourth son 'after three quarters of an hour's comparatively slight suffering.'[57] Given the baptismal name of 'Augustus Frederic', to his family the boy was known as 'Geraint'.[58] It was touching revelation of her affection for the story. The work came out just in time for the 1840 meeting of the *Cymdeithas Cymreigyddion Y Fenni*.

Intriguingly, even when her engagement with the *Mabinogion* had advanced a long way, her understanding of what the title actually encompassed remained fluid. The fact was that the *Llyfr Coch* was, in effect, a cornucopia of narrative, and included many stories which, although written in Welsh, were not Welsh in origin. It was not until 1843 that she decided to omit the tales of 'Amyc and Amlyn', 'Bown – or Bevis – of Hamtoun', *'Chwedlau seith doethion Rufein'* ('The Seven Wise Masters') and *'Historia Charlamaen'* ('The History of Charlemagne') on the grounds that they were no more than 'mere vapid translation from some Norman original'. Even then she toyed with the idea of publishing them as an appendix, a sort of *Mabinogion* Apocrypha, although she did not think that they had much merit. Before she had finished translating 'Amyc and Amlyn', she dismissed it as 'not ... very interesting', which is mild censure for a singularly gruesome tale, and 'Bown' she thought 'nearly as dull'.[59] It left eleven canonical stories:– the 'Lady of the Fountain' (appeared in 1838); 'Peredur, son of Evrawc' (1839); 'Geraint, son of Erbin' (1840); 'Kilhwch and Olwen' (1842); the 'Dream of Rhonabwy' and 'Pwyll, Prince of Dyfed' (appeared together 1843); 'Branwen, daughter of Llyr', 'Manawyddan, son of Llyr' and 'Math, son of Mathonwy' (appeared together 1845); 'The Dream of Maxen Wledig' and the 'Meeting of Lludd and Llevelys'(appeared together 1849). With these last two tales, perhaps because she thought twelve tales an appealingly round number, she included the 'History of Taliesin'. The hero's namesake, Taliesin Williams, who may have been a difficult man to whom to say 'no', had expressly provided her with a working copy of the Welsh text drawn from a manuscript which had apparently belonged to his late father, Iolo Morgannwg.[60]

Carnhuanawc, for the record, favoured its inclusion on the ground that the evidence from the *Myvyrian Archaiology* suggested that it had originated much earlier than the late fourteenth century – supposedly the period of its composition. How well she got on with this erudite bard and clergyman is a slippery question. So little correspondence survives to attest to the part he played in shaping her work on the Mabinogion that it is difficult to form much idea of their way of working together. On the one hand, her readiness to explain the connection between the dragons of 'Lludd and Llefelys' with the dragons of Merlin's vision suggests that she had much respect for his learning. At the same time, she had little compunction about using him as a research assistant, not to say academic errand-boy. In a note of 6 May 1843, for instance, he tells her that he cannot find any mention of the 'Greal' in the *Cymmrodorion* Catalogues, which she has evidently asked him to check, but thinks it may possibly be among the manuscripts at Hengwrt, home of the Vaughan family. Asserting his clerical dignity, he then suggests that since the newspapers have just announced Sir Robert Vaughan's death, she ought to consider when, or whether, it would be appropriate to pursue enquiries with Vaughan's brother and executor.[61] Surprisingly, she made no acknowledgement of his efforts on her behalf, not to mention his regular appraisal of her work, in her prefatory material. The omission may be owing to his having died in 1848, before publication of the three volume edition, but the absence of any mark of appreciation is surprising and sad. Not only would it seem fitting for Charlotte publicly to express some appreciation of his contribution to the completed work, but also it would be rewarding to have some sense of just how much her edition of the stories owed to his distinctive scholarship and interpretation.

Once she had trumped Villemarqué by bringing out her 'Peredur' before his French edition appeared, her work settled into something approaching a routine pattern of transcription, translation and annotation, while Netherclift and the engravers furnished illustrations to her specification. The full work appeared first in seven parts, issued at intervals between 1838 and 1849. Modestly priced and presented in provisional covers of light board, the publishers evidently made the tacit assumption that purchasers would collect the sequence as it appeared, and later have the separate parts bound in a more robust binding of their choice. When the three volume edition appeared in 1849, it proved to be a sumptuous production, the elegance of its appearance catching the critics' attention as readily as its content. 'It is with no miser's hand that the table is spread and the materials provided for the literary banquet at which we are here made guests', wrote an anonymous reviewer in the *Morning Chronicle*, for instance. 'Verily, the mythic beauty of those old legends of faery land and chivalry is sweet as the song of the birds of Rhiannon.'[62]

How far it justifies such fulsome appreciation is a subjective matter, for Charlotte's *Mabinogion* – like any ground-breaking literary work – has its detractors. Much of their censure turns on what they regard as a certain Victorian squeamishness in dealing with any episode that concerns sexual relations. Infamously, in 'Pwyll', Pwyll and Arawn, king of Annwfwn, each disguised as the other, exchange places for a year and, perforce, wives. The Welsh text describes how Pwyll, sharing a bed with the wife of Arawn, sleeps with his back to her and keeps silence, but Charlotte omits it from her translation. When Arawn comes home, in bed with his wife, he asks why she will not talk to him, and she not unreasonably explains that for the past year when they have been in bed together, he has said nothing. At once, Arawn explains about changing places with Pwyll, at which she marvels both at the agreement that the men have made, and at Pwyll's steadfast integrity in the face of temptation. But Charlotte omits these passages in their entirety. Whether it was her decision to leave them out, or whether her clergy advisers suggested it is unknown.

Not only does Charlotte sanitise the *Mabinogion* bedroom-scenes but she clearly dislikes the idea that the chivalric mediaeval world could include anything resembling squalor. In 'The Dream of Rhonabwy', her phrase 'mire of cattle' tiptoes round the sheer stench that must have hit Rhonabwy and his companions when they entered Heilyn Goch's filthy hall. She is also wary of blunt speaking. In 'The Lady of the Fountain', when Owain is trapped behind the portcullis, the maiden Luned tells him outright that he strikes her as an ideal young man for a woman; a true friend and a good lover, which is why she is ready to help him. In Sioned Davies's 2007 translation, her frank Luned announces with heartfelt warmth,

> God knows, I have never seen a better young man for a woman than you. If you had a woman friend, you would be the best friend a woman could have; if you had a mistress, you would be the best lover.[63]

Charlotte swathes the utterance in courtliness. 'Every woman ought to succour thee,' her courtly maiden tells the hero, for I never saw one more faithful in the service of ladies than thou. As a friend thou art the most sincere, and as a lover the most devoted.

What her interpretation of Luned's remark gains in decorum, it lacks in passion. In the light of her dislike of anything that smacked of 'coarseness', perhaps a species of chaste purity was just the quality which she considered appropriate for Owain's female rescuer.

In its complete form, the publication initially gave Charlotte such status and authority that she found herself hailed as a 'patroness of Welsh Literature'.[64] But in 1877, bookseller and publisher Bernard Quaritch set her work on a new and less austere trajectory. By omitting the Welsh text and the facsimile sources, and presenting Charlotte's translation as a stand-alone English version of the tales, he proved that there was a ready market for them among general readers, as well as scholars and antiquarians. Not long after, American Sidney Lanier, a Southern-states blockade runner with a taste for chivalric adventure, published a version of the stories that he judged suitable for youth under the title *Knightly Legends of Wales, or The Boys' Mabinogion* of 1881. It took its place in Lanier's *Boy's Library of Legend and Chivalry* alongside *The Boy's Froissart* and *The Boy's King Arthur* to give the stories footing within the popular, commercial sphere.[65] Rather than nurse any grievance in the matter, Charlotte, whose interests had undergone many shifts by the 1880s, seems to have been flattered to think that her work and the legendary characters whose exploits she had found so absorbing kept their place in the public eye.

Nevertheless, the accolades heaped upon her publication would, in time, give rise to some nationalistic dispute. Early in the 1920s, a letter signed 'Ap Dowlais' appeared in the *Western Mail* asking what truth there was in the rumour, lively in Merthyr Tydfil, which maintained that the *Mabinogion* translation credited to Charlotte was actually the work of one Thomas Stephens, a scholarly chemist of Dowlais whose scientific and historical research the Guests had encouraged. 'We are joyfully prepared to accept our fathers' joyful assertion that it was a Welshman who gave to the world these translations,' wrote Ap Dowlais, 'and not the intellect of another race.'[66] For the Englishwoman Charlotte to have pirated the Welshman Stephens's work might have made a colourful, if unlikely, story, but it turned out to have no foundation. Between them,

Swansea librarian David Rhys Phillips and Charlotte's daughter Blanche, who was by this time the Countess of Bessborough, demolished the notion; Blanche by tracing her mother's journal references to her work in progress and Mr Phillips, who felt strongly enough upon the subject to publish them.[67] As an Englishwoman's response to Welsh culture and narrative, Charlotte's *Mabinogion* is a remarkable tribute.

Merthyr Tydfil. Alphonse Dousseau (1769–1875) *Souvenirs Pittoresque de mes Voyages de la Pays de Galles, 1830–69.* (Courtesy of the National Library of Wales)

Above left: Lady Charlotte Guest, from a painting by Richard Buckner, engraved by William Walker. (Courtesy of the National Library of Wales)

Above right: Josiah John Guest, from a painting by Richard Buckner, engraved by William Walker. (Courtesy of the National Library of Wales)

The Old Castle Inn & Hotel, Merthyr Tydfil. (Courtesy of the trustees of the Alan George Archive)

Dowlais House 1900. (Courtesy of the trustees of the Alan George Archive)

Thomas Revel Guest, undated, artist unknown. (Courtesy of Glamorgan Records Office)

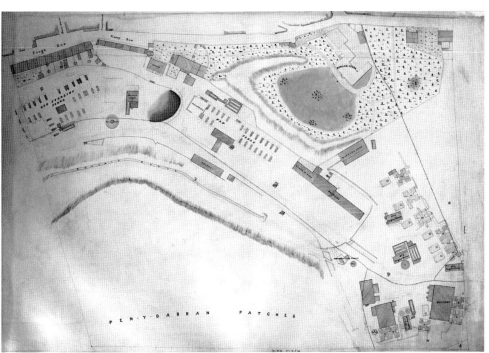

Plan from 1836 survey by Peter Henderson, Cardiff, and 13 Maddox Street, London, showing Dowlais House's proximity to the Ironworks. (Courtesy of Glamorgan Records Office)

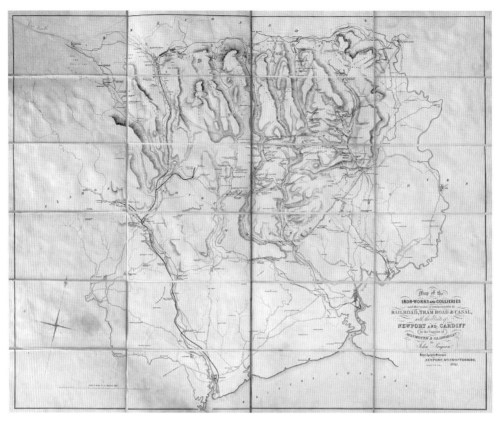

John Prujean, Map of the Ironworks and Collieries, and their means of transport, by rail road, tram road and canal, 1843. (Courtesy of Glamorgan Records Office)

Dowlais Iron Works c.1840 from a painting by George Childs (1829–94). (Courtesy of the trustees of the Alan George Archive)

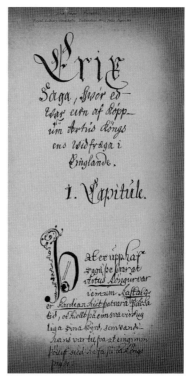

Above left: Title page of Pt IV of the *Mabinogion*, Kilhwch and Olwen. (Courtesy of the Wellcome Library)

Above right: Facsimile of Erik saga from the Royal Library, Stockholm, made by Joseph Netherclift. (Courtesy of the Wellcome Library)

Below: Canford Manor – house and garden with Nineveh porch to the right. (Photograph by author, August 2019)

Above left: The Guests' intertwined initials, CEG and JJG, carved in the stone vault over the entrance to Canford Manor. (Photograph by author, August 2019)

Above right: Photograph of Lady Charlotte Schreiber addressing staff and pupils of Dowlais Central School, c.1870. (Courtesy of Glamorgan Records Office)

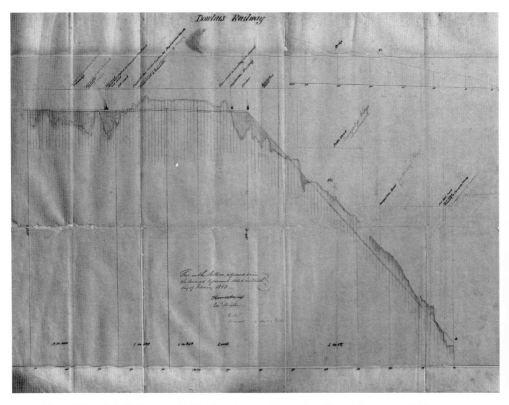

Plan of Dowlais Railway, c.1850, showing gradient of incline. (Courtesy of Glamorgan Records office)

Above left: William Menelaus 1818–1882, by Parker Hagarty (1859–1934). (Courtesy of Cardiff University and the South Wales Institute of Civil Engineers)

Above right: John Evans, Dowlais Works Manager, d. 9 March 1862, by William Edward Jones (1825–1877). (Courtesy of Cyfarthfa Castle Museum and Art Gallery, Merthyr Tydfil Leisure Trust)

Page of Lady Charlotte's journal, 20 July 1853. It includes her exchange with John Evans at the beginning of the strike. 'My question was, "Peace or War?" He answered "War!"'. (Courtesy of the National Library of Wales)

George Thomas Clark,
1809–1898, photograph by
Arthur Pendarves Vivian, 1854.
(Courtesy of the National
Library of Wales)

Undated photograph of Lady Charlotte, with two of her sons and Charles Schreiber at
Canford. (Courtesy of www.EliotsofPortEliot.com (Port Eliot Collection))

Chapter Seven

Lord Bute and the Dowlais Lease

It was a matter of good fortune to the Guests that, ever since its inception in 1759, the Dowlais Ironworks had occupied its site on extraordinarily favourable terms. The founding partners initially purchased a number of leases and sub-leases from the Dowager Countess of Windsor which gave them mineral rights over her land. In 1763, they took out a further lease from Lady Windsor for an additional 22 acres of land, on which to put up blast furnaces, forges, mills, engines, storehouses, kilns and coal-houses. At the same time it was agreed that all the leases would expire in 1848. Either through her own inexperience or from lack of foresight on the part of her lawyers, Lady Windsor never claimed any mineral royalty payable on the coal and ore extracted from her land. In time, although the Iron Company's yearly profit might be in the region of £50,000, they paid something closer to £100 by way of annual rental. Not surprisingly, as the heir to Lady Windsor's lands, John Crichton Stuart, Second Marquess of Bute, found this situation acutely frustrating.

Relations between the Guests and Lord Bute were, if not openly hostile, always strained. The speech he made at the opening of the 1834 Cardiff Eisteddfod left Charlotte unimpressed (she considered it 'miserable'), but when she met him socially at Singleton Abbey in Swansea, home of John's friends the Vivians, she forgot his shortcomings as an orator. Sitting at opposite ends of a long dinner table, the eye-disease which afflicted Lord Bute, combined with her own acute myopia, somewhat frustrated the courtesy of their drinking one another's health.[1] In consequence, they sat 'nodding to each other like [...] Chinese mandarins', each unable to discern whether his or her bow was returned.[2] But Charlotte was charmed. She thought Lord Bute was 'delightful' and was in ecstasies over the perfection of his 'manners and refinement'. In time, she would change her mind.

John's commercial enterprise had led him to take measures which Lord Bute found provocative. In the 1820s he had leased land from the Bute estate and conveniently close to the Glamorgan Canal on which he had established a glassworks, the Cardiff Glass Bottle Company, its three cone-shaped chimneys forming a distinctive landmark on the Cardiff skyline. As a business it was precarious and by 1830, no fewer than three of John's partners– Adam Stodart, James Bowden and William Henry Land – had resigned.[3] Undaunted, John took sole charge and, despite its never being very successful, he kept the glass-bottle works running throughout his life.[4] To Lord Bute, who wished to develop his land in Cardiff and capitalise both on its geographical location and on the fast-growing coal trade along the canal, John's refusal to relinquish what he called his 'glasshouses' looked plain mischievous. Lord Bute, to exacerbate matters, always stood rigidly upon his dignity in all his dealings with the Glamorgan industrialists whom, in the view of Cardiff historian John Davies, he expected to treat him 'not as a fellow business man, but as an aristocrat to whom special deference was due'.[5] It is a shrewd remark which throws much light on the trouble that accompanied renewal of the Dowlais lease. What should have been a straightforward business transaction between lawyers acting for the Iron Company on the one hand, and the Bute Estate on the other, degenerated into a war of words in which both parties levied unreasonable demands and despatched intemperate letters amid an atmosphere of mutual suspicion and acrimony.

On 8 October 1839, the Guests attended the opening of the imposing new dock and ship canal which Lord Bute had built with the intention of making Cardiff a leading commercial port.[6] Seeing the Bristol steamer, the *Lady Charlotte*, draw through the sea lock and head towards the inner dock, with John extending his arm by way of assistance, Charlotte leapt on board, to shouts of 'cheers for Lady Charlotte' from the spectators. Many of them followed her lead, which was rather perilous because the influx almost caused the vessel to capsize, but no one appears to have come to any harm. John attended the dinner in the evening, where he inadvertently annoyed the Bristolians present by pledging that Cardiff would soon eclipse the port of Bristol.[7] It was a tactless remark, but did not cloud the event's success. With music playing, flags flying, crowds of excited spectators and visiting dignitaries happily wandering under the ornamental evergreen arches and enjoying the dahlias, for Lord Bute, the fine, formal celebration to mark his dock's opening was a great coup.[8]

A year and a day later, on 9 October 1840, the Taff Vale Railway opened from Cardiff to the Navigation House at Abercynon, which gave the Guests the opportunity to demonstrate that they too could put on a good show. In Cardiff, church bells rang, flags flew, spectators thronged the trackside, and the band of the Glamorganshire Militia played 'a variety of marches, quadrilles, etc.', amid bursts of jubilant cannon fire.[9] At midday, what Charlotte terms 'the great opening train' pulled out of Crockherbtown Station *en route* to further junketing.[10] The engine crew defied the railway company's 12mph speed restriction to cover the twelve miles from Cardiff to Newbridge – present day Pontypridd – in exactly half an hour, and at Abercynon the passengers, among them the Taff Vale directors and their friends, enjoyed 'roast and boiled-flesh and fowl' at the Navigation House, with 'sherry, port, and champagne, without measure', which John had provided for their refreshment.[11]

In the afternoon Charlotte and John led the party up the Inclined Plane, which Brunel had introduced near Treharris to enable the railway to accommodate the 1-in-22 gradient. Dowlais works' manager Thomas Evans served as the party's official escort and the Treforest Band provided background music. Although the ascent proved 'rather … severe' for many of the well-fed participants, it afforded ample reward in terms of spectacle.[12] Not only did it offer fine views along the Valley of the Taff, but it gave them access to the Cefn Glas tunnel, which TVR resident engineer George Bush had specially lit for the occasion, and thence to the Goitre Coed Viaduct, which the *Monmouthshire Merlin* pronounced 'stupendous', and Charlotte thought 'beautiful as ever'.[13]

On their return to Cardiff, stricken with what she terms 'violent face-ache', she spent a peaceful evening at Sully in the company of Isabella Hutchins and her sister Clara. For the gentlemen, there was to be no such respite. After 'an elegant cold repast' they moved onto toasts and speeches. John toasted the Lord-Lieutenant of Glamorgan, in other words Lord Bute, on whose good will the railway relied, and apparently everyone present drunk his health 'most enthusiastically'.[14] Coal-owner and Taff Vale promoter Walter Coffin proposed a toast to 'the prosperity of the city of Bristol', to which two Bristolian shareholders,

Mr Ruddell and Mr Hall, replied in fulsome appreciation. Edward Hutchins discoursed upon the mineral wealth of the Taff Valley and then the line's engineers, and the towns and trade respectively of Merthyr, Newbridge and Cardiff, all came in for tributes. Even an unsuspecting Netherlands army officer, a visitor to the Dowlais Iron works, found himself thrust forward and invited to address the company. William A. Bake named as 'Captain Back' in the *Monmouthshire Merlin*'s report, was the unsuccessful promoter of a railway intended to connect the cities of Amsterdam and Cologne by way of Arnhem. John Guest had befriended him in the belief that the Dutch government had asked him to inspect railways throughout this and other countries; apparently Bake made an off-the-cuff speech in perfect English.[15]

In Dowlais, the optimism did not last long. 'We have but slender chance of a new lease', reflected Charlotte some six months after the railway's opening; 'Lord Bute dislikes our politics too much.'[16] If John, with his glass bottle business and his one-upping railway celebration, set out to tease Lord Bute, stray sentences in Lord Bute's correspondence reveal the scorn and suspicion with which he regarded his tenant. Lord Bute wrote to his agent Richard Roy in March 1839,

> You should understand distinctly that I will not take up anything for Sir John until he <u>has done something</u> to make up to me for the unnecessary system of injury and insult both private and public which he has been endeavouring to pursue towards me for the last three or four years.

Three years later, writing again to Roy, he advanced the view that 'Rich ironmasters ought to be treated like any other trespassers.'[17] To all appearance, he treated the renewal of the Dowlais lease as an opportunity to pursue a personal grievance.

On their side, in land management terms, the Dowlais Iron Company had done themselves few favours. Determined to maximise their advantages while they lasted, the company endeavoured to extract coal and ore for the iron-making operation by the fastest and cheapest possible means. The company colliers followed the 'patch method' of extraction; in other words, they dug straight into the ground at any point where outcrops of coal or ironstone were clearly visible. It made for rapid working, but at the cost of much wastage and despoliation. If the accumulated spoil from mineral extraction blighted the landscape, the consequences of ruthlessly rapid working could be perilous underground. Used to relying on the 'stall and pillar' system of working, to extract as much coal as possible as fast as possible, the colliers extended the length of the stalls and reduced the number of pillars. It made for frequent collapses and, besides the danger, the rock falls blocked access to the more distant coal measures.[18]

It was against this unpromising background that the respective parties tried to settle fair terms for the Dowlais Iron Company's continued occupancy of its site. Understandably, perhaps, they tended to negotiate through deputies, and at intervals over the early 1840s, Lord Bute's agents Robert Stephenson, Richard Roy and John Geddes all tried to reach a consensus with the Evans brothers who represented John Guest. Their early efforts repeatedly foundered but in 1842, Robert Stephenson for Lord Bute and Thomas Evans for Guest drafted terms for a new fifty-five year lease, under which Dowlais would pay both a fair market rent and mineral royalties based on the market price of iron. Charlotte, who watched the proceedings with keen if anxious interest, commented that as far as it went, the matter looked as though it was settled. Only in her journal did she admit to misgivings; there were too many areas which invited disagreement between the respective parties for her to have any confidence in the outcome of their talk, although she hoped that her pessimism would prove groundless.[19] Unfortunately, at the end of the year, a Dowlais agent named Griffiths made the mistake of shipping a consignment of iron from the 'Little Dock'- that is, the Taff Vale Railway's dock-instead of from Lord Bute's Dock from which Dowlais had agreed to despatch all its material. Trivial in itself, Griffiths's error scuppered the negotiation-in-progress. Lord Bute sent word to the Guests through his brother, the Lord James Stuart, sometime MP for Cardiff Boroughs and Constable of Cardiff Castle, to the effect that he had no intention of ratifying the lease on the terms that Stephenson and Evans had outlined the previous July.[20]

The pattern of anticipating an agreement, only for it to vanish, mirage-like, before it actually came into being was one with which the Guests soon grew familiar. At intervals, it would appear that terms for the lease's renewal were, in effect, on the table, only for Lord Bute to sweep them away at the ratification stage. Charlotte, increasingly drawn into ironworks concerns, gives a graphic sense in her journal of the sheer frustration that arose from his manoeuvrings. In June 1843, Robert Stephenson wrote to Thomas Evans coolly admitting that throughout their previous discussion, he had never actually had authority from Lord Bute to propose terms for the lease's renewal. His statement, Charlotte observed, not only contradicted everything he had said previously, but was so completely out of character that she did not know what to make of it.[21] John, meanwhile, received two letters from Lord Bute in rapid succession. In the first, he raised a relatively small point about boundaries, admitting relatively easy resolution. But the second took a completely different line. In it, Lord Bute stated that he wished to add nothing to his previous exchanges with the Dowlais Company, but if they wanted to contract for an entirely new lease, 'he would desire his Mineral Agents to attend to it.'[22]

Stunned at finding him so capricious and high-handed, but reluctant to sour relations further by taking legal proceedings, the Guests reluctantly accepted that the settlement which they thought they had reached in 1842 no longer had any validity. John, Charlotte reflected, had done everything in his power 'to bring matters to a satisfactory conclusion', but there was 'a point of conciliation beyond which it would be unworthy to go'. They stood in a dilemma. All that deterred Charlotte from urging John to tell Lord Bute to find a new tenant was the question of what would happen to their employees if the works should close. 'We walked to the furnaces after dinner,' she recorded, 'and I afterwards went round the bank in front of the house to catch my favourite view of the dear old forges. A tear dimmed my eye as I turned from it for the last time....'[23]

It was not the 'last time', but other matters soon caught her attention. The Guests' third daughter and eighth child, Mary Enid Evelyn, was born ten days later on 1 July 1843.[24] Charlotte reckoned that the birth had caused her 'as little pain as it is possible to suffer on such occasions.' 'Dear Merthyr,' she added, 'was surprised and a good deal overcome. The baby is a nice little strong thing. – The only peculiarity about her was her being born in a caul –. She has [...] a quantity of long black hair.'[25]

By now, Charlotte was worried about her husband's health. Early in 1844, they stayed with the Duke and Duchess of Bedford at Woburn and during the visit, she happened to wear the bracelet which held his miniature portrait – one of the pair which Alfred Edward Chalon had painted after the Guests returned from their honeymoon. When another Woburn visitor remarked on the picture, so shocking did Charlotte find the contrast between John's 'present worn and anxious look, and the gay smile he wore ten and a half years ago' that she wept. The illness told upon his temper as much as it did upon his appearance. There were house-party theatricals which she adored until he complained that she was over-acting. Stricken, for his censure always cut her to the quick, she burst into tears again. John was not, she thought, 'in his usual spirits'.[26]

Although he agreed to consult Joseph Skey (1773–1866), sometime physician to the armed forces and inspector-general of army hospitals a week later, Charlotte appears not to have been satisfied with the outcome. Taking matters into her own hand, at the end of January 1844 she discussed her husband's symptoms with John Ludford White, the new Dowlais Works surgeon who had replaced John Russell. 'I had a long and most painful conversation with him,' she recalled. 'I pressed him very much and besought him to be candid.' Putting aside all questions of medical confidentiality, Mr White confirmed Charlotte's worst fears. 'He owned that the recent symptoms led him to suspect that my darling husband's complaint was a fatal one,' she recalled, 'and, he said, if his forebodings proved correct, his days were numbered.'[27]

It would be at least another fortnight before there was any of chance of seeking further medical advice. In agonies of anticipation, Charlotte nevertheless picked white violets for John's birthday and tried to concentrate on preparing 'Lludd and Llevelys' for the press. On 16 February, no fewer than five consultants arrived at 8 Spring Gardens – the Guests' new London home – to consider John's symptoms and essay a diagnosis. Hearing them greet one another, Charlotte realised that since one of their number, Dr Prout, was deaf, they all raised their voices when they spoke to him. By taking her needlework into the room next to the one where John was resting, she heard most of their deliberation and was able to learn a great deal about his condition which the medical men might not have wished to tell her in person.[28]

They identified his trouble as 'calculus in the kidney' – in other words, kidney stones. Two days later Sir Benjamin Brodie (1783–1862), President of the Royal College of Surgeons, confirmed the diagnosis. If her husband was not in quite such alarming straits as Charlotte first feared, he was still seriously ill. Treatment took the form of lithotrity, a procedure by which a surgeon inserted an instrument known as a lithotrite into the patient's bladder so as to crush the calculus (stone) and enable its expulsion. It was both painful and demeaning, and Charlotte referred to her husband's lithotrity sessions euphemistically as 'operations'. For the first operation, Mr White remained with the Guests overnight by way of precaution and in the following days, Charlotte did her best to keep John quiet. Many people wished to see him. There was a 'Mr Poole about the Railway'; Thomas Evans up from Dowlais about the Iron Company; Brownlow [Layard], his business unknown; 'Mr Divett & (from Uffington) Mr Pyne', presumably on some Bertie family matter, and Pegus and Brownlow in connection with Mary Pegus's imminent marriage.[29] Dutiful and efficient, she dealt with them all, in tacit recognition that the decisions which John had taken in the past would fall to her for the future. Despite, or perhaps because of, John's condition, in April 1844 Charlotte and he made a fortnight's trip to Belgium and the Rhine together with Lindsey and Bertie, and eldest children Maria and Ivor. On their return, they resolved to purchase a country house, well away from the works. The clear intention was that it should serve John as a place of retirement, in every sense of the expression.

In August 1844, an overture reached the Guests from Lord Bute's agents and legal advisers. They offered, Charlotte noted, to 'reopen the negotiations for the renewal of our lease'. It was a significant development, but she disliked the Bute faction's assumption that Dowlais, 'as a matter of course', was 'ready to treat with them'. Experience made her wary. 'Important as I consider it that no opportunity for an arrangement should be neglected by us,' she wrote, 'I cannot help feeling some resentment at the recommencement of a correspondence which is sure to give us a great deal of trouble and will very probably end as unsatisfactorily as the last.[30] In the short term, John was inclined to postpone discussion of the lease and concentrate instead on securing fair terms for the Taff Vale Railway to lease wharfs at the Bute Dock. Here, after all, was a victory which lay within his grasp. It was in Lord Bute's interest to ensure that the railway company should preserve his profitable Cardiff trade by using his dock, rather than build a dock for itself around the outfall of the River Ely, as it had repeatedly threatened. What was more, it promised to benefit all the trade on the railway, whereas any breakthrough made in relation to the lease would be of use only to Dowlais. Sure enough, John's efforts paid off; in December 1844, Lord Bute announced 'his assent to the Railway Co's terms regarding the rates at his docks.[31]

By this time, Merthyr Tydfil was in the throes of a Winter measles epidemic which soon spread to the Guests. All the children had measles; Maria took a long time to recover and for a while, it looked as though Merthyr *bach* would not survive at all. Constance Rhiannon, ninth child and fourth daughter, had been born on 17 October at the end of an afternoon which Charlotte spent walking up and down in the garden learning German poetry.[32] Worried about the 2-month-old baby, Charlotte was appalled to learn from Mr White that one of the wet-nurse's children died from the disease on Christmas Eve. Her terse sentence 'Suddenly checked' tells its own tale.[33]

While the measles ran their course, 1845 also witnessed a further attempt to reach a settlement regarding the lease. It proved fruitless from the outset. On 22 July, Charlotte related with some asperity that Lord Bute had considered the matter, settled on what he considered to be fair terms, and had them posted in his office in Cardiff. 'They were as we expected quite preposterous,' she expostulated, underlining the words in her journal to express her dismay at the extortionate sums which Lord Bute proposed to levy:- '4/6 per ton Royalty on Pigs and 7/- on Bars. Dead rent of £9,000 per annum … and a fine of £80,000 for renewing the lease.' 'Of course,' she added, 'it was at once determined that such terms could not be entertained for a moment....'[34]

To all appearance, it was a deadlock, but in November John defiantly made the logistical arrangements necessary for production of '1100 tons of rail and 130 tons of bar per week' to complete outstanding orders for Russian and Polish Rail and from the German Lower Silesian Railway Company.[35] That the quantity, as Charlotte observed, went 'very far beyond what any other work can manage', suggests that facing an uncertain future, John's defiant response was to extend and expand the works exponentially.[36] On the brink of a metaphorical abyss, profits rocketed; Dowlais sales agent Thomas Evans received a salary of £1,000 pa; his brother John, the works manager, £750 pa, and engineer Samuel Truran £200 pa.[37] The works, meanwhile, at once valiant and vainglorious, reached immense proportions, employing some 7,300 men and operating eighteen blast furnaces.[38]

Meanwhile, the Guests had been house-hunting. Difficult to please, they rejected several distinguished dwellings out of hand. John, for instance, thought that Woodchester in Gloucestershire would be too cold, while Londesborough Hall in Yorkshire reminded Charlotte of the bleaker aspects of her Lincolnshire childhood. She would, she observed,

> rather live in the smallest cottage in any part of my own dear beautiful Glamorgan than in the finest palace that could be built at Londesborough. I often think if I lived in a flat country again, I should pine away and die.[39]

But they liked Canford Manor in Dorset from the outset. John paid £335,000 for the house and a further £19,000 for the 17,000 acre estate.[40] Engaging Charles Barry, designer of the gothic Palace of Westminster, to renovate the house that Edward Blore had modified over the 1820s and 1830s for long-term owner Lord de Mauley, would be a further expense. At the same time, the purchase brought them some significant advantages. Their new home was elegant, well-appointed, a refuge from the cholera, and only five hours' travel by railway to London. Barry's plans would, in effect, remodel much of the building while retaining the surviving part of the mediaeval manor. The effect was to create a dwelling which paid affectionate tribute to the past, while introducing modern amenities. By dint, for instance, of removing some internal walls, Barry redesigned the area of Blore's building which housed various pantries and butteries, to create a comfortable Victorian version of a 'Long Gallery' – an airy room which lent itself to reading, entertainment and conversation.[41] He also introduced a Great Hall and accompanying tower and, with Charlotte's encouragement, contrived to express his clients' shared social status through splendid decoration. As Erica Obey argues, possession of a self-supporting landed estate counted for much with the Guests, and their entwined initials which appear in the form of an elegant device carved in the vault of the entrance, give conclusive stone-and-mortar rebuttal to any foolish notions about the 'taint of trade.'[42] If Dowlais, with its prospect of the works, spoke of wealth, Canford, with its gardens and grounds, manifested the grace, munificence and hospitality which that wealth supported.

Since John spent an increasing amount of his time in Dorset, it fell to Edward to oversee operations at the ironworks. Seasoned by his travels and settled within married life, the Guests had every reason to think that he must have acquired steady and purposeful habits. In May 1846, just when John, Charlotte and their nine children were beginning to acclimatise themselves to Canford, the Hutchins ménage, Edward, Isabella and her sister Clara, moved into Dowlais House.[43] The terms of their occupation were slippery, and it is not certain whether there was a formal lease, or whether the Hutchinses occupied the Guests' old and much beloved home on a grace-and-favour basis. Nevertheless, in his letters to the Iron Company agents in London, Edward always gave his address as 'Dowlais House, Abergavenny.'[44] An efficient-looking arrangement at the time of its making, the consequences of Edward's management would only become apparent later.

Meanwhile, the war of attrition between the Guests and Lord Bute dragged on. For a time, the Guests pursued the possibility of joining forces with Thompson and Forman of Penydarren, so as to run the two works together in the form of one joint stock company, but the plan foundered in the face of Lord Bute's quibbling over the respective boundaries.[45] At the end of 1846, Bute agent Geddes sent John what Charlotte termed a 'curious, Jesuitical' letter, in which he announced that he had been 'obliged', by way of making a pre-emptive move on the Bute Estate's behalf, 'to advertise' the Dowlais minerals – ore and coal – for sale.[46] Three months later, he called on the Guests in London with Lord Bute's final offer. Charlotte was present to record their exchange: 'Merthyr,' she wrote,

> told Geddes firmly that unless he could get the Royalties on fair terms, he would not think of taking a new Lease, and that he would positively pay no £80,000 renewal fine. Geddes said his ultimatum was 10 1/2d per ton for the coal and thereupon Merthyr expressed his determination to give no such sum. So Geddes said it was no use going further into the matter, upon which they parted, Merthyr having expressed his willingness to dispose of his plant at a fair value either to Lord Bute or any person to whom he might grant a lease of the minerals.[47]

It was, to all appearance, the end of the matter, a 'Day of Doom to Dowlais' thought Charlotte, who found the prospect of relinquishing all connection with the place 'very bitter, very heartrending indeed'.

There was a short joyous interlude when Grand Duke Konstantin Nikolayevich (1827–1892), second son of Czar Nicholas I, in Britain on a state visit, suddenly announced that he wished to see the Dowlais Works. After all, when the St Petersburg-Pauloffsky Railway, otherwise known as the Tsarskoye-Selo Railway opened in 1837, its trains ran upon on rail that had come from Dowlais and years later, a grim joke would have it that the last words to be read by Tolstoy's tragic Anna Karenina were 'Guest, Lewis & Co., Dowlais.'[48] For the Guests, whatever difficulties Lord Bute and his agents might cause, the Grand Duke's visit was an immense accolade – a tribute to John Guest's commercial instincts; to the skill of his workface and to the quality of their product, which now formed the foundation of railways worldwide. Excited, the *Morning Advertiser* reported that Konstantin intended to stop at Dowlais 'for the purpose of inspecting the extensive ironworks at which some of the most extensive Russian contracts have been taken'.[49] Charlotte briskly installed herself at Dowlais House with Isabella Hutchins and her sister, ready to mastermind the works necessary for the accommodation of a Russian Grand Duke and his retinue, having first entrusted the catering arrangements to the rather smart firm of Gunters in Mayfair.[50]

Her account of Konstantin himself suggests that he did not entirely impress her. A note of special pleading runs through her description: 'He is short, but has a good deal of dignity', she concedes before adding the detail that 'his features are slight, but they are delicately chiselled', and remarking that 'there is much firmness of purpose in the profile and the thin upper lip'. Phillip von Brunnow, the ambassador who accompanied him, proved to be rather a stick-in-the-mud; he barely glanced at the Works at night – the sight that Charlotte always found exhilarating – and declined to join Konstantin in inspecting the rolling mills, hard at work in producing rail destined for the expanding railway network of Imperial Russia. Charlotte determinedly persuaded him to let her take him round the old works in which he evinced no curiosity whatever. By contrast, Konstantin had at least acquainted himself with the broad idea of the railway phenomenon. A courteous man, he presented her with the lump of coal he had cut in one of the works' collieries, amiably requested to hear some Welsh music and went into raptures over the women's singing. Overall, Charlotte decided that the visitation 'had all gone off very well', and she thought the duke 'gratified with what he saw & with his reception generally'.[51]

The episode shows both Guests' determination that if they were to lose Dowlais, they should go out in style. They would, of course, do everything in their power to keep it – everything, that is, except pay the extortionate royalties and lease-renewal fine that Lord Bute demanded. In July 1847 after a bout of illness and pain which necessitated another of Brodie's 'operations', John took the serious step of revising his will. Under its amended terms Charlotte, supposing that she outlived him, would take sole charge of the management of his property, 'unshackled by the authority of trustees'.[52] Her response was solemn and heartfelt. 'I pray,' she wrote, 'should I be called upon ever to exercise this trust, that I may faithfully and judiciously discharge it, in the same noble and affectionate spirit in which it is confided.'

But by now, she had reconciled herself to severing her links with Wales and adjusting to life in Dorset, and by way of establishing herself upon the local scene, she soon interfered over the liturgy at Canford Parish Church. The theology of John Henry Newman, Edward Bouverie Pusey and John Keble had begun to colour Anglican worship, with clergy wearing stoles over their surplices, lighted candles appearing on church altars for the celebration of the Eucharist, and a move towards introducing devotional customs like fasting on Fridays. Charlotte thought it an anathema. When she heard Rev. Walter Ponsonby, Rector of Canford intoning parts of the service and noticed his preference for a crucifix rather than a plain cross on the altar, she made an appointment with John Sumner, Archbishop of Canterbury, to talk over her distress at this 'Popish' flavour of worship.[53] She also persuaded Rev. Evan Jenkins to visit from Dowlais to set Mr Ponsonby straight. On the secular side of things, she took the chance to attend 1846 meeting of the British Association at Southampton and set in motion improvements both to the estate – house, garden, park and farmland – and to the nearby schools. John would donate a large silver trophy, the 'Canford Cup', for award at the Poole Regatta, but defying his illness, he made a point of standing for re-election as MP for Merthyr Tydfil.[54]

*

He was returned unopposed, and soon afterwards, a deputation of workmen brought him what they called a memorial, that is, a statement setting out the disastrous consequences for the town if he and Lord Bute failed to come to terms. Neither party was willing to yield any ground, but both clung doggedly to their respective lines. Bute indicated that he owed nothing to the people of the place, but if the Dowlais Iron Company cared to renew their lease on his terms, they need only apply to his mineral agent. John meanwhile maintained that Bute's terms ruled out any question of renewal; besides, he claimed that he wished to move into 'the quiet of private life' which, on the eve of his re-election as Merthyr's member of parliament, seems rather a surprising disclosure. Clearly, the strife was set to continue.

Acutely conscious of the responsibility which he owed both to his workforce, and as the largest employer in the district, to the tradesmen of Merthyr Tydfil, John nevertheless remained unwilling to pay the vast sums which Lord Bute demanded. In November 1847, Charlotte set out the arithmetic of the impasse. 'Say that the profits have been £50,000,' she conjectured,

> of this the Royalties demanded by Lord Bute would absorb £25,000 leaving the other £25,000 for the leases. But the capital &c., in the works if withdrawn would yield £15,000, so that the £25,000 to be expected on renewal would only give a gain of £10,000.[55]

Loyal Edward Divett, John Guest's fellow MP, adviser and longstanding friend, also counselled against payment. Lord Bute's terms rendered any return from the ironworks inadequate to compensate for the 'risk and anxiety' involved in renewing the lease, particularly in the light of John's advancing age, his children's youth – Maria, the eldest, being at this time 13, and Blanche the youngest, just 3 months old – and what Charlotte termed 'the great difficulty of finding people to manage a concern of this magnitude'.[56] All that was certain was the unreasonable, slippery nature of Lord Bute's dealing and the Guests' wish, having recently acquired Canford at great expense, to enjoy a life of relative leisure in the gentle Dorset surroundings where the weather was kinder to John's health than the high winds and heavy rains of the valleys.

In January 1848 there was a rash of robberies in South Wales – the result, the newspaper pundits argued, of increasing unemployment. 'To make matters worse,' lamented the *London Daily News*, 'it is expected that the Dowlais Ironworks will soon be stopped'. It also remarked that the High Sheriff of Glamorgan had already requested that increased numbers of policemen be made available.[57] 'With regard to the state of affairs at Dowlais,' the *Bristol Mercury* reported a few days later, 'nothing can be more deplorable. […] The trade of the district is in a measure paralysed, no man buying but for daily consumption. […] No less than 1500 miners were yesterday discharged from the Dowlais works.'[58] Anticipating that huge numbers of families would soon be 'thrown upon the poor rate', the paper expressed a powerful wish to see Lord Bute and John Guest 'consent to a friendly arbitration'. Guest, it appeared, was willing to make public all this correspondence on the subject, to demonstrate that he had done everything in his power 'to avert the calamitous results that will ensue upon the stoppage, or even the temporary suspension, of the works'. Edward, meanwhile, took the drastic step of dismantling the engines. When three of the furnaces were blown out, the works' closure looked inevitable. In the febrile atmosphere, worried people seized on any comfort they could find, regardless of whether or not it had foundation. When a misleading rumour arose to the effect that John Guest had purchased George Crane's Ynyscedwyn Ironworks, the *Cardiff and Merthyr Guardian* soon stifled it.[59]

Just when all hope of Dowlais's survival appeared to have gone, Fate intervened. Visiting friends in Bournemouth, Charlotte heard someone say that Lord Bute was dead. As soon as she could get away, she returned to Canford agog with her news and took John through to his private room bursting to confide, only to discover that he already knew what had happened. Soon, the full story came out in the newspapers. Lord Bute had been staying at Cardiff Castle with his second wife and much adored baby son. On 18 March, he had inspected his new dock, to all appearance in robust health and buoyant spirits, and in the evening, entertained local dignitaries to dinner. Only later did his valet find him supine in his dressing room. He never recovered consciousness. At the subsequent inquest, the jury gave the verdict that 'he had died by visitation of God, in a natural way'.[60]

The unexpected speed of the event left Charlotte aghast. 'For years,' she wrote,

> Lord Bute had been the person to thwart and annoy us,
> perhaps I should say was the only enemy I felt conscious of
> possessing. […] his conduct towards us was certainly more
> like a persecution than anything else. Now to feel that one's
> only enemy was removed so suddenly was awful indeed….[61]

Lord Bute's body was taken to Kirtling in Cambridgeshire for burial. The funeral was grand and solemn, the crowds of mourners outnumbering those present at the funerals of the late kings George IV and William IV.[62] The tradition that none of the Glamorgan ironmasters attended the obsequies does not stand up to scrutiny. Rowland Fothergill of Llwydcoed, together with a couple of representatives of the Rhymney Iron Company, were on the dockside to watch the dead marquess borne away on his final journey and Francis Crawshay of Hirwaun, although not present himself, despatched fifty of his workmen to swell the Cardiff procession.[63] The Guests, however, were conspicuous by their absence. Since the fate of the lease now rested in the hands of Lord Bute's trustees, Onesiphorous Bruce and James McNabb, arrangements for the terms of its renewal could proceed in an atmosphere of professional detachment rather than grudges and guile.

Chapter Eight

Edward Hutchins

Having explored the ruins of Mosul and Kuvunjik in Assyria and excavated the site of the city of Nineveh, Charlotte's cousin Austen Henry Layard returned to Britain in April 1848, and visited the Guests at Canford. Henry, as they called him, endeared himself to all the family. Adventurer, explorer and scholar, he had seen – written in cuneiform – Sennacherib's record of the biblical siege of Jerusalem.[1] The discoveries that he had made in the company of Assyrian archaeologist Hormuzd Rassam promised to thrill the nation. It was no surprise that bookish, well-informed Charlotte should have revelled in his company. When Henry arranged to meet John Murray – publisher of *On the Use of Hot Air in the Iron Works of England and Scotland* – remembering her experience both of etching the Dufrénoy illustrations and commissioning the lithographic images for her *Mabinogion*, she was quick to offer advice on the best method of publishing Henry's 'on the spot' drawings.[2] If John, preoccupied with clarifying indistinct boundaries and labyrinthine subleases for the Bute Estate lawyers, not to mention shouldering the vast expense of Barry's work at Canford, should have resented Charlotte and Henry's carefree performance of the music of Mozart – she at the piano and he with his flute – it was understandable.

On the last Sunday of the month, instead of going to church with the children, Charlotte, feeling mildly unwell, stayed at home looking forward to 'a pleasant ramble' on their return. In the family's absence, John confronted her with an appalling accusation. It was not unusual for her to grow 'overset' and tearful at his rebukes, but this time her anguish was devastating. 'In the innocence of my heart,' she remembered,

> how little could I have anticipated these cruel, unjust suspicions – It was as though a thunderbolt had fallen at my feet. All that I suffered in those two hours, no one can

guess, and though now the wound has scarred over, I feel that it can never be effaced.[3]

Ignoring her tears, he compelled her, by sheer force of character, to join him and the children for a walk. 'I prayed to remain alone to compose my thoughts & feelings till tea time,' she recalled, 'but he insisted so much that at last I consented. They were all out, in gay, happy spirits, while I could not even hide my tears.' In the course of the outing, he recovered his temper. But nothing that he could do served to mollify Charlotte who cried and cried, and then spent a chilly evening watching the sunset from the Canford garden before retiring to bed. The next day, things were no better. 'Mayday though beautiful in itself brought no sunshine to me', she lamented, and ceased to write her journal for a full three weeks. Precisely what exchange occurred between John and herself over that time is unknown, except to say that it left the Guests once more reconciled.

In July, with the works' future secure, they made a triumphal return to South Wales. The train on which they travelled down from Cardiff was decked out with 'ribbons and flags and flowers' in their honour; the Dowlais friendly societies came out in force to join the procession and the police, under Superintendent Wrenn (on horseback), attended it in numbers, though whether their role was to keep the peace or augment the dignity of the occasion is not entirely easy to determine. Seeing the Guests, the townsmen wanted to unhitch the horses from their carriage and haul it through the streets themselves – an offer which Sir John declined. At the same time, he heard and accepted an engrossed copy of the fulsome address with which the Rector Evan Jenkins welcomed Charlotte and himself, and in response, while acknowledging that times for the iron trade had turned harsh, he pledged to do the utmost that he could for all who sought to follow their fortunes in the Dowlais works. The inns of the town stood open; Charlotte, in a burst of emotion, proposed a fond toast to *Yr Hen Wlad* – the old country – and John gave orders to put the out-of-commission furnaces back into blast.[4]

Keen to improve the living conditions of their workforce, in order to get some sense of what was achievable, late in the summer of 1848, the Guests visited Worsley in Lancashire, home of the Earl and Countess of Ellesmere, to see the various social amenities that they had provided for their labourers. Worsley, after all, was an estate village of an industrial character. Site of extensive coal mines, Lord and Lady Ellesmere's efforts to supply the colliers and their families with ample means of 'moral and intellectual improvement' had earned them a reputation for enlightened management. Their initiatives included building churches; opening schools, including one which specialised in 'training female servants'; stocking a reading room, and making a six-acre field available as 'recreation ground'. It had an 'ornamental building' at its centre, where the estate labourers received their fortnightly wage. Underlying the generous provision of facilities was a powerful wish to combat the menace of drunkenness and, unlike Dowlais, 'few public houses and no beer-shops' existed on the Ellesmere Estate.[5]

It is hard to gauge quite what the Guests made of their visit. Floating up to Worsley on the Bridgewater Canal, historic source of much of the Ellesmere wealth, was delightful, but when it came to viewing the actual estate, Charlotte was not entirely impressed. Like parts of Canford Manor, Worsley New Hall, where the Ellesmeres resided, had been designed by Sir Edward Blore. Charlotte thought it messy – 'full of incongruities' is her description, although she could not help but admire its situation. Inspecting the 'recreation ground', Charlotte observed a few children at the 'swings' and 'gymnastic poles', in the field, but remarked with some disappointment that the grounds were 'not very much frequented'. About Lady Ellesmere's 'servants' school' she had mixed feelings. While she was ready to concede that it had a 'very charitable' objective and appeared 'well-managed', she did not believe that it had any great utility. Training up twelve girls for servants' duties was, she thought, unlikely to make much impact upon the high levels of unemployment in a heavily populated area. Since they visited on a Saturday, she had no chance of observing lessons in the schools, but she admired the parish church and enjoyed visiting the henhouse that Lord and Lady Ellesmere had built to amuse their daughter, Lady Brackley. She also noted John's delight in the workshops and sawmill, complete with 16-horse-power engine which was, apparently, 'in beautiful order'.[6]

The Guests did not need the Earl and Countess of Ellesmere's example to make the case for social reform. Both John and Charlotte set great store upon nurturing the wellbeing of the workforce – something which they understood chiefly in the sense of promoting education. Even before the Worsley visit boosted Charlotte's zeal, she had already begun to set up schools, and the promise of the lease's renewal strengthened her commitment to the task. The Dowlais schools did not offer training in the tasks of domestic servants, but provided an expansive curriculum including reading, writing, arithmetic, geography, religious instruction, music, and English grammar and history for boys and girls alike.[7] Some of the senior boys, destined for employment in the ironworks, also learned algebra, mechanics and science. The Commissioners of Enquiry into the State of Education visited the Dowlais schools in 1846 and praised the 'discipline and good order' that they found there.[8]

There was some irony in this commendation, for their reports, known as the 'Blue Books', came to be infamous in Wales for their denigration of the Welsh language, which they described as 'a vast drawback to Wales and a manifold barrier to the moral progress and commercial prosperity of the people'.[9] Assuredly, the observations that the English clergy inspectors made upon the language and, by implication, its speakers, were hardly flattering. Carnhuanawc's scholarship came in for an almighty snubbing from commissioner Jelinger Symons who, in a contemptuous footnote upon the *Cymdeithas Cymreigyddion y Fenni*, related that one of the members had 'written a history of Wales, but couched it in such antique phraseology that its sale has never repaid the expense of publishing it'.[10] To add insult to injury, Symons went on to remark that there was 'no Welsh literature worthy of the name' – an ill-informed comment which Charlotte, with six parts of the *Mabinogion* already published and a seventh imminent, did not deign to dignify with a response.

Instead, pleased with the commissioners' broadly favourable account of education in Dowlais, over the autumn of 1848, she gave much time and attention to encouraging good practice at the existing schools, established some new ones and organised night-classes for adults employed at the works. She soon realised that she had embarked on an educational project on a truly epic scale. 'I think our present schools – boys – girls – infants – are thriving,' she wrote, trying to gauge the sheer extent of the task she had set herself.

> They will take in 5 to 600 children, but there are more than double that number yet unprovided for, half of them just the age to require schools, the other half probably either too young or too old – say altogether some 800 ready to be

educated. I must try what can be done. It is very difficult and in the present depression of trade and the very sad state these Works are in owing to their recent dismantling for the expiring Lease, it is almost impossible to accomplish anything just at this moment. I am promised another infant school towards Gellifaelog, and I am trying to organise a night school for the young females employed in the Works.[11]

Demand for tuition ran high, notably among the young women 'without any sort of education', who had come from West Wales in search of employment. Other prospective pupils were the daughters of Dowlais employees who had been to school as infants, but received 'very little instruction'.[12] To get some idea of what was available to them, Charlotte called at the existing girls' school in Merthyr Tydfil and found it in 'a sad state of neglect and ignorance'. The one teacher, wife of the boys' schoolmaster, to whom the post had fallen apparently by default, appeared to know 'nothing of what she was about'. There were some 220 girls registered, but – perhaps fortunately – only half that number actually present in class. 'This school,' wrote Charlotte, 'and one for the boys of about the same extent are all the schools that exist in Merthyr with a population of from 40 to 50,000 souls.'[13] Three days later, accompanied by Emily Kemble, the Guest daughters' governess, she opened her night school to the young women of the works. Out of the 177 present, twenty claimed to be able to read and write. She divided them into classes of about thirty-five pupils and put them to work under the supervision of the existing teachers and some of the agents' wives. They very much enjoyed the singing which opened and closed their instruction and were, she discovered, 'most anxious to learn [and] most grateful to be taught'.[14] Before long, visiting the schools became a regular part of the pattern of her own and her older daughters' evenings in Dowlais, unless John wanted them at home. At Christmas in 1848, the Guests invited all the night-school pupils to Dowlais House where they admired the hothouse fruit – pineapples, grapes and oranges – had tea and cake and cheered one of the teachers who had just got married.[15]

Charlotte would, incidentally, maintain an enduring interest in the education, not only of the school-age children, but also of the adult workforce at Dowlais, through lectures and establishment of libraries.

Successive school inspections yielded broadly favourable reports. As the years passed, the inspectors began to remark on cramped conditions, which suggest that the schools fell victim to their own popularity. A remarkable early photograph shows Charlotte, dressed in white, presiding in front of a mixed class and front row of teachers and works managers, beneath a gothic window in the school-buildings that she had commissioned Charles Barry to design. The building, with its elaborate tracery, has proved less durable than the image; sadly, it no longer survives.

While Charlotte busied herself with the Dowlais schools, John set about restoring the works to full efficiency and order. By February 1849, rebuilding of the out-of-blast furnaces was well in hand.[16] Now that the lease's renewal was no longer in doubt, the Dowlais Iron Company had every incentive to build on its commercial activity of the early 1840s, when orders for rail from different railway companies had flooded in. But John had failed to appreciate the degree to which, under Edward's supervision, standards had slipped.

The company clerks' correspondence gives a strong sense that Edward lacked the necessary skills for the job. On 11 April 1846, R.P. Davis, one of the senior clerks at the Dowlais Iron Company's London House in Lothbury, wrote to Edward in Wales to advise him that 'Goldschmidt's order' was now 'fully confirmed'.[17] Behind this brief detail lay an order from the banking house Bischoffsheim and Goldschmidt, on behalf of the Hungarian State Railway and the Thuringian Railway Company, for the supply of 2,208 tons of iron rail in total. The Thuringian company had also requested 'Pattern Rails' – that is, samples giving the rail profile – which, Davis explained, would leave London for the port of Bristol that evening, with the firm's nominated inspector scheduled to view them at Dowlais during the following week. Three vessels, Davies added, would be in the docks at Cardiff at the end of April ready for loading in the expectation that the entire consignment would be ready for shipping by the middle of May. Two days later, thanking Edward for his attention to the Hungarian order, Davis emphasised that the banking house regarded it as being of particular importance.[18] After another two days and further correspondence with the bank and their client, he instructed Edward not to wait for the inspector's report and not to concern himself about the risk of the rails' going over the specified weight; there would, admittedly, be an extra charge to pay, but it would not exceed 1*s* per ton. What mattered in executing the order, he emphasised, was achieving absolute accuracy in the rails' dimensions – they were to be 'rolled exact to template and no mistake' – and punctuality in supplying them.[19] As the weeks passed, Davis reiterated the imperative need to make haste with the Hungarian order, which rather suggests that there was some delay at Dowlais. On 22 April 1846, Davis passed on an instruction from John telling Edward to go 'as hard as he can' with the Thuringian and Hungarian orders, even if it meant delaying work-in-progress for the Cork and Bandon Railway in Ireland, which was evidently another Dowlais customer.[20] A day later, it emerged that there had been some unspecified set-back. Davis said that he was 'confident' that Edward would do all that he could to get the Thuringian, Hungarian and Chemnitz rails shipped before rolling any others; at the same time he castigated his failure to prepare more than one set of rolls for the Thuringian rails. It was, in his view, a piece of downright negligent oversight, especially since the Thuringian Railway Company had paid for them three months previously.[21] Edward's side of the correspondence does not, unfortunately, survive. For what it is worth, in his next missive, dated 28 April 1846, Davis promised Edward that he would 'enquire about the pictures'; in the thick of an exchange about the need for prompt fulfilment of an order for iron rail, this allusion to artwork is rather surprising.[22]

Early in May, there was some unrest among the workforce, and Davis wrote to express his hope that Edward's men were 'going on better'.[23] But things continued to go wrong. Soon, the London House received a complaint about 'a mistake over the Chemnitz Co's contract', specifically, that the Iron Company had supplied 'too large a proportion of short rails'.[24] By November 1846, the sheer volume of letters from aggrieved customers had grown to alarming proportions. Davis and his Lothbury colleague William Purnell contrived to answer the complaints diplomatically before conveying their gist to Edward. There had, apparently, been several objections to the effect that 'nail rod bundles' – that is, bundles of off-cuts from iron plates suitable for forging into wrought iron nails – were not of the specified weight; Davis instructed Edward to ensure that the weights be adjusted.[25] Messrs Goldschmidt sent a 'serious' letter indicating that despite repeated overtures, their order remained incomplete. Failure to forward the remaining rails would result in 'a heavy penalty' being levied upon the Dowlais Iron Company and – in all probability – rejection of the shipment already made.[26] Edward, it appeared, had priced the company out of the market for supplying double-headed rail for the GWR's line to Cheltenham.[27] There had been a delay in despatching a Mr Jevons's order to Cardiff and Davis requested that it be sent immediately, since he had assured Jevons that the iron had been ready for some time.[28] At the end of the month, a disappointed Irish customer complained so vehemently about the sub-standard bar iron which he had received from Dowlais, that Davis wrote to Edward to insist for the future that all iron be tested before it left the works, 'and no bad quality [....] be sent off'.[29]

Despite this precaution, things would get worse. Among the contracts secured by George Kitson, Dowlais's energetic agent in Europe, was one to supply iron rail for the Genoa-Turin Railway. In December 1848, Kitson intimated that he had some apprehension that his 'mission to Turin' was not proceeding entirely well, and that if he were not 'more successful at Genoa', all the rails would be 'thrown on our hands', in other words, rejected.[30] By way of response, Edward offered to obtain a testimonial as to the rails' quality from the Russian ambassador Baron Brunnow, although whether Brunnow had sufficient specialist knowledge to pass authoritative judgement upon iron manufacture is doubtful and, unsurprisingly, Kitson said that it would not help.[31] In Kitson's opinion, the promoters of the Genoa-Turin railway were 'a parcel of ignorant Jacks in office', and he did not care for their high-handed way of dictating terms.[32] At the same time, he knew that they suspected Dowlais of trying 'to foist upon foreigners goods that are not saleable in our own country' and, being a loyal man, wanted to see the company redeem its reputation with a high quality product. It was not to be. When the ship *Champion* docked at Genoa with her cargo of rails, the railway company tested them right on the quay with lamentable results. They proved to be 'as brittle as glass'.[33]

John might look upon his nephew's errors of judgment with a degree of forbearance, but Charlotte's patience began to wear thin. In January 1849 John had been reading the paper and dozing when, for a short time, he lost consciousness and she had been unable to rouse him.[34] The episode shook her, bringing the question of what was to happen to the works in the event of John's death to the forefront of her mind. John, of course, dismissed it from his thinking. Soon afterwards, he and Edward – 'carrying on business in co-partnership under the name or style of the Dowlais Iron Company' – jointly petitioned parliament for leave to bring in a Bill for making a branch of the Taff Vale Railway to Dowlais.[35] Behind their decision lay a vexed tale of failed attempts to construct the branch, and lapse and renewal of the authority granted by the TVR's enabling Act of 1836.[36] By the end of the 1840s, John was determined that Dowlais, both the village and ironworks, should have the benefit of an efficient rail connection with the TVR. Since his health was in palpable decline, promotion of the Dowlais Branch looked likely to be the last major initiative of his life. It was a time when Edward should have been a bulwark; instead, he was a liability. In June 1849, the parliamentary committee which had been examining the Dowlais Railway Bill and petitions opposing it from Penydarren and Plymouth, persuaded John to compromise over aspects of his original plan. Surprised that his counsel had recommended him to concede a number of points, Charlotte attributed the change of strategy to Edward, whose outlook she considered craven. She was, she wrote, 'most hurt at the way Merthyr had allowed himself to be put aside by Ed. Hutchins', and complained, in the privacy of her journal, that she could not understand how John, 'who used to be so firm', had allowed his nephew's 'weak counsels and want of spirit' to sway his judgment. 'This I shall never get over', she added.[37]

In 1850, for the first time in Charlotte's marriage, the Dowlais Iron Company made a loss. It distressed her beyond words, particularly since her husband was on the point of purchasing William Wyndham Lewis's share in the business for the substantial sum of £200,000. The following year, the Hutchinses' occupancy of Dowlais House would become a major flashpoint for controversy between them and the Guests. The Guests, after all, had made no formal written agreement with the Hutchinses as to when and in what circumstances they might make use of their old home. They probably thought it unnecessary: John because he was on good terms with his nephew; Charlotte because she considered that she had an inalienable right to stay there if she chose. Having decided to visit South Wales early in 1851, they rashly assumed that there would be no obstacle to their staying in the house where they had once lived.

It soon emerged that, far from being the only visitors, their trip would coincide with the visit of Rev. Thomas Joseph Brown OSB, Catholic Bishop of Newport and Menevia. He was to preside at the confirmation service at the Catholic Church of St Illtyd in Merthyr Tydfil and Isabella Hutchins, herself a Catholic, had offered to have him and his chaplain to stay while they were in the district. Being hospitable, she was ready to welcome and entertain the Guests at the same time.

But the 'No Popery' sentiment weighed heavily, not only with the Guests, but also upon the public mood. Cardinal Nicholas Wiseman had inadvertently stirred things up by introducing new Roman Catholic dioceses throughout England and Wales, which centred upon industrial towns. It caused an extraordinary amount of resentment and Lord John Russell, he of Reform Act fame, brought in an Ecclesiastical Titles Bill which purported to outlaw the new creations. Although it became law, no one was ever prosecuted under its clauses, and after twenty years it would be repealed. Nevertheless, its enactment said much about the anti-Catholic spirit of the times, a spirit with which Charlotte was roundly in tune.[38] The prospect of meeting Bishop Brown ignited all her indignation.

No sooner had the Guests reached Dowlais than they learned that he was 'expected on the morrow'. There was no time for them to alter their arrangements, and little scope for execution of Charlotte's secret plan to cut short their stay. Realising that she had no escape, she took Edward sternly to task, told him that there could be no question of John and herself meeting the bishop, or by their presence affording 'any sanction to his being there'. She then retreated to her room, smarting over the way that John and she found themselves stymied.[39] The next day she joined John on a walk around the Works, nursing her grievance every step of the way and bitterly resentful of Edward's following them. Briefly, she toyed with the notion of requesting John Evans to put them up overnight, but – despite Evans having made his own objections to the Hutchinses' visitor – she soon dismissed it. A meeting of the local Sanitary Commission occupied the afternoon, but then came the 'severest blow'. Charlotte's unspoken intention had been for John and herself either to decline dinner entirely, or to request that it be served to them in their bedroom. To her alarm, John was not willing to play along with her scruples, but intended to dine with the Hutchinses and the bishop. The shock upon finding her loyal ally turn traitor hit her with visceral force. 'I never felt so deserted,' she wrote, 'so completely cast aside and flung back upon myself.' While John dined with Bishop Brown, Edward and Isabella, Charlotte remained upstairs, crying, eating nothing and seeking balm for her wounded spirit by reading the Book of Proverbs. It was not her finest hour.

Over the remainder of the Guests' stay, Isabella tactfully used illness as an explanation for Charlotte's almost total invisibility. On the one occasion when she found herself in the same room as the bishop – he came into the dining room while she was eating breakfast – she rose at once and went out. As events turned out, he left Dowlais before the Guests did, apparently in response to a letter, although Charlotte preferred to believe that it because he 'suspected how uncongenial' she and her husband found his presence.[40]

The episode crystallised all Charlotte's resentment of Edward, of the position that he held in the works and of his occupancy of what she, not entirely fairly, continued to regard as her rightful home. When John and she left, despite parting 'kindly' with Isabella, she could not bring herself to bid Edward farewell. To her thinking, his conduct had sealed his fate. The following month, Francis Bircham, the Guests' solicitor, called on them at 8 Spring Gardens. In a rather cautious, roundabout passive construction, which declines to identify who actually said what, Charlotte reveals that in the course of discussing business, 'something was said of the discomfort of our connection with Edward Hutchins in the Works'.[41] The words, whoever said them, paved the way for decisive action. Bircham promptly recommended measures that would secure Edward's removal from the Dowlais Iron company's management. John, in other words, would buy him out.

When Bircham broached the proposal with Edward, he raised surprisingly little objection. His only stipulation was that 'some mutual friend' should be brought in to assess the value of his holding. In fact, the valuation question proved more vexed, and lengthier in the resolution, than either Edward himself or John, who initially wanted to organise the whole share transfer privately through Bircham, could have foreseen. Indeed, despite having agreed to purchase Edward's shares in the Company, John seems to have had second thoughts, or, as Charlotte expresses it, 'doubts … whether it is wise to incur the increased responsibility'; she herself wondered whether the agreed strategy would ever take effect. Although she expressed herself evasively, she recognised that John – acutely unwell – was beginning to contemplate the prospect of leaving the works to a successor. 'If … it pleased God to deprive us of his controul [*sic*],' she conjectured on paper, 'of what avail would be the presence of one whom it required all his [John's] knowledge and experience and standing to keep straight?' It is an obscure sentence, but its sense would seem to be that if John should cease to manage the works, what use would Edward, who needed all John's support, be in his stead? 'Rather would it not be one constant scene of struggle and contention, of grief and humiliation, to such as my dear husband might leave behind him?'[42]

Both Charlotte and Bircham had enough intuition to recognise John Guest's unspoken dislike of the entire arrangement. 'There is no new movement respecting Edward Hutchins' business and I begin to feel anxious', fretted Charlotte early in March, and later the same month, Bircham took the precaution of persuading John to agree to the appointment of a Mr Locke as arbitrator to rule on the value of Edward's holding, should John and he prove unable to decide the matter between themselves.[43] John's discomfiture with the process was entirely understandable. It presupposed his tacit recognition that Edward, the beloved nephew, political ally and – it is likely – *quondam* heir, was not up to job of running the works. Admittedly, not only Charlotte – her views coloured by prejudice – held this opinion; Bircham shared it and Divett took the blunt view that removing Edward from Dowlais was 'indispensable' to the Guests' 'future comfort & well-being'.[44]

The matter hung over them through the early summer of 1851.To Charlotte, sunny with the excitement of watching Queen Victoria open the Great Exhibition, Edward's vacillation and manoeuvres threatened trouble for the future; one day he appeared happy with the terms reached and the next, he would insist that his interest in the company was worth more than John had offered. By July, he was starting to talk of letting the time allowed for arbitration run out so that he could retain his interest in the works by default.[45] John, fond and indulgent, was inclined to humour his caprices, but Bircham took a firm line. On 5 July, after much hesitation, John made Edward what was to be his final offer. Teasingly, he asked Charlotte whether she would be 'angry' if he paid out £60,000, knowing that she would be only too glad to see an end to the matter. It meant that John became sole partner in the business, with the proviso that in the event of his decease, the works should be committed to Charlotte's sole charge, 'for the children' to inherit in time.[46] For the future, Charlotte would cease to be a spectator where matters of business were concerned, and become an active and committed player. The tenor of their marriage had imperceptibly but irrevocably altered.

Chapter Nine

A Good Death

Having run the Dowlais operation down while its future had looked uncertain, as soon as he was confident of the lease's renewal, John had set in hand a programme of upgrade and transformation. The dedicated branch-line, giving Dowlais its the vital transport link with the Taff Vale Railway was only one part of the improvements which included opening new coal pits to augment the fuel supply and, by way of increasing the works' overall capacity, installation of a vast new blowing engine and no fewer than eight Cornish boilers to provide blast to some eight furnaces.[1] There would also be a new rolling mill. But the time was less than propitious for such large-scale, costly improvements. The market had slumped and the dearth of orders hardly boded well for the future.

Marking the sombre portents, Charlotte recognised that, whatever his inclinations might be, despite having secured sole charge of the Dowlais Iron Company John's illness would, sooner or later, get in the way of his management of the concern. Always alive to the chance that he would read her journal, she avoided any speculation upon the consequences of his declining health. At the same time, it is likely that appraisal of his condition led her, tacitly – perhaps unconsciously – to make decisions which would have far-reaching consequences both for herself and for the works.

One such episode appears to have unfolded on 16 July 1849, when the Guests were at 8 Spring Gardens. John had spent the morning in exchange first with Edward, and then with Francis Bircham. Knowing that he had to undergo one of Sir Benjamin Brodie's unpleasant 'operations' in the afternoon, Charlotte soon intervened to curtail their conversation. Nevertheless, by the time that Brodie arrived, his patient was already exhausted. Worried, he had a brisk consultation with John which convinced him that delay would only exacerbate the pain, and that it would be best to go ahead at once. When the procedure was over John, faint and feverish, went to bed and Charlotte sat and sewed at his side. Hearing him begin to talk confusedly she realised, appalled, that he was delirious. At a loss, she hastened after Brodie, who was confident that John would soon regain consciousness, but nevertheless returned to help her nurse him through the night. 'No one,' Charlotte reflected, devoutly relieved that the children were all at Brighton, 'suspects how ill he was […] nor is he in the least conscious of it himself.'[2]

She could not entirely banish anxiety from her mind, but it did not cloud her capacity for taking an active interest in the events of the time. Walking or riding in Hyde Park, she observed the construction of the Crystal Palace in readiness for the Great Exhibition. Although she was ambivalent about the merits of Paxton's design – she thought it had 'all the flatness of a greenhouse' – the notion of a display of the Works of Industry of All Nations appealed powerfully to her imagination.[3] In February 1851, under her patronage, an Excursion Society formed itself at Dowlais with a view to coming to London later in the year to visit the spectacle, the members each subscribing £1 10*s* for their travel and accommodation.[4] Determined to give them the chance to make a full tours of the sights of London during their stay, she arranged accommodation for the party at the Ranelagh Club, otherwise known as the Mechanics' Club, at Thames Bank in Pimlico. Owned and run by one Thomas Harrison, whom the Exhibition must greatly have enriched, it offered sleeping accommodation for up to 1,000 men – there appears to have been no provision for women. Lodging cost 1*s* 3*d* per night. There was a smoking room; a reading room; concerts in the evenings; breakfast at 6*d* or 4*d*, and an evening meal at 8*d*.[5]

On 21 July 1851 the Dowlais contingent reached Paddington, ninety-strong, at about half-past five in the afternoon. No sooner did their train stop than the members of Dowlais Brass Band began to play. Predictably, they caught a great deal of attention and it was only by exercising all her powers of persuasion that Charlotte induced them to cease so that she could welcome them and despatch them to their lodging. She was careful to arrange that they should 'drive down the whole length of Regent Street, past the Houses of Parliament and Westmr Abbey on the way.'[6]

The following day, to reassure herself that they knew how to reach the Exhibition, she made a point of asking them to call by 8 Spring

Gardens for directions. By some misunderstanding their designated leader, Mr Howard, fell into line behind a regiment marching on its way towards St James's Park, but the Guests' butler, John Luff, intercepted them before they became totally lost. With his assistance, they found their way to the Crystal Palace, leaving Charlotte and her daughters to meet and greet the Canford estate workers and agricultural labourers, whom she had also invited to join in her scheme, and who were due to arrive at Waterloo shortly, via the South Western Railway.[7]

Over the following days, the visitors went all over central London. Not only did they visit the Great Exhibition and Westminster Abbey, but also St Paul's Cathedral, the Tower of London, the Monument, the Thames Tunnel, the Coal Exchange on its site near Billingsgate fish market, the National Gallery, Vernon Gallery, the British Museum, where Henry Layard showed them the marbles that he had brought back from Nineveh, the Royal Polytechnic Institution in Regent Street and the zoo.[8] It rained intermittently and John, who was, by now, in constant pain, made no secret of viewing the whole excursion-enterprise with the deepest pessimism. It almost made Charlotte lose heart. 'The responsibility of all these people,' she admitted, '(& with my dear husband telling me every moment that what I had proposed for them would not do at all, and that it must end ill) seemed too much for me–.'[9] But she could hardly send them home early and instead, determined that nothing should prevent them from having a good time that they would always remember.

One of the highlights she had planned was a visit to the new, purpose-built Houses of Parliament.[10] When they arrived, a difficulty confronted them which must have appeared to bear out all John's misgivings. The Lord Great Chamberlain of England – the officer of state entrusted with the care and custody of the Palace of Westminster – who was at this time Charlotte's relative Peter Drummond-Burrell, 22nd Baron Willoughby de Eresby, refused them admission. The Houses of Parliament, he insisted, were open to groups of visitors only on Sundays. By Sunday, Charlotte protested, her party would have gone home. It was to no avail. Lord Willoughby insisted upon keeping the rules.[11]

Baulked, Charlotte resorted to guile, and with great initiative, sought out Charles Barry. After all, not only had he been responsible for renovating and modifying Canford Manor, but he had also collaborated with Augustus Welby Pugin in designing the new Palace of Westminster. It was an inspired stroke. Architect Barry invoked his privilege of access to lead the entire party – 200-strong – 'through all the new works' and, Charlotte happily remembered, gave them 'many kind explanations and remarks' in the course of their tour. Having first visited the House of Commons, which was 'already prepared for a first sitting', he then showed them the House of Lords, 'which delighted them still more'. Touched by the men's interest in the building, he removed the covers from the throne and 'chairs of State' so that they could 'gratify their laudable curiosity' by a close-quarters inspection. Charlotte's stratagem for getting past a pompous official proved a triumph, and she thought she had never seen 'people better pleased, nor more rational withal' than the Dowlais and Canford tour parties.[12]

The high point of their London visit was to be a meal in the Guests' garden. Charlotte had intended that it should take place in the evening of 24 July, but it rained so hard all day that she reluctantly decided to postpone it; 25 July dawned clear, but a new difficulty arose. When she had first mooted hosting the open-air banquet, John had liked the idea. As soon as it promised to take solid shape on the lawn at 8 Spring Gardens, he became peevish and discouraging. It put Charlotte in a dilemma. On the one hand, she could not bear to upset him; on the other, having promised the men their celebration, she could not bring herself to disappoint them. Wretched with the knowledge that whatever course of action she adopted must lead to trouble, she put the matter before John: if he 'seriously wished' her to cancel the dinner, despite the good weather, she would do so, and assume full culpability for the let-down. Grudgingly, since illness seems to have eroded his old generosity of spirit, he allowed her to go through with her plan, but made no attempt to hide his frustration at what he regarded as her foolishness.

Trying not to lose heart, she escorted the Welshmen both to the British Museum and the zoo before returning to Spring Gardens, where she directed Luff and the other servants to set out tables in garden – one on either side of the broad walk, and a circular one for the Band at the end, ready for the children to decorate with flowers and fruit. By now the weather was 'brilliant'. When the men arrived, Charlotte took the head of one table and 'prevailed upon' John to take the head of the other. Husband and wife carved, while Lady Lindsey, Bertie, Henry Layard,

Anne Divett, tutor and governess Mr Newton and Miss Kemble, served and waited upon the company with help from the older children in an inspired Victorian Saturnalia. After-dinner speeches followed, the visitors cheering each toast so exuberantly that Charlotte half suspected that the police might arrive at any moment thinking that a riot was imminent. Once the party had ended, John took Charlotte aside, complimented her on the day's success and gave her 'his entire forgiveness'. Wisely, she avoided entangling herself in any question about what error she had made for which she needed to be forgiven. 'Poor thing,' she reflected,

> it is his state of health that makes him so averse to every exertion, not only on his own part but on that of others–. It makes me venture to take more on myself than I otherwise should do. In this case at least, the event proved that I was in the right & such he was only too ready to own.[13]

The following month the Dowlais Railway, which had caused Charlotte such consternation at the Parliamentary Committee stage, opened to traffic. The 1849 Act which authorised its construction allowed the Iron Company five years to complete it. It was, in fact, ready in three. Conceived primarily as a mineral line, in the early years it also carried both general goods and passengers. The extreme gradient of its route up Twyn y Roden Hill meant that its lower part operated as an inclined plane, for which the Newcastle firm of R and A Hawthorn designed a stationary engine capable of drawing trains of up to six carriages in length and 33 tons in weight, up the 1 in 12 slope. Watching the extensive work required for the engine's erection, a correspondent to the *Cardiff and Merthyr Guardian* drily enquired whether the railway was intended to run 'from Dowlais to the extreme point of Anglesey'.[14] In fact its total length was one mile and sixty-eight chains (2977.28m).[15]

Modest it might be, but royalty would grace its opening. Three days before the ceremony, just as John and Charlotte were about the set off on a carriage drive, the horse-omnibus had drawn up outside Dowlais House bringing Henry Layard on a visit, and with him, his friend Nawab Ekbal ed Dowleh, to whom the newspapers referred as the 'ex-King of Oude.'[16] With the help of John Evans, Charlotte planned and managed every stage in the celebration, from welcoming a party of Taff Vale Directors who had travelled down from Cardiff for the occasion, to pairing up her children to walk in the procession: 'viz. Ivor and Maria; Merthyr bach and Katharine; Montague and Enid; Geraint [Augustus] and Constance; Arthur and little Blanche'. Flanked by the local police, probably as much for show as for protection, they made their way to the station, which had been decked with greenery, with the schoolchildren and company agents following, to be joined on their way by 'the trade of Merthyr and Dowlais'. The combined bands of Cyfarthfa and Dowlais provided music for the occasion. Having boarded the train, they travelled to the top of the incline where there was a brief delay before they descended and went on to Merthyr. Some of the party ventured on by the TVR to Abercynon, but the Guests returned to Dowlais to prepare for the breakfast, speeches and dancing that were to take place at the Ivor Works.

At first, all went well. John proposed the opening toasts, and the Nawab set the seal upon the day's pleasures by responding with expressions of delight at the hospitality he had received in Dowlais, and asserting that he had never enjoyed himself so much as he had during his 'brief sojourn' in Wales.[17] But soon afterwards, John retreated from the fray and quietly went home, leaving Charlotte to pledge the health of the Taff Vale Directors, and initiate the dancing part of the proceedings. John's behaviour worried her – not so much his departure from the party, but his failure to any interest in 'all that was going on'.[18] She was not the only person to mark on his decline. The *Silurian*, which had covered Layard's lecture on Nineveh a few evenings earlier, noticed that on that occasion also, John Guest left the event early and remarked that he did 'not appear to be in good health'.[19]

Still she cherished the hope that he might get over his illness or, even if he did not make a full recovery, that Brodie's 'operations', to which he so stoically submitted, might relieve the constant pain. But in September 1851, when the Guests were at 8 Spring Gardens, Brodie's assistant Charles Hawkins called unexpectedly and, without evasion, told Charlotte that John's condition would neither stabilise nor improve. She does not report their conversation directly, but her journal account leaves little doubt of her recognition that her husband's decline was terminal. 'Mr Hawkins […] had a very long talk with me', she wrote, treading a path between outward poise and inner turmoil,

> He told me all I had to avoid, and all I had to dread. It was
> as much as I could do to bear it, but I dared not give way to

any appearance of feeling. I had, as soon as he was gone, to drive out with Merthyr. It was a glorious day – but what a drive it was! We went round the Park & near the Exhibition and the sun shone and all nature looked gay, but my heart was so full I felt it must almost burst.[20]

There was nothing further that either she or the medical profession could do, except to ensure that John should live out the rest of his life in peace, and die a good death.

Towards the end of the year circumstances manoeuvred her into exerting all her active authority in the ironworks' management. There was always a need for skilled staff, and in March 1849, John had recruited one William Wood, sometime manager of bar production at the Abersychan Works, to oversee manufacture of bar iron at Dowlais. Edward, who had been present at Wood's interview, pronounced him 'less aged & unwieldy than he had conceived him to be', which does not sound much of a recommendation. Admittedly, at the time he added that Mr Wood was likely to quarrel with John Evans and that the £1,000 salary with which John wooed him was far too high, but his warnings went unheard. John engaged Wood on the spot and promised him that since Thomas Evans had died the previous year, he should have Evans's old house to live in.[21]

It proved to be a rare error of judgement. Before long, just as Edward had anticipated, John Evans (Thomas's brother) made it clear that he was not prepared to take Wood's orders. John, who had known Evans for years, wrote him what Charlotte considered a 'kind and warm letter', in which he tactfully agreed to go along with his wish that Wood and his respective roles might be 'clearly defined' and that he – Evans – should be answerable for his orders to Guest alone.[22] But Wood appears to have been a magnet for trouble and in 1851 a simmering disagreement between him, Evans, and new recruit William Menelaus erupted into open strife. By this time John was too frail to intervene, so it fell to Charlotte to resolve matters.

Menelaus had previously worked for Rowland Fothergill, for whom he managed the small iron works at Llwydcoed and Abernant. At some point in 1850, John had noticed how shrewd a manager and skilled an engineer he was, and persuaded Menelaus to take up employment at Dowlais by offering to double the salary that he had from Fothergill.[23]

In his new position, Menelaus found himself expected to oversee the 'boiling and blooming' that went on at the Ivor Works, while at the same time maintaining the works' machinery. Since the machinery took up most of his time, it fell to William Wood to ensure that the supervision of the Ivor Works was adequate at all times.

Early in December 1851, Evans and Menelaus called on Charlotte at Dowlais House. Iron production at the Ivor Works was, apparently, drastically low. The cause of the shortfall appeared to be that in Menelaus's absence, the labourers were left 'to manage themselves'. Evans's view of the matter was that, by rights, Wood should have taken some initiative in resolving matters, either by overseeing the Ivor Works himself when Menelaus was caught up in his other duties, or by putting one of the on-site foremen in charge. He had, in fact, done nothing except keep quiet and leave Menelaus to take the consequences. Anxious not to be seen to take sides, Charlotte confined her scorn for Wood's readiness 'to throw the blame of mismanagement on another' to her journal, while promising to find Menelaus some 'assistance at the machinery' for the future.[24]

But the matter did not end there. In financial terms, the poor production rate of the Ivor Works gave rise to some bleak accounts. Three days after her exchange with Evans and Menelaus, Charlotte and Evans had a meeting with Dowlais accountant James Walkinshaw; Wood, whom she had also requested to attend, arrived late and out of temper. Having adopted a 'dogged and surly' attitude throughout the discussion, he ignored Charlotte's attempts to 'check' his 'snarling and unconciliatory manner' and began to bait Evans, against whom he appears to have nurtured a deep-seated grudge. A full-out quarrel ensued with the upshot that Wood handed in his three-month notice, before anyone could sack him. 'It had,' remarked Charlotte, 'been an exciting scene'.[25]

Perhaps unsurprisingly, Wood did not work out his notice. A couple of days after Charlotte's meeting with the accountant, Menelaus visited her to say that 'from Mr Wood's thrashing him', he found it 'impossible' to fulfil his supervisory duties in the Ivor Works and begged her to 'relieve him of all charges'. For answer, she austerely ordered him 'to do his duty and mind nothing'. At the same time she steeled herself 'to act boldly and let [Wood] go at once'. Since Wood owed his appointment to John, it was a large step for her to take, but finding Walkinshaw and Evans in total accord with her decision, she sacked him. 'This settled, and a plan for the future sketched out,' she wrote, 'I proposed to drive with Merthyr.'[26] As a manager, the episode marked her coming of age.

George Kitson wrote from Russia to say that he had reached a provisional agreement with Count Pyotr Andreevich Kleinmichel, Imperial Russia's Minister of Transport, for the supply of a large order of rail, at £6 10*s* per ton. Provided that the Tsar approved the agreement, he explained, the contract would, in effect, be sealed. While thinking the price on the low side, Charlotte found his news heartening enough to pass it on to John.[27] To her dismay, three days later, a further missive of Kitson's arrived to announce that Kleinmichel insisted upon discussing the 'necessary finance for the affair' further with the Tsar.[28] Telling John that the deal still hung in the balance upset her considerably when he was so ill, although on hearing the news, he accepted it with what she thought 'wonderful equanimity'.

Early in January 1852, there was a worrying development. Kitson reported that, with the Dowlais contract unconfirmed, rival company Bailey's – that is to say, Joseph and Crawshay Bailey's business at Nantyglo – had bid for the work on more favourable terms. Dreading the possible effect of this news upon John 'in his shattered state', Charlotte decided to say nothing until the order's fate was known.[29] After a week's uncertainty, another letter arrived from Kitson in which he proposed that if John were to request the Russian Ambassador Baron Brunnow to pledge that the Dowlais Company was best equipped to deal with the large Russian order, it might prove persuasive with the Russian authorities. Since there was no question of John's writing to the ambassador himself, Charlotte decided to make Purnell her emissary. She wrote a letter of introduction for him to present to Brunnow, explaining about John's illness by way of background, and trusting him to make a strong case for Dowlais's getting the order.[30]

John, in the dark, grew more impatient by the day and eventually decided that his wife must know more than she cared to admit. When he confronted her, Charlotte could no longer hide the truth about Kitson's letters and the arrangement that she had brokered between Purnell and Ambassador Brunnow who, incidentally, had written to her in most flattering terms. A reference for the Dowlais Iron Company would, the ambassador considered, be unnecessary since their name was 'as familiar in Russia as Barings'. Besides, to remind Kleinmichel and the Tsar of their 'standing and position' would 'seem impertinent'; Dowlais's professionalism, after all, spoke for itself. With John, these fulsome sentiments cut little ice, and Charlotte could see that the entire episode 'greatly vexed' him. Nevertheless, with a burst of his old acumen, he instructed her to inform Purnell that he proposed making terms with Bailey's by which the two works would 'divide the order' amicably between them, as opposed to 'running one another down.'[31] It was not the end of the business, but by drawing tactfully on the skills of Kitson and Purnell, Charlotte had at least set it on its way.

She had to meet a different kind of challenge when Ivor's housemaster wrote to recommend – in effect, to demand – the boy's immediate removal from Harrow School on account of his using 'wicked language' and being 'a promoter of evil in others'. Whatever the truth of the accusation, Charlotte could never bring herself to think that her eldest son could be in the wrong. The 'frank and affectionate kiss' that Ivor bestowed upon her as soon as he reached home was all that she needed to convince herself of his unimpeachable character. Although John insisted upon Ivor's accompanying him to the library for a serious conversation, within quarter of an hour he too was 'perfectly satisfied' that nothing was badly wrong with the boy or his morals.[32] To complete his education, the indulgent parents decided to send Ivor on a continental tour in the company of his sometime tutor, Mr Flamank. It ended prematurely after only a couple of months after their departure, when Flamank wrote to insist upon relinquishing his post, leaving Charlotte with no choice but to look for a suitable replacement bear-leader for her much-adored son.[33]

Politics also intruded upon her thinking. February 1852 brought the opportunity to re-nominate John's protégé Henry Danby Seymour to stand for re-election at Poole. Seymour had won the seat in 1850 at the by-election which followed the death of former Poole MP, George Richard Robinson.[34] He almost forfeited the Guests' favour, making no secret of his support for the creation of the new Catholic dioceses, like Menevia, and voting against Lord John Russell's Ecclesiastical Titles Bill.[35] Initially, John and Charlotte flirted with the idea of introducing Henry Layard to stand in his place, but Henry had by now found his political feet in Aylesbury which elected him as its MP in 1852.

Seymour, meanwhile proved popular with the Poole townsmen, which convinced John of the merits of his candidature. They joined forces to promote a Bristol and Poole Railway and John pledged to support Seymour at the 1852 poll, although Charlotte thought that their 'long and rather excited conversation' about the campaign did her husband 'no good'.[36] Nevertheless, the two men became friends as well as colleagues and before long, it began to look as though their friendship might have a remarkable outcome.[37]

In the summer of 1852, a number of West Country newspapers indicated that Seymour was about to marry one of the Guest daughters – Maria, whose eighteenth birthday fell on 3 July 1852, being the only plausible candidate.[38] Charlotte always had strong opinions about her children's prospective marital alliances and years later she took ruthless steps to end Merthyr bach's relationship with Georgina Treherne (born Georgina Thomas, later Georgina Weldon), whom she considered most unsuitable as a prospective wife.[39] It is difficult to believe that Seymour, being a partisan of the Catholic cause, would have been her husband of choice for Maria. Quite what happened between the Guests, their eldest daughter and the Poole MP is unknown. Certainly no marriage between them ever occurred and it is quite likely that the newspapers which predicted it had collectively jumped to a wrong conclusion.

In July 1852, despite being too weak to canvass, John was re-elected as Merthyr Tydfil's MP.[40] He was unable to attend the town's celebration of his success. To witness his decline, physical and mental, Charlotte found painful beyond words. All her instincts suggested that he would be happier in Wales than in London, but she knew that he would not find a long journey either peaceful or comfortable. Any stimulation, be it the visit of a friend or the prospect of a change of scene, left him so tense that she hesitated to make any arrangements for travel. Reluctantly, she agreed that they should start for Dowlais on 17 September, but faithful Edward Divett, 'passing through town' the day before, had called to see John, who became so 'excited and nervous' that she could 'hardly pacify him'.[41] She postponed their return to South Wales by a week and they reached Dowlais on 23 September.

In his old home, John recovered something of his former strength and gusto. The day after their arrival, Charlotte and he walked through the works and inspected the new Blast Engine, which had been four years in the making and which William Menelaus had 'just got to work'.[42] Another day, they met and chatted to Mr Cartwright, one of the engineers apparently recruited to assist Menelaus.[43] John agreed to the establishment of a Savings Bank in Dowlais and undertook to underwrite it for the first year of its existence.[44] Towards the end of September, they drove together down the valley to Troedyrhiw, once a beautiful spot, but now, Charlotte complained in high indignation, 'being destroyed by the ruthless cupidity (rather Barbarism) of Mr Lewis to whom this property was ceded in part payment at the settlement' – that is, as part of the agreement by which Guest had bought him out.[45] As the days went by, they picked up the familiar rhythms of the past, its preoccupations and prejudices alike. Charlotte remarked on George Kitson's having glimpsed the prospect of a large order from Warsaw; noted with satisfaction that the price of bar iron had 'run up to £7 per ton', and observed with less pleasure the governess Miss Kemble's attachment to the 'Puseyite' Mr Milton. Except for the detail that the new lease had not yet been ratified and finalised in readiness for John's signature, the string of experiences might fit within any year of the Guests' residence.

They went out in the carriage together on 17 November, as they had often done in the past, but the following day, John was too weak to get up. Charlotte sensed that his life was near its end and at once the tempo of her journal changed.[46] In place of bustling entries in which each day's activities – business; children; visits; reading; accounts and 'work' among them, – followed one another, hugger-mugger, at great speed, she tracked his ebbing life from hour to hour, as though by putting the experience into words upon the page, she could grasp it, like her pen, in her hand. 'He [John] slept all night & till 9 this morning,' she wrote on 22 November,

> when we woke him & tried to give him his breakfast but could not get him to take much. He seemed to take less notice today though he once asked me if Ivor were returned. Mr White helped me with Luff and Hillyard to make his bed comfortable and then Mr Jenkins saw him. Merthyr at once recognised him and after a few words, Mr Jenkins asked if he should pray. Merthyr answered, 'I have no objection' and Mr Jenkins gave us a short but most eloquent prayer.

Dear Merthyr cordially joined in it. His lips frequently moved – & when the Lord's Prayer was ended he audibly said Amen. After Mr Jenkins had left the room, he spoke of Christ and of looking to him – I could hardly catch his words but said enquiringly 'You do look to him?' He answered 'Yes, but not as much as I should do.' He had now been awake so long that we wished him to sleep. He did so, and I went down & saw Evans on various matters pertaining to the Works.[47]

He lingered on for three more days. On 24 November, John Evans brought the infamous lease which had just arrived in the post from Francis Bircham to the library at Dowlais House. Renewed, ratified, in its legally binding final form, it awaited only John's signature, but he was too weak to hold a pen. Evans, whose loyalty to his long-standing employer was akin to devotion, could not at first understand the difficulty. Only when Mr White explained the full medical gravity of Sir John Guest's condition did he grasp, shocked, the truth of the matter. Belatedly calling to mind his long service, Charlotte suggested that he come up to the sickroom to see John before he died. 'He accepted my offer most eagerly & followed me upstairs,' she wrote later,

But he hardly looked at him – & touched his hand – when he was so over-powered by his feelings that he was obliged to leave us hastily. Poor honest old man! How soon his own time may come – & then what a loss his fidelity will be to me![48]

On the following day, late in the afternoon, Merthyr bach, Montague, Augustus and Arthur arrived, permitted by their respective schools to come home while their father remained alive. Two by two, first the elder pair; then the younger ones, they watched for a time by his bed in farewell. For much the day, she and 15-year-old Katharine had kept him quiet company, needlework in hand. In the evening, Edward arrived to make his own stricken farewell to the uncle who had brought him up. 'He was,' wrote Charlotte, for once compassionate towards a man about whom she is seldom charitable, 'deeply affected.'[49] Over the morning of 26 November, all of John's children, except for Ivor who was abroad, kissed him and said a final 'God bless you'. Charlotte remained at his side, sitting on the bed with her left hand clasped in his, with Ann Hillyard, the children's nurse beside her. Around noon, John's breathing changed and he became quite still. Reaching to take his pulse, Charlotte could find none. He sighed and she kissed him, and then he sighed again, and was gone. For a time, the two women gazed on him together. Then Charlotte removed the gold and emerald ring that she had given him long ago from his finger, and put it on her own. 'My darling had passed away,' she wrote later, 'and I was left desolate.'

Chapter Ten

The Ironmaster

On 4 December 1852, John was buried in Dowlais – the place which he loved and whose people loved him. The local collieries and ironworks halted their operations and the shops, many of which had been partially closed since his death, shut for the day. For the funeral procession, the ironmasters Antony Hill, Crawshay Bailey and Robert Thompson Crawshay walked at the coffin's side together with Edward Divett MP and the lawyer Francis Bircham. Edward and Pegus took their places among the chief mourners alongside Merthyr bach and Monty. George Kitson and Mr Purnell came down from the London House, to join Henry Danby Seymour MP, Henry Layard MP and John Evans, who had been amazed to discover that John had remembered him in his will. No fewer than five clergy presided at the service: the bishop of Llandaff, the rectors respectively of Dowlais and Merthyr; the vicar of Aberdare and the curate of Dowlais. Schoolmaster Matthew Hirst conducted the Welsh and English choirs, who sang suitably solemn music as John was laid to rest in a vault below the communion table of St John's Church.[1]

According to the custom of the time, it was not until the day after the burial that Canon Jenkins preached the funeral sermon. It was an opportunity for him to pay public tribute to John's virtues and beneficence. Not only had he provided Dowlais with its church, library, mechanics' institute, schools and savings' bank, but he also withstood the fury of the 'misguided and misled multitude' during the 1831 Rising; taken measures to counteract drunkenness – 'the sin that so much degrades already corrupt and sinful human nature', and, by renewing the lease, had ensured the continued employment of 'tens of thousands' of local people'. Towards the end of his eulogy, Canon Jenkins offered some rather more personal reminiscence. John, he recalled, was 'by nature, nervous, timid and reserved' – words which suggest that, left to himself, he found the solitude of the Sully marshes more to his liking than brokering deals in the London House or resolving disputes among his workforce at Dowlais. Yet, the clergyman continued, 'in the creation of plans and projects, the executing of which he knew would necessitate him to lay out thousands upon thousands, he was as bold as a lion.'[2] Since the congregation remembered how close to closure the works had recently come, this reminder of John's readiness to invest in their revival was fitting.

Telling herself that there was 'nothing disrespectful or irreverent about routine's reasserting itself,' Charlotte ordered herself to 'Work – Work–'.[3] Her grief, she resolved, should not interrupt the rhythms of family and business life and she sketched out a pattern to follow; prayers and bible reading in the early morning, letters and calculations to occupy most of the day with an interval for 'dinner at one' if she could spare the time, and the evenings to be spent with the children.[4] Before long, with her encouragement, Merthyr bach, nearly 15 years old, took the significant step of dressing as a grown man rather than a boy, and was 'elated' at the transformation of his appearance.[5] When Ivor, abroad at the time of his father's funeral, came home, he presented a more sophisticated challenge. Since he could not get along with Mr Flamank, it was imperative to find a replacement tutor with whom he might study before he went up to Cambridge. Rather surprisingly, she put Pegus 'on the lookout' for a suitably scholarly individual and, equally surprisingly, he soon produced a most promising candidate.[6]

Walking home through the dusk with Maria, Katharine and Ivor one December evening after they gone to pray beside John's tomb, Charlotte observed the new tutor's arrival at Dowlais House. His credentials certainly impressed her; beyond his academic distinction – 'a Fellow of Trinity – has taken high honours' – people who knew him spoke well of him.[7] The following morning, she sent him on a walk through the Works with Ivor and they got on so well that she engaged him straightaway. 'He is to give up all other pupils – to remain with [Ivor] to prepare him till he goes to Cambridge & continue his Tutor while there. He is to have £400 a year,' she noted in satisfaction. Mr Pegus was delighted. 'My Dear Charlotte,' he wrote on Christmas Eve, 'I congratulate you upon securing […] a conscientious safe man to entrust your Boy […] and who will do his best to keep him in the straightest path.'[8] The new tutor's name was Charles Schreiber, and at the time of his appointment no one imagined quite what an impact he would make within the family.

Although they did not greatly impinge on her attention, she could not ignore civic and political matters; 14 December was the day of the by-election to fill the vacancy left by John's death, and the sorrow which Charlotte had tried to suppress almost overwhelmed her. 'How sad a Merthyr election seemed to me,' she wrote, 'the first in which my own darling has not been the principal person concerned.'[9] On the day of the poll, a bellman went through the streets of the town to summon the electorate to vote; at her behest, the Dowlais agents instructed the workforce to stay away. In the event, the successful candidate was Henry Austin Bruce. Since he had to relinquish his role as stipendiary magistrate, appointment of his successor was a matter of some interest to Charlotte, since John had been one of the moving spirits behind the legislation which secured for the town the services of an impartial justice.[10] The new stipendiary would be John Coke Fowler, and when it emerged that his appointment had not been formally ratified, Charlotte wrote in some annoyance to Lord Palmerston, the home secretary. 'If you can consistently confirm him [Fowler] in the post,' she explained, 'you will confirm a boon on a large population.'[11] She owed it to John's memory, so closely bound up with Merthyr Tydfil's wellbeing, to have the matter resolved.

She was already so familiar with the day-to-day tasks associated with the ironworks' administration, that after the months of John's illness they offered her the solace of routine. The essence of her management strategy emerges from the pages of her 'Works Journal', which she treated as a stark, dispassionate companion to her more colourful personal journal. Only a portion of it survives and not even in hard-copy form. Running from 6 December 1852 to 11 April 1854, it exists on a reel of microfilm which an enterprising staff member at Glamorgan Records Office made just before one of the Guest family took the original to the USA.[12] Fragmentary as they are, the entries suggest that her Works Journal served both as a memorandum book and a chronicle of collective corporate experience. Within it, she records Company requirements and activities; decisions taken or contemplated; contracts pending and agreed; and various proposed improvements, both within the works and on behalf of the workforce. Compiling her entries contemporaneously with writing her personal journal enabled her to view the same events from slightly differing perspectives. The entry in her personal journal for 21 December

1853 includes the brief statement, 'Colliers doing no work – much drunkenness – and the Works almost stopping.'[13] In her Works Journal, Charlotte expands this information and the more detailed account indicates how, rather than enter into dispute with the drunken colliers, she took advantage of their stupor to get ahead with some maintenance. 'Colliers working very badly,' she commented,

> beginning to keep Christmas – Little or no coal coming out. Arranged at once to stop Plate Mill (now, Middle Forge) and No. 6 furnace and make the alterations required in their engines – which we had contemplated deferring till next week.[14]

To all appearance, she wrote as she thought, impulsively and without much correction or re-working. Writing gave her scope both for reflection, and to probe the thinking of her lieutenants. In spring 1853, for instance, the market for iron experienced considerable fluctuation which led Richard Makin, Dowlais's sales agent in America, to make some serious miscalculations. 'I do not know what to think of the prospects of the Trade', mused Charlotte, musing over Makin's experience.

> We have on the books about 12,000 tons of Rails to make, besides 8,000 tons of the Russian contract for this year. The prices are not high [....] The 3000 tons were taken by Makin in America who, though having authority from us to take seventeen thousand tons more at or near £9 10 had such faith in the market that he declined several orders above that figure. He was, I fear, too sanguine; indeed, from the last letter from him received last week, it would appear the price in America had receded to £8 15s[15]

She had good reason to be anxious. The uncertainty of the market, which would continue for many months, would have some drastic results.

But other matters, such as the need to review the works' available motive power took up her time. By the end of 1852, the truly parlous condition of the existing Dowlais Railway locomotives was impossible to ignore. Shortly before Christmas 1852, her first Christmas as a widow, Charlotte ordered three new tank engines 'for mineral traffic' from

Neilson & Co of Glasgow, each costing £780.[16] It would be some months before they were available and the shortage of reliable locomotives for haulage meant that in the meantime, the works faced a coal-famine.[17] By mid-February 1853, there was so little fuel available that Charlotte sanctioned the despatch of the passenger locomotive *Ivor* 'up to the coal roads'. *Ivor* does not appear in John Owen's definitive list of Dowlais Ironworks locomotives. It is possible that the name was given informally to a 0-4-0 engine purchased from Sharp Brothers in 1851, and numbered 13. Whatever the passenger locomotive's provenance, Charlotte was quick to seek the assurance from Locomotive Superintendent Mr Barry that one of the other worn-out engines of Dowlais's disintegrating fleet would be repaired, and made ready for work while John Evans arranged for all the available horses to be harnessed ready for coal-haulage as a stop-gap measure.[18] Knowing that it would be many months before the Neilson tank engines arrived, Charlotte wrote to the London House to authorise immediate acquisition of 'two good second-hand locomotives, if such could be found' to be despatched to Dowlais 'directly for immediate use'.[19]

In the short term, this directive yielded no result, but being in London herself a week later, Charlotte seized the initiative and took her own steps to arrange the purchase. Of her negotiations she says nothing, but on 9 March she noted that 'One of the second-hand engines – the *Windsor* – arrived today, purchased from Wrights'.[20] *Windsor* cost £850 – rather more than the Company would pay for each of the Neilson engines – which suggests that the vendor may have driven a hard bargain. When Charlotte came to inspect her new acquisition in the engine shed at Dowlais, she thought it had a 'rather clumsy' appearance.'[21] By 19 March 1853, a further second-hand locomotive, this time purchased from the 'North West Co' arrived on the docks at Cardiff destined for Dowlais. With '4 wheels coupled for mineral traffic' it was, perhaps, one of the 0-4-0 goods engines that Edward Bury designed for the London & Birmingham Railway, later part of the LNWR. It cost the Iron Company a relatively modest £600.[22]

Supplementing the available locomotive stock was a useful measure, but it did not solve the problem of the coal shortage. Production of one ton of pig iron required something in the region of three tons of coal; to produce a fair week's make, the amount of fuel required was positively gargantuan. Although coal supplies around Dowlais were extensive, even in the early 1850s, methods of mining were far from efficient. In the weeks immediately preceding John's death, consumed with zeal to maintain Dowlais's profitability, Charlotte blamed some 'falling behind' with the make on an 'inadequate' amount of coal. It was apparently 'only 7,300 tons', instead of the 9,100 tons required to produce a make of '1,500 tons of finished iron per week'.[23] The shortfall hardly came as a surprise; towards the end of the 1840s, John had asked Thomas Errington Wales, the Dowlais mines engineer, to make an investigation of the work methods in use in the Iron Company's pits.[24] At the root of John's concern was the fact that it cost the Iron Company dear to access its own coal and he hoped that Wales would find some means of enabling the pits to be worked more economically.

By now, Charlotte had to make her own decisions. For a time, she had the support of George Thomas Clark, John's sometime adviser and the Guests' close friend, but he went abroad in February 1853, probably to attend the opening of the Great Indian Peninsular Railway.[25] Clark had a gift for dispensing counsel that was both sympathetic and, in Charlotte's opinion, 'sensible'. It was hardly unreasonable if he chose to join the first passenger train to make the twenty-one-mile journey between Boree Bunder in Bombay and Tannah – which, incidentally, it completed in less than an hour – since he had been in the Railway Company's employ over the years 1843–47, but his absence hit Charlotte hard. On the day of his departure she prayed fretfully for 'strength and sense' to sustain her while he was away.[26] By bad luck, at much the same time, Sir Stratford Canning despatched Henry Layard, who might also have been a heartening companion, to Constantinople. Convinced that Canning wished to get Layard 'out of the way and make him work for him, that he may get all the end of it … just as he was entering on the career of English public life', Charlotte ascribed the decision entirely to spite.[27]

Reviewing Wales's comprehensive pit-by-pit report, she realised that, despite the existence of plentiful coal deposits, the Dowlais Collieries were in a bad way. Typical entries include 'Lower Four Feet No 1 – Nearly reached the boundary & very little coal left. In a bad state. Ventilation weak. 8 horses'; 'Ras Las Right Level – Very unsettled due to working of the Brewhouse Big Coal above. Expensive to keep open. Ventilation very bad. 8 horses', and 'Great Cross Measure Drift – Very wet & arching bad in many places.' Wales also observed that the colliers' working days were not designed to maximise production and recommended that if, instead of having all the men start their twelve hours shift at 6am, half of them were to begin at 2am, staggering the shift would have the effect of getting double the quantity of coal from the same area over each day. He also proposed that it might make for greater efficiency if they were all to work in the same area, rather than over 'many seams at the same time'.[28] To improve the means of moving coal from the workings to the pithead, he advocated replacing the heavy iron trams with light wooden carts, reasoning that the energy of the horses was better spent in hauling coal than weighty wagons.[29]

Such remedies, while well-intentioned and not impracticable, could not offer a complete solution to what had become a major supply problem. In the short term, Charlotte resigned herself to sanctioning the purchase of coal from other mines of the district, such as Aberdare and Troedyrhiw.[30] Asked to revisit the issue in 1852, Wales concluded that the only effective means of ensuring that Dowlais had adequate coal for its needs was to sink new pits in to the Big Coal Level and the Upper Four Feet Level.[31] Wary of the likely expense involved, Charlotte decided to approach Northumbrian mines engineer Nicholas Wood for a second opinion on the matter.[32]

Wood's lifelong interest both in coalmining and in locomotive design may have encouraged her to regard him in a friendly light. What was more, he had been one of the judges at the 1829 Rainhill Trials, intended to make the case for the superiority of locomotives as opposed to fixed engines as the Liverpool and Manchester Railway's source of motive power, and John's and her journey along the Liverpool and Manchester line in 1833 had been one of early adventures of their marriage. Besides requesting him to comment on how best to maximise her available resources, she also asked him to revise Wales's survey of the Dowlais coal reserves, and to report on their working.

Wood spent about a month at Dowlais, engaged upon a thorough inspection of its pits. Broadly, his advice was consistent with that of Wales. Agreeing that it made sound sense to sink new pits on the Big Coal and Upper Four Foot Levels, he recommended suitable locations for them, together with additional pits on the Soar Level; for reasons of economy, he strongly advocated using engines rather than horses for haulage, 'both above and below ground level' Charlotte noted. He also recommended the purchase of a dedicated 'hauling engine' to operate on the Brewhouse Level. He suggested installing barrel-shaped coking ovens for coking the relatively uneconomic small coal, and promised to despatch a foreman to erect and manage them. Rather than appoint two coal agents to share responsibility for keeping up the supplies, he thought it preferable to have 'one responsible head' with a deputy to arrange for transport of the coal to where it was needed. In rather the same way, he preferred to see one managing engineer take charge both of the blast engines and what Charlotte calls the 'mineral engines', presumably the engines which were located at the mines as opposed to the furnaces. At the same time, he suggested that a 'superior foreman' be appointed to help the current works engineer Samuel Truran. By and large, he found much to approve in the operation of the Dowlais Mines, that is, the ironstone workings, which he considered to be in rather 'better order' than the collieries. Conducting what appears to have been an informal employment appraisal, Wood pronounced himself 'satisfied' with Mr Wales's competence; further, that if at the year's end, he appeared to have exerted himself to good purpose, his salary would rise by £50 at the end of the year.[33] In the meantime, Wood proposed to take Wales, Truran and mining engineer George Martin on a field trip round the mines of the North so that they could see the innovations he recommended in operation. Charlotte, appreciative of his clear-headed and authoritative appraisal, requested him to inspect the Dowlais coal pits twice a year.

Not only were the collieries grossly inefficient, but by the early 1850s maintaining supplies of ore was an equal challenge. Besides the local ironstone, the works required large amounts of red ore, or haematite, the best of which came from Cumbria. Carriage costs always added to its expense and as Dowlais agent John Wolrige explained to her, the price of shipping it from North West England to South Wales inevitably rose amid the winter storms. 'Freight for Red Ore much enhanced,' noted Charlotte in her Works Journal, having just read one of his letters.

> From Whitehaven 5/9; Barrow 5/- (or if Barrow ore shipped at Ulverstone then 5/6 on account of difficulty of loading). We have to advance to these rates though without much hope of getting vessels, which are very scarce in consequence of adverse weather etc.[34]

At the time, she hoped that she had sufficient reserves in hand to tide her over until the weather improved and shipping costs fell. But although John Evans contracted to purchase 20,000 tons of Northamptonshire ore early in February 1853, it was slow to arrive.[35] By Spring 1853, when the shortage of red ore was extreme, far from decreasing, the transport costs had risen. On 11 March, Wolrige wrote from Liverpool to say that he had contracted with one Mr Treweek to ship 25,000 tons of iron ore from Whitehaven to Cardiff docks 'at 6/6 per ton–'. Since available 'freights' – that is, vessels – were scarce, the arrangement looked satisfactory, not least because it promised to safeguard Dowlais against any recurrence of what Charlotte termed 'the great inconvenience we have been suffering from the want of a sufficient & regular supply of Red Ore.'[36] But in midsummer, Mr Treweek, through his agent, protested that he could not fulfil his part of the contract, 'owing to the extreme scarcity of vessels'. Freight carriage rose to 9s per ton, and by now Charlotte was growing desperate.[37]

She had some prospect of extending the Dowlais's iron-ore holding at Edge Hill near Cinderford in the Forest of Dean.[38] At the end of 1852, John Evans had offered to purchase the land adjoining the Dowlais mine for £3,300. Since it lent itself to ease of working, the acquisition potentially counted for much. Unfortunately, the owner's brother claimed that he had a share in the site with which he was unwilling to part.[39] It was an acutely frustrating discovery, since the mine had looked as though it might be a useful resource. 'Our workings in the Forest are in a sad state,' wrote Charlotte,

> The water has gained upon us to such an extent that all our operations are stopped. There has been unusually wet weather and many other people are similarly inconvenienced, but we are very badly off, and this coming at a time when we have been unable to get in Red Ore from the north owing to the scarcity of freight, is a most serious matter.[40]

By the following summer, she had resigned herself to the need to invest in a pumping engine to bring the Forest of Dean mine into efficient productivity.[41] Whether it was ever installed on the site is uncertain.[42]

Despite these setbacks, she had considerable aptitude for retaining the loyalty of her key personnel. When first she took charge of the Works, foreseeing a significant regime change, both Samuel Truran and Thomas Wales showed signs of discontent. Although Charlotte, who cannot have wished to lose either a competent engineer or her company coal agent, gave only the briefest account of her dealings with them, she appears to have been ready to listen to their grievances. Acknowledging that Truran was 'uneasy and about to leave', she added laconically that she had 'spoke to him', and was to see him again, the gist being that she had urged him to reconsider his decision.[43] Three weeks later, she wrote 'Saw Truran again – He stays with us.' The background detail that she supplies for his change of mind sketches both the reasons for his discontent and the tact and resourcefulness with which she addressed them. 'I would not accede to his demands for an advance,' she notes,

> However, I promised to allow him a poney [*sic*] & to give him a present of £50 if he put the new mineral engines to satisfaction – which will probably be a yearly allowance. The poney is necessary for him to get readily to his work which is far scattered over the mountains [...][44]

Provided with a bonus and the 1850s equivalent of a company car, Mr Truran remained in the Dowlais Iron company's employment until his death in 1860.[45] On the same day that Charlotte asked Nicholas Wood to inspect the Dowlais collieries, Thomas Errington Wales applied for his salary to be raised from £250 to £350 per annum. Having given the matter some thought Charlotte told him frankly that if she were to agree to his terms, it would set a 'dangerous precedent' at what, for the Company, was a volatile time. 'He therefore leaves us', she wrote, adding that he was 'a good man' and that she was 'sorry' to see him go.[46] But her journal does not tell the whole story, for Wales appears to have remained at Dowlais at least until 1855.[47] In July 1853 he was on hand both to escort Charlotte through the coal workings and, together with Evans and Bruce, to interview a deputation of striking colliers.[48] His continued presence at Dowlais may have owed something to her quiet persuasion and diplomacy. Later, he took up employment with the Abersychan Iron Company at their Ebbw Vale works and would in time join the Mines Inspectorate.[49]

*

Besides overseeing the operation of the Works and keeping herself informed about their stocks of materials and condition of the machinery, Charlotte – perhaps even more than John – was concerned with the social and educational facilities available to her workmen. Always interested in learning, when renewal of the lease became a certainty, she had been quick to increase school provision both for the Dowlais children and for adult learners. Widowed, she asked John Evans to solicit estimates for the cost of establishing what she called a 'Workmen's Room' – in effect, a reading room and library with smoking room annexed – and had it open and in use by March 1853.[50] Following Lord and Lady Ellesmere's example, she also provided her workforce with a recreation ground and attempted, by instituting the pattern of paying the labourers individually rather than in 'lists', to discourage widespread pay-day drunkenness. As a social reformer, she directed her energies towards education with great zeal, but in John's lifetime, both he and she had been strangely slow to recognise what peril lurked in the squalor of Dowlais. It was a filthy place, in common with the rest of Merthyr, as successive Reports to the Local Board of Health – by William Ranger Rammell in 1850, and William Kay in 1854 bear out.

Well supplied with water, much of what poured along the Taff served, through ingenious channelling and diversion, to power the Cyfarthfa works. For years, the need to make water available for domestic use somehow escaped attention, but by 1848 when the Public Health Act came into force, it was too pressing to ignore any longer. Owing much to Edwin Chadwick's championship, the Act promoted provision of piped sewerage systems and improved drainage; arrangements for cleansing streets; the appointment of medical officers in every town and – crucially – provision of wholesome drinking water. While it laid a framework for improvement open for local authorities to adopt, it did not make adoption compulsory. Essentially, either the ratepayers in a district could request an inspector to attend if 10 per cent of them signed a petition, or, its local Board of Health could convene an enquiry if the prevailing death rate exceeded 23 per 1,000 people. On the strength of an inspection or enquiry, a town could pay for and authorise its own water supply without the need to obtain an Act of Parliament first.

Quick to see the potential benefits for the people of Merthyr, Charlotte also acknowledged the strength of entrenched interests. 'The Ironmasters are averse to every improvement on the score of expense', she observed clear-headedly. Although she had misgivings about the extent of the influence she could bring to bear upon the matter, she nevertheless resolved to try to 'promote an amelioration of matter'.[51] Towards the end of his life, John had got into the habit of attending meetings of the local Board of Health specifically to discuss what Charlotte optimistically termed, 'Our proposed water company for Merthyr and Dowlais'. On Sunday 28 September 1851, while she took Edward Divett to watch the Dowlais Railway's inclined plane in operation, John attended a formal debate about the proposed waterworks, where he discussed the locations of reservoirs and talked up the health benefits of piped sewerage systems.[52] The day had ended on the rosiest of notes. 'The Company for the Water is formed & everything put in progress,' wrote Charlotte happily, 'for which, for my people's sake, I am most grateful.'[53]

But in autumn, her mood changed. In October, she admitted in her journal that she was concerned lest the project should be 'jobbed' – that is, evaded – 'or perhaps lost for this Session'. 'I do hope that all is now going straightforward', she wrote fretfully. 'I pray God it may be so for the sake of my people.'[54] Just before John had set off to attend the November waterworks meeting, a Mr Lynch called to tell him that 'everything seemed going wrong'. It appeared that shares in the new concern were under-subscribed by some £4,000. Generous as ever, John had promptly doubled his £2,000 subscription and persuaded William Crawshay to follow his example.[55]

Soon afterwards, weakened by illness and on the orders of his physicians, he withdrew from the fray. Admittedly a Merthyr Water Works Bill passed its third reading in the House of Commons in June 1852, but little came of it, except for complaints about the 'exorbitant' bill of Mr Lind, the lawyer who shepherded it through the House, and a raft of objections from the local ironmasters and the proprietors of the Glamorganshire Canal who all viewed the water works as a threat to their continued survival.[56] All the early promise of the scheme evaporated, while the cholera, which repeatedly ravaged the insanitary town, was a recurrent reminder of its necessity. Although a Water Works Company existed, the parties on whose goodwill its efficacy relied, objected to the plans for water extraction and rendered all the planning for a joint project ineffectual. Determined to take some definitive action, Charlotte proposed that the Dowlais Iron Company should provide the people of

Dowlais with their own supply of piped water at a cost of about £3,000 to be refunded by the Board of Health. It was almost a triumph, with the local paper impulsively declaring that she deserved commemoration with a statue for this inspired idea, but the Board of Health declined to cooperate and the whole enlightened enterprise withered on the branch. It would be some years before George Thomas Clark provided Dowlais with a reliable water-supply.

Through vision, resolution and energy, in spring 1853 Charlotte nevertheless succeeded in setting in motion the beginnings of a new regime. Foremost among her changes was the modification of the ironworks' pay-schedule. Under the system that she had inherited, the men received their pay as a lump sum handed to a 'list', or group. It was a practice which encouraged them to head for the nearest inn to divide the amount, accompanying the transaction with copious drinking. Disliking the haphazard procedure she determined that the men should be paid individually.[57] It might seem a simple and obvious initiative, but it caused considerable trouble. For one thing, it presupposed that the Merthyr Tydfil branch of the Brecon Bank would have sufficient coin available to furnish each man's wages. Charlotte managed to persuade local bank manager Mr Evans to furnish the iron company with enough cash for the 21 May payday, but her resolution 'to make enquiries in other directions how we can be best and cheapest supplied', suggests that his cooperation came at a cost.[58] In view of the sheer sums involved, it was not entirely surprising. On the first day of its operation, the new system did not run smoothly. The money, when it arrived from the bank, needed sorting into separate 'boxes', which had to be placed in 'compartments' for collection – a time-consuming task for the company clerks. Other unforeseen difficulties arose, which Charlotte does not describe, and the pay did not begin until fifteen minutes after the scheduled time. But she brushed every unanticipated obstacle aside. Once it began, the remuneration process went ahead fast and efficiently, and Charlotte was confident that the arrangement that she had set in hand would 'be productive of much good effect' for the future.[59]

As another reform, she requested monthly updates from her sectional managers responsible for 'Coal; Mine; Furnaces; Forges & Mills; Mineral & Blast Engines; Forge & Mill engines & machinery; Locomotives; Dowlais Branch & Traffic; Stables; Farrier; Houses & Buildings and Forest of Dean Mines' about their works in progress.

It would, she reasoned, avoid any wasteful duplication of existing projects. Before authorising any new work, her managers were to report on the 'estimated cost of labour and the description & quantity of the materials required for the same, with any suggestions for improvements, and other remarks that may present themselves.' On receipt of their bulletins she would, she resolved, consider their proposals and estimates of costs. 'From these estimates', she planned to determine 'how much it will [be] expedient to put in hand at once for the month [...] and to which of these it will be advisable to give precedence'.[60] Like her introduction of the new payment arrangements, the monthly report-writing was aimed at improving a lax, old work-practice which as manager, she regarded as no longer acceptable. It is, admittedly, debateable whether the busy stables, locomotives and mill-managers would have welcomed the new requirement to compile a monthly costed appraisal of works planned or in progress, complete with list of materials, possible improvements and other 'remarks', but Charlotte was confident that her scheme had sufficient merit to justify its implementation. She did not foresee the consequences of the market for iron's falling slack while the price of provisions rose.

Chapter Eleven

'...the right on our side':
The Strike of 1853

Between January and December 1852, the price of rail rose from £5 0s 0d to £8 10s per ton and early in 1853 some of the Dowlais workmen who had marked the rising market asked for a wage-increase.[1] The managers agreed to meet their demand but insisted that the pay-rise should not take effect until March, which did not entirely satisfy the workforce, since the cost of provisions was mounting fast. In February a number of them applied to the Company for 'relief' – that is to say, financial assistance for hardship. Naively, they even suggested that it might be helpful to have a Company shop, a proposal which Charlotte dismissed out of hand as being too much like truck.[2] Instead, she instructed them to find out the difference between the price of provisions in Dowlais and elsewhere, reasoning that if the local shopkeepers were taking advantage of her workforce, she would see what measures she could take to help.[3] As 1853 advanced, wages at Dowlais and the other Merthyr ironworks initially rose, but the market for iron slumped. It made the level of remuneration unsustainable and paved the way for a summer of strife.

The first intimation of trouble came in May 1853 when Charlotte, who was in Brighton at the time, received a letter from Robert Thompson Crawshay of Cyfarthfa. Skilled labour was in short supply and Crawshay, concerned about losing men, announced that he had increased the wages of the Cyfarthfa miners and colliers to the same amount that their Dowlais counterparts received.[4] As he must have known, where he led, the other ironmasters were likely to follow. For Charlotte, his move was contentious because Dowlais had a history of paying higher wages than the other works. It dated back to the 1820s when Plymouth, Penydarren and Cyfarthfa had all cut their wages, but Dowlais had maintained its rate of pay.[5] In local memory, the detail burned bright and the company valued its reputation as a generous employer. Among Charlotte's workforce, the 'Dowlais differential' was sacrosanct, but when times turned hard, the tradition gave rise to potentially unrealistic expectations. Recognising that the recent increase in the price of iron owed more to a short-lived boom than a stable market, she questioned whether current conditions justified Crawshay's action. It would, she foresaw, 'lead to another general advance', which the Merthyr Ironmasters could not comfortably afford. By way of economising, she promptly cancelled her contract for the installation of Ball Courts in the Works' new Recreation ground.[6]

Before long, Benjamin Martin, agent to William Thompson and William Forman of Penydarren, and Anthony Hill of Plymouth simultaneously sanctioned a wage-increase of 10 per cent. Anxious, Charlotte foresaw that that Dowlais would have to follow.[7] If she took a less than sanguine view of the matter, she was not alone. Hill called on her in June, ostensibly to discuss railway matters, but in reality, to express his concern at the possibility of pay spiralling out of control. In the light of the pay rise that he had so recently authorised, it was high-handed, but nevertheless he had good reason to emphasise the importance of all four Merthyr iron works adopting a concerted approach towards offering future advances, so as to avoid any question of the labourers playing one employer off against the others. Specifically, Hill asked Charlotte to take no steps over wage-rises without first consulting with the other Merthyr iron manufacturers. Although she was well aware of her own inexperience in the field of industrial relations, she could not help viewing his advice with some apprehension. 'I don't know whether the masters have cause to stop any further rise of wages,' she observed, 'but I am quite confident that if the four Works would agree to act together and keep faith with each other, it would be better for them, and for the men also.'[8]

The Penydarren Works proved to be a powder-keg, explosively precipitating the summer's storm. Some of Thompson & Forman's colliers never received Martin's promised a 10 per cent increase in full, and in protest, they threatened to withdraw their labour unless and until they were paid the monies owed. A small number of Dowlais colliers went to the Penydarren meeting in a spirit of support and, as a precautionary measure, Charlotte arranged for a policeman to 'see what was going on'.[9]

At the time, her thinking was on other matters. George Kitson had just written from London to urge her to ensure that the consignment of Dowlais rail destined for St Petersburg should be sent without delay. Political tension between Russia on the one hand and Britain, France and their allies on the other was rising fast, which promised to have rather more serious consequences than anything which emerged from an indignation meeting in Penydarren. Concerned, Charlotte gave instructions to the Iron Company's Cardiff agent for the rails' immediate despatch.[10]

While she mused over the Crimean conflict's likely consequences for her Russian trade, Charles Schreiber sickened with a fever. Close to delirium, he experienced something between a nervous breakdown and a crisis of conscience, and begged Charlotte to come to him to hear out his woes. At first, native scruple made her hesitate. To engage in intimate bedside conversation with the young tutor would, in her view, be indelicate. Thinking again, she decided that he must regard her as an aged crone in whom he could confide without arousing any improper suspicion. It was not an interpretation of Schreiber's thinking that flattered her vanity. 'It is,' she wrote, 'difficult for me who was comparatively a young woman last year, to feel and believe myself, as I am, an old woman now.' Although a widow, she was only 40 and even if her bereavement was recent enough to be raw, she always cherished the company of intelligent men, as Clark and Layard could have testified. But recognising that Schreiber believed he was near death, she put all thought of etiquette aside, went to his bedroom and let him pour out to her his 'fears'; his 'anguish at ever having sinned'; and his remorse at having 'forgotten God' and having 'neglected so many opportunities'. When he had finished, she prayed with him and comforted him with words from the Bible. Unwilling to dwell in her journal upon what she described as 'a very trying scene' she briskly summoned Mr White to assess Schreiber's medical needs and wrote asking Mrs Schreiber to come at once to look after her son.[11]

Charlotte tried to turn her full attention to her uneconomic collieries. On a wet day at the end of June she persuaded Thomas Wales to escort her through the underground workings – the Drifts, the Ras Las workings, the Cross measures and the Upper Four Foot Level – show her the ventilation system and explain the short-comings of the stall-and-pillar method of coal extraction. Once they had inspected the pumps and the underground stables, they emerged at ground level near the Bargoed Big Coal Pit. By good fortune, one of the more reliable Dowlais Railway locomotives was waiting near the top of the Bargoed Incline, so Charlotte climbed onto the footplate, sat down on a stray lump of coal, and rode home through the pouring rain.[12]

But the threat of unrest did not recede. Understandably 'dissatisfied' with the shortfall in the advance they had been promised, on 29 June the Penydarren men resolved to strike. When their intention became known, Anthony Hill decided that the ironmasters of Merthyr needed to meet and decide on a plan of 'concerted action'.[13] Charlotte, he assumed, would send John Evans to represent Dowlais's interests, but he underestimated her commitment and tenacity. She determined not only to attend the meeting, but also to host it.

It took place at 8 Spring Gardens on 1 July and shocked her rigid. Hill proposed if the Penydarren men had not returned to work by 9 July, then he for Plymouth, Crawshay of Cyfarthfa and Charlotte at Dowlais would give notice to stop their works a month from that date. The effect would be to mobilise local opinion against the aggrieved Penydarren labourers. In her Works Journal, Charlotte recorded with dry precision that, 'It was proposed that the men of the Working works should be seen on Monday & told that if by Saturday 9th [July] the Penydarren men were not at work, all the men of the district might expect notice to stop that day month.'[14] In her personal journal, she made no attempt to hide her repugnance for Hill's measures, saying that it struck her as 'monstrous [...] to tell our steady, good men that unless [...] they compelled their refractory neighbours to go to work we would revenge it upon them and throw them out of bread.' Concepts like 'revenge' and throwing people 'out of bread' had little place in the other ironmasters' understanding. Wondering uneasily whether her scruples amounted to nothing more than 'woman's weakness,' in the haste with which the meeting closed, Charlotte demurred over putting her name to Hill's resolution. 'Until I had signed,' she reasoned, 'I was not pledged [...] and could, after reflection, withdraw.'[15]

She was busy throughout the rest of the day. She engaged a 'chemist' – perhaps closer to a metallurgist – named Riley to analyse the content of the foreign ore which the Iron Company purchased. Edward Riley would also carry out the first experiments at Dowlais in the Bessemer process.[16] Later, Henry Layard called to discuss the increasing threat from Russia, and after he had left, Charlotte called on her mother who was now 73 years old, yet 'all her dress as soignée as a girl's'.[17] But she could not forget or quell her misgivings about the direction of the ironmasters' talk. At eight o'clock the following morning, as soon as John Evans arrived at Spring Gardens she told him definitively that she would not consent to join Hill and the others in a scheme that she considered 'Unjust, wrong and [which] could not prosper.' Thinking that he observed her change of heart with some relief, she sent him to tell Hill and Robert Crawshay that although she would assist in subsidising the Penydarren Works while the operatives were striking, she was not prepared to enter into what she called their 'horrible compact'.[18]

On her return to Dowlais, she discovered that Mrs Schreiber, having hastened to Dowlais to watch over her son's convalescence, was beginning to think he might make a good recovery. The two women walked around the village together, and Charlotte took the chance to show off the market and recreation ground.[19] But business, specifically a letter from William Thompson of Penydarren, soon reclaimed her attention. Remembering Charlotte's distaste for the tenor of the ironmasters' recent resolution, Thompson insisted upon the 'propriety' of the heads of the other works taking his part against the strikers. If they would not support him, he added with Charlotte in his sights, he would pay his men what they asked.[20] It would, as Charlotte recognised, precipitate demands for a wage rise at Plymouth, Cyfarthfa and Dowlais. Just as she began to draft a reply, John Evans called, bringing Penydarren agent Benjamin Martin with him. Thinking that she owed Martin a full and direct explanation, Charlotte courteously told him that, whatever opinions might prevail at the other works, she was not going to make herself party to a scheme which, in her opinion, contravened every principle of common justice. The Dowlais men, she said, had 'worked well and faithfully in times of much difficulty & temptation'. She could see no cause to hold them responsible for their striking neighbours at Penydarren, let alone threaten to terminate their employment if they did not 'induce or compel' the Penydarren to return to work.[21]

To expect Martin to grasp the force of her reasoning was vain endeavour. A company agent, he was caught between the stubborn Penydarren labourers on the one hand, and the high-handed demands of his masters Forman and Thompson on the other. In response to Charlotte's argument, he pronounced himself 'beaten' and made ready to authorise the advance which the Penydarren workforce demanded. It left Charlotte in a quandary, but she could not abandon her conviction that to gamble on closing her works as a means of quelling the unrest at Penydarren would be wrong. The consequences of putting her works, central to the livelihood of 'a population of some 40 to 50,000 people' out of commission did not bear contemplating.[22]

The middle of July found the Plymouth colliers and miners struck for an advance of 7½ per cent. John Evans received a letter from old William Crawshay and a visit from one of Anthony Hill's agents demanding to know if there was any truth in the rumour that Charlotte had promised the Dowlais men a 3½ per cent advance with an additional amount of 'charity money'.[23] To both of them, he gave a terse, negative answer. The probing, Charlotte reasoned, suggested that the men of both Cyfarthfa and Plymouth would shortly receive an advance.[24] The wage spiral continued its upward twist, and it was only a matter of time before the Dowlais men also demanded a pay-rise. The question of whether or not she would allow it, was not one that she cared to pursue. 'Of one thing I am quite resolved,' she wrote, 'if the men threaten, or make any demonstration of a strike, I will resist them to the end.[25]

By now, Mrs Schreiber thought that her son was strong enough to travel, and planned to take him to Brighton to set the seal on his recovery. To Charlotte, their departure was a blow. Lonely, she had enjoyed Mrs Schreiber's company. In the evenings, they had strolled together in the Dowlais House garden, or visited the church and the reading room which Charlotte had established in John's memory. Once Charles was well enough to get up, she warmed to his 'pleasant, animating discourse'.[26] After their departure, she spent a desolate afternoon watching the monumental masons erect a marble slab over John's tomb.[27] 'I am now left quite alone, not one mind [*sic*] near with whom I can exchange an idea', she lamented. She still hoped that the Board of Health would press ahead with measures to provide the town with adequate clean water, but their July 1853 meeting gave little ground for optimism. Evans reported Hill, the Crawshays and the Glamorganshire Canal Company all opposed proposals to build a Merthyr Tydfil waterworks on account of the threat that it posed to their water supplies. They intended, he gathered, to resist its establishment for as long as possible. At the prospects of future cholera epidemics, Charlotte nearly despaired. The only means by which to combat the menace, she reasoned, was to treat Dowlais independently from Merthyr, ensure that it should have its own water supply and, in her expression, 'get the cleansing of our district into our own hands'.[28] It would mean surveying, planning and drafting a whole new proposal.

Although she knew that a strike at Dowlais was pretty much inevitable, she almost missed the incipient signs of trouble stirring among her workforce. On 18 July, she went underground again with Mr Wales to familiarise herself with her collieries and found a small boy 'keeping a door' – in other words, opening a ventilation door to let coal carts through, which was typical of the type of job allotted to young persons employed in mines. Knowing how stringent the law had become – under the 1842 Mines Act, it was illegal for any child younger than 10 to work underground – she demanded to know his age. To her consternation he gave the frank answer that he was 'going his nine'. 'Poor infant' was her instinctive reflection, although she realised that his wage must make a crucial contribution to his family's income. Resigned and pragmatic, she resolved to find him 'an easy berth above ground'.[29]

As she and Wales walked on through the workings by candlelight, Charlotte's thoughts probably still with the infant, a number of colliers suddenly approached, demanding to know from Wales what level of advance they were to have.[30] Charlotte was not at first sure whether the men who accosted Wales and herself came from Dowlais or one of the other works, but she did not care to see her escort quizzed about remuneration in her presence. Knowing her views, he asked her whether the figure agreed was not 20 per cent. How he arrived at this amount was a mystery, not least to Charlotte, but she knew better than to encourage any off-the-cuff parleying. Instead, she told Wales to instruct the colliers to depute some of their number to see him about it in the evening.[31]

As soon as she was above ground once more, she appears to have put the incident to the back of her mind and chatted to the men about the Benefit Club and the recreation ground with its skittles and quoits. If she imagined that these subjects would distract the colliers from the questions of whether and when they would get an advance and how large it should be, she was mistaken. News of the recent exchange with Wales about their possible pay rise spread fast, its details garbling in the process. That very afternoon, Robert Crawshay asked John Evans if it was true that on her recent visit to her colliery Lady Charlotte had, allegedly on her own initiative, informed the men that they were to get 7½ per cent over and above anything that the other works were willing to pay. Evans hotly denied it, asserting that Crawshay's allegation had 'no shadow of foundation'; that the men had made no request for enhanced payment, but continued efficiently in their work and that for Lady Charlotte spontaneously to announce an advance in the manner that Crawshay suggested would be completely out of character. But in a febrile atmosphere, rumours could be remarkably difficult to quash. Evans, it emerged, had to parry questions from the Dowlais colliers 'about the amount of their advance' all the way home from his meeting. 'He told them 10 per cent – they muttered something about the 17½ per cent – but he told them we were giving them as much as we could possibly afford', wrote Charlotte, reflecting that the 1,655 tons of coal that the Dowlais Colliers had sent out the previous Saturday hardly represented an expression of discontent.[32]

In the evening, Wales called on the colliers' leaders as he had promised. In a bid to scotch some of the wilder allegations which had done the rounds, he told them point blank that they could expect an advance of 10 per cent. Evidently, they did not think it adequate because some of them went to John Evans afterwards to tell him that they would not continue working unless they received an advance of 17½ per cent. In the long summer dusk, the town crier went through the streets summoning all the Dowlais miners, who dug ore, and colliers, who dug coal, to a meeting at the top of the Drift, at 8 o'clock the next morning, to discuss strike action.[33]

Before 8 o'clock the next morning, John Evans arrived at Dowlais House, his ears ringing with the Dowlais women's jeers and taunts about the imminent stoppage. Wales came in soon after, and in consultation with Charlotte, they agreed that they must 'adopt the firm, bold course'. Specifically, it meant resisting any threat from the strikers, and as Wales observed, if they gave any ground to their opponents, it would jeopardise their chances of retaining control of the works and the men. In tacit agreement, Charlotte tallied up her accounts, so as 'to put the works in perfect order', while Evans worked out the likely cost to the works of sustaining a strike – the arithmetic suggested that they should have to allow for expenditure of 'about £1,000 per week without getting any return'. At his request, she also took the precaution of contacting Merthyr's new MP, Henry Bruce, for advice and support.[34]

Around mid-morning, a deputation from the meeting at the Drift came to the works office to ask Evans what level of advance the company was willing to offer. When he told them that the Dowlais Iron Company's offer stood at 10 per cent, they protested that since Cyfarthfa, Penydarren and Plymouth were paying 17½ or even 20 per cent, by virtue of Dowlais's traditional differential, they should be paid more. Unimpressed, Evans replied that with a recent down-turn in the market, the company could not improve the offer that it had already made; if they chose not to accept it, their best course was to give a month's notice. After all, he continued taking a more emollient tone, in that time the trade might improve which would raise the possibility of a more generous advance. If, on the other hand, the market remained stagnant, under the terms of their notice they could leave their employment in good standing. Seeing the force of his arguments, the miners and colliers' deputies thanked him, expressed their appreciation of the chance to have a 'reasonable conversation' and left to relay his gist to the assembly at the Drift. An hour later, a less deferential delegation arrived at the office and told Evans that unless they received the higher advance, they would not work. Preferring not to head into fruitless debate, he informed them that the company would not sanction it, and that he could say no more. Apparently, they tried to goad him into dispute, but taking his cue from Charlotte, he told them that if they went on strike, the furnaces would be blown out. It would, as he must have known, be a drastic step. By virtue of its construction, once a blast furnace has gone out, returning it to utility tends to be a major challenge and involve a rebuild. It evidently swayed the thinking of the miners, since they decided that their best course was to return to work. But the colliers remained set upon striking and in the face of their obduracy, Evans abandoned any further discussion and returned to Dowlais House.

'Peace or War?' asked Charlotte as he approached.

'War!' he answered.[35]

The afternoon was overcast and drizzly. Charlotte, having warned Menelaus about the latest developments, took solace from the reflection that all along, she had acted in accordance with her conscience and convictions. 'I am so grateful,' she wrote, 'that we have the right on our side, that this quite outweighs every other consideration.'[36] Her words invite some probing. After all, only a few weeks previously she had been at pains to praise her 'good, steady men', and eloquent in her objection to threatening them with unemployment if they failed to coerce their 'refractory neighbours' at strike-torn Penydarren back to work. Now that her colliers had shown themselves to be neither as good nor as steady as she had assumed, she no longer found the prospect of starving them into submission so objectionable. It was, by her reasoning, the fair outcome of their resolution to strike. Admittedly, the presence of the Dowlais differential muddied the waters of justice somewhat. To strike for a living wage might be one thing; to strike for the entitlement to receive a high wage because your employer had a reputation for paying more than her competitors looks rather different. It was not a theme that Charlotte explored, and nor did she look closely into the factors behind the colliers' decision. On their side, they took little reckoning of the prevailing economic climate in which the price of iron fell fast, and they either never read, or else dismissed out of hand, the local press's admonition to the effect that if wages rose unchecked, the net result would be a total exhaustion of the employers' capital.[37]

Committed to her course, in the evening Charlotte accompanied Evans out to the works. News had just come that Hill, 'in a pet', had sanctioned an advance to his men of 20 per cent, which was even more than Thompson and Forman had allowed at Penydarren. It was just the time when the 'turn', or shift, was changing. Evans summoned the men and told them that all charging of the furnaces was immediately to cease, except for No 17 at the Ivor Works, which had to be kept in blast because it was firing badly, and No 18, which was required for the supply of essential castings. While he gave the order, to demonstrate that he had her full backing, Charlotte deliberately stood nearby, talking to Menelaus. For the fires to burn themselves out would, she anticipated, take around forty-eight hours.[38] The following day she observed that 'the glow of the condemned furnaces [...] seemed to flame with surpassing brilliancy as their materials sank'. Watching, the spectacle recalled to her all the greatness that Dowlais had known in the past. It was, she wrote, 'the most magnificent sight' that she ever saw.[39]

*

On 22 July, Charlotte gave her workforce a month's notice to quit, and signs announcing the news went up throughout the works.[40] Foreseeing trouble, she agreed that fifteen policemen should be on hand at the next pay-day as a precaution. Lest their presence should suggest that she was 'afraid of the men' – something which she vehemently denied – she declined to accommodate them anywhere near Dowlais House, but instead sent mattresses for them to rest on in 'the large room of the works office'.[41] But there was no disturbance. Her workmen were 'perfectly peaceable & as quiet & respectful as possible', and she thought that she 'never saw the people more civil and better behaved'.[42]

Henry Bruce hastened down from London in answer to her summons and they walked together through the works, which were now dauntingly quiet, discussing the threat of legal action by the strikers. In their haste to make a stand, the colliers' leaders had given little thought either to the calendar as it charted Charlotte's 'long pays' or to the consequences of embarking on a strike some three days before pay-day. In Bruce's opinion – being a former stipendiary magistrate, he had a keen appreciation of the law – by striking, the colliers had forfeited the wage owing to them for the past six-weeks' work.[43]

Despite their talk, which Charlotte found 'very strengthening', she harboured much doubt in her own ability either to weather the present storm or to manage the works for the future. Breezy, well-meaning Henry Layard, she remembered, was apt to say that she took upon herself too many tasks that she would do better to delegate to other people. 'Now this sounds very feasible,' she wrote in frustration, 'but who is there to take the Head of a Work like this?' To leave Dowlais in the care of agents, like Thompson and Forman's Penydarren, would be to invite disaster and anyway John had always considered that an ironmaster should exercise active managerial oversight of his works. Besides, it was most unlikely that independent-minded John Evans – 'our invaluable old veteran', as she described him – would ever agree to work with a paid agent. True, she did not imagine that her present system of supervision was perfect: 'An able Principal, with practical and theoretical knowledge combined, would doubtless do much more than I can, who am only a woman and know nothing,' she wrote, reiterating her old grievance. At the same time, she could not see any realistic means of improving things. When it went well, she found the work satisfying; it had, what was more, sustained her through 'a load of misery', but that was not why she persevered with it. 'If but for the sake of the works, & the people & my children, the system could be amended, my private feelings should never stand in the way of doing what I thought advantageous for these, the care of whom has been so solemnly left to me,' she ended.[44] But her *cri de coeur* stayed silent, unheeded and hidden within the pages of her locked journal.

Rather than remain aloof and solitary in her great house overlooking her idle ironworks, she decided to go to Canford, where she would be 'better employed' in the company of her children.[45] But before she went to Dorset, to clarify her understanding of how things stood with the other Merthyr ironmasters, she took the opportunity to go into Cardiff on 26 July knowing that there was to be a canal meeting. It was a chance both to confer with Hill, the Crawshays and Ben Martin for Penydarren and to demonstrate that, whatever indecision she might have shown over the 'horrible compact', with her striking colliers she would be inexorable.

By good fortune, when the Cardiff train stopped at Troedyrhiw, Mr Hill got into her carriage. Having engaged him in conversation, Charlotte made a point of impressing upon him 'the necessity of the other ironmasters giving [Dowlais] their assistance in fighting this great battle.'[46] On reaching the Cardiff Arms Inn, where the meeting was to take place, she found herself surrounded by members of the Crawshay family, which made her think that it might be best if she waited in one of the upstairs rooms until the canal business was finished. It turned out to be a room in which she and John had often stayed and for a time she was overcome with tears. When John Evans arrived to tell her that the meeting had finished she composed herself enough to let him know that Hill had promised her his support, and make him, in effect, her messenger with Crawshay. Evans proved a most adroit deputy, and much to her relief, all the other ironmasters agreed to subsidise Dowlais while the strike ran its course. They would divide its 'make' of 1,350 tons of iron per week among their furnaces 'pro-rata' at an agreed sum of £7 10*s* per ton for rails – £1 below the market price – or pay £1 per ton for the quantity they should have made, if they were unable to supply it.[47] With this outcome, Charlotte was delighted. Not only had she secured a deal that would tide her works over a difficult time, but also – admittedly with

Evans's assistance – she had held her own with her iron-making peers, to sound practical purpose.

Having caught the mail train to London, she reached Paddington in the early hours of the following morning. By 5am, she was at Spring Gardens to hear the clocks strike the hour, snatch an early breakfast, and rest before George Kitson called. Wanting the reassurance of knowing that Dowlais was in secure hands while she was away, Charlotte despatched him to to act as 'a species of counsellor and adviser' to John Evans who would, she judged, appreciate the presence of an authoritative colleague. Their prime objective would be to ensure that the men who remained in the Iron Company's employment had useful tasks to engage them for the duration of the notice period. Their jobs included taking No 5 Blast Engine to pieces prior to a refit; repairing the Big Mill Boilers, and draining the Cae Harris Pond, all of which were no doubt necessary, if rather too menial to afford much satisfaction to a highly skilled workforce.[48]

No sooner had Kitson left for South Wales by the earliest train, than a succession of friends and relatives came in his wake, among them Henry Layard and his mother, and Edward Hutchins. Hutchins thoughtfully sent his carriage to take Charlotte to the station, which was just as well because the London cabmen, like the Dowlais colliers, were on strike. She caught the train, slept as far as Basingstoke, and on reaching Canford, found 'all the children assembled' to greet her.[49]

The leisure of Canford, with its gardens, proximity to the sea and her children for company pleased her less than she had expected. A visit from Henry Layard was welcome, but brief. The letters which arrived from Evans at Dowlais and William Purnell or George Kitson in London came in for her keen consideration and careful response.

Before long, the Company faced various legal challenges from its employees. A couple of days before their payment had fallen, two colliers went to the office to ask Evans if they were to receive their 'draw' on the morrow. He replied that they would not. By withdrawing their labour, he explained, they had breached the terms of their employment.[50] Their response was to bring a test case against the company.

On 1 August, John James, a Dowlais collier, sued the Company for his unpaid wages for the period immediately before he went strike. Under cross-examination in court, Mr James manged to tie himself in verbal knots by alleging on the one hand that he did not know it was the custom to give a month's notice before withdrawing labour, and on the other, agreeing that that he had heard the requirement read out aloud. Eventually he admitted that, contrary to custom, he had left his work without giving or receiving notice and was therefore in breach of the contractual conditions of his employment. Not surprisingly, stipendiary magistrate John Coke Fowler, found in the Company's favour by declaring James's wages forfeit.[51] It makes rather pathetic reading. The facts that first, the Dowlais Company appears customarily to have issued its notices in English (to judge from examples in Glamorgan Archives) and second, that at the hearing, the Welsh-speaking John James required the services of an interpreter (one of the Bench was a bilingual clergyman), suggests that a language barrier existed between himself and his employers. Whatever the precise terms of the law, there is also something unsettling about the spectacle of a man who admitted, upon oath, that he could not read and does not appear to have known whether he was being paid to cut coal by the ton, or work by the month or week, trying conclusions with a large and powerful company.[52] Mr James represented himself at the hearing; Dowlais had the services of Cardiff barrister John Bird. Having said that, the plaintiff probably did himself no favours by insisting in the proceedings that he knew 'nothing about anything except cutting coal by the ton'. Wisely, the Company did not ask for costs.

On 25 July the Dowlais iron puddlers had struck for a wage of 10/6d a ton – an increase of more than 3s upon their old wage of 7/2d a ton, on the basis that in the absence of coal, the Welsh pig could not be made, and the Scotch pig, which the Company purchased to tide the works over during the colliers' strike, turned out to be significantly harder to work. Puddling was skilled work. It involved working up pig iron in a furnace so as to rid it of the excess carbon content that made it brittle. When the facts behind the Dowlais puddlers' claim emerged, Dowlais's counsel, Welsh advocate Morgan Lloyd, advised Charlotte that the decision might well go against the Company.[53] Having endeavoured to broker a compromise, which the puddlers refused, she came back to Dowlais on 8 August. If outwardly resolute, her spirits were far from buoyant. The previous night, she all but admitted in her journal that her early zeal for the works, for the iron trade, for the world of commerce and industry that she had so much relished in John's life, was fast evaporating. 'While the first excitement of the novelty of my position lasted,' she reflected, her appetite for business, for improving the works and riding the currents of the (global) market had been formidable if not boundless. Without John, for so long her 'comfort and support', the excitement had gone. Lonely, her responsibilities had become her 'greatest trial'. 'Much as I love my children,' she wrote, 'I cannot entirely form every thought & feeling to them – they could not understand – they could not sympathise.'[54] Among her loyal and trusted friends, Henry Layard stood out, but they met 'too seldom' for him to give her the encouragement she sought, and besides, she thought him 'too full of politicks' – his own interest, in other words – to grasp the full extent of her concerns. She also thought George Clark 'might help her', except for the fact that he was abroad at this time. A few days previously, she had disclosed that he was in Versailles which, being accessible even in the 1850s by sea and rail, was hardly remote.[55] If she did not care to be seen to require his assistance, it was a misjudgement. Clark complained later that she had kept him 'in the dark' about the state of the Dowlais Works.[56]

The puddlers' case came before the court on 17 August. Evans, as witness, claimed that the change of pig-iron would be insignificant – it was no such thing. The court upheld the puddlers' claim for a higher wage on the basis that the Scots pig iron was so unlike the familiar Welsh pig iron and was so much more laborious and time-consuming to work into malleable wrought iron, that it more or less behaved like an entirely new and different substance.[57] It was a defeat for the iron company, which Charlotte could not help but take to heart. Under the provisions of John's will, youngest son Arthur should not come into his share by way of inheritance until he reached the age of 25; at the beginning of August 1853, he was not quite 12. 'Duty' to safeguard the family heritage demanded that she remain head of the works for many years to come. Somehow, she could find little zest for the prospect.

The notice which Dowlais had given its men expired on 19 August – at which every man employed in the works could either leave or be discharged. Charlotte, by this time, had marked signs that the colliers' resolve was weakening. As early as 31 July some of their wives had asked Evans for a 'draw' because they were starving; on 4 August, a number of the men told him that they 'were most anxious to work but that if they returned unconditionally, the other men would call them turncoats'. On 17 August, they sent messengers to Charlotte, saying much the same thing. She marked what they said, but declined to bargain with them.

On 29 August, the colliers approached Evans again, begging for their forfeited wage. They suggested that payment of a very small bonus per head would induce most of them to return to work. Charlotte noted the event, but gave no ground. Meanwhile, the increasingly penurious shopkeepers of Dowlais had met and compiled a rather desperate 'Memorial' in which they deprecated the strike – it had hit them hard – and expressed the hope that good relations between master and men might resume. Charlotte replied to the effect that it was her intention to act 'with firmness and justice', and that the interests of masters and men were 'identical'.

The strike dragged on until the local clergy, mindful of the hardship around them and conscious that winter was approaching, took decisive action. They agreed, among themselves, to get up a subscription for reward in the shape of an unspecified sum of money to be paid to the colliers at the end of a week's work. After a six-week strike, the colliers were more than ready to return to work – for nothing more than 'a minute bonus and no rise'. By this time, they had neither money nor the support of other Dowlais workers, let alone a union. Quite what sentiments lurked under the 'quiet, respectful demeanour' that Charlotte observed on passing them in the streets is open to question.

She revisited Dowlais at intervals over the following months, still intent upon securing for the place a decent supply of clean water. Despite her efforts, a mix of Board of Health inertia and active opposition by other ironmasters – since they were on the Board, the two things went hand in hand, the scheme failed to materialise. To add to her gloom, there was an ugly accident on the Dowlais Incline at the end of 1853, when someone failed to attach a rope to a descending carriage; it came down the precipitous slope with seven passengers inside and no control whatever. Somehow, six of passengers survived but the inquest's searching questions about traffic management on the Dowlais Railway cannot have lightened Charlotte's spirits.[58] But by now, something had overtaken Dowlais, its ironworks and all the supporting network of communication and amenities, in her thinking. That summer afternoon spent listening to a young man's sickbed confidences counted for more with her than she recognised at the time. She had fallen in love with Charles Schreiber.

Chapter Twelve

Lady Charlotte Guest and Charles Schreiber

In the immediate aftermath of strike, Charlotte stayed in London or Canford. 'They do not think it prudent that I should appear amongst the people for a few days, until matters have settled down a little more,' she wrote, and then added, 'but as soon as all apprehension of this kind is at an end, I must hurry back to Dowlais.'[1] Although she does not identify who 'They' were, the advice may have come from the clergy who encouraged the men back to work. From Lothbury, William Purnell wrote gloomily to draw attention to the 'heavy liabilities' that the Company had incurred over the recent weeks of inactivity, but at Canford, Charlotte's children congratulated her on the strike's resolution. Arthur, who had been unwell for most of the most of the summer, was beginning to recover and was at last, noted Charlotte, having previously said nothing about his paralysis, 'able to walk a little'.[2] Having written to the newspapers to correct the widespread misapprehension that she had 'employed' Rev. Evan Jenkins to broker an agreement with the strikers on her behalf, she requested Schreiber, or 'Charles' as she was beginning to think of him, to help her to draft an account of the recent unrest for possible publication in *The Times*.[3]

By 9 September, the news from the Works was sufficiently positive for Charlotte to return to Wales together with Ivor and, to his consternation, Charles. 'I think he a little dreads the idea of being at Dowlais', she reflected, and no doubt to the Cambridge scholar, the prospect of re-visiting the distant town, its inhabitants embittered by their strike's failure, cannot have been inviting. How much his inclusion owed to his scholastic duties, and how much to Charlotte's wish to have his company is debateable. After all, tutor and pupil had only recently been reading together in Bournemouth, so it is not entirely easy to see why uprooting themselves to travel to South Wales was strictly necessary.[4] Trying to

clarify her thinking, Charlotte only enmeshed herself in introspection.
'How it is to be, I even yet hardly know –', she wrote,

> Of one thing only I am certain – that is that I am intensely
> selfish and do what I will – with every effort to put self
> aside – I find thoughts of my own desolation <u>will</u> rise up in
> every picture for the future. My mind is in a very unhealthy,
> unsettled state. Even work does not seem to bring the relief
> it did – & ought.[5]

Such melancholy was hardly the dynamic outlook needed to restore
Dowlais's confidence for the future. But John had been dead for less than
a year. Only nine months previously, not long after she had signed the
new Dowlais lease, she had thrown her arms around his marble statue
in the library at Canford and kissed it over and over in a storm of tears.
In the collective memory of Dowlais, which would before long seek to
commemorate him with a library, he was irreplaceable. No wonder that
his widow should feel apprehensive.

The party from Canford arrived in South Wales on 13 September,
Charlotte's old affection for the hills and valleys, tips and furnaces
surging as she travelled along the Taff Vale Railway. On one side of the
line, the full moon rose above the Brecon Beacons; on the other, the
sun was setting. Once more in Dowlais, to all appearance, she devoted
herself to business matters with all her old zeal, meeting John Evans,
John Wolrige, Nicholas Wood and William Menelaus in succession on
her first morning. To show that the old routines and discipline held
good once more now that the strike was over, she inspected the steam
shears and 'spike machine' at the Ivor Works, and deliberately walked
back to Dowlais House past the tops of the furnaces and through the
forges and mills.[6]

Not everything went according to plan. One of her new 0-6-0
locomotives arrived from Neilsons and made a trial run on the metals
at the foot of the Incline. Just as Charlotte arrived to watch her new
acquisition's progress, the engine derailed. It was not an auspicious
beginning, but from her coign of vantage, Charlotte took the opportunity
to have some conversation with Wood and his assistant Mr Armstrong
on the subject of heat transference. As a result, not long afterwards the
two gentlemen bore John Evans off on a visit to Tredegar to inspect the

heat transference system which the Harfords of Ebbw Vale, who owned the Tredegar Iron Company, had recently introduced. The principle, as Charlotte noted in her Journal, was that hot gas from the furnaces was re-purposed 'for all heating purposes'. Having seen the Tredegar system for themselves, Evans, Armstrong and Wood gave Charlotte such a glowing report of its operation that she prepared to install similar apparatus at Dowlais.[7] It looked as though her old spirit would revive.

From her tours of inspection of the mills, engines, foundry, pattern shop, stables, Charlotte found 'everything […] in these Departments […] in the utmost confusion'. 'The sooner a new system is adopted the better', she decided, complaining that the sheer expense of running the works on their present chaotic footing was 'ruinous'.[8] Any notion of giving Ivor the chance to familiarise himself with the concern that it was his destiny to inherit seems to have escaped her. Instead, to all appearance, she set out to reassert her own authority both at the works and in the surrounding district.

Early in October, John Evans's nephew William called at Dowlais House to report that cholera had broken out once more. Shocked, Charlotte swore him to secrecy until the circumstances should be confirmed.[9] It reignited all her zeal to provide the local people with a supply of clean water, but the less-than-encouraging response with which the local ironmasters and the Board of Health had greeted her previous attempts to promote the project made her think carefully. Rather than take any action herself, since George Thomas Clark was visiting, she gave him the news. It was probably a piece of deliberate opportunism. The previous week the *Cardiff and Merthyr Guardian* had carried a story of the disease ravaging north-east England, and in the same edition, a letter signed 'M.R.C.S' remarked acidly upon the filth of Merthyr's streets and courts. Clean water, suggested M.R.C.S, for which there was pressing local need, might be taken from the Taf Fawr – big Taff – north of Cefn-coed-y-cymmer, and from the Taf Fechan – little Taff – near Morlais Castle and stored in a reservoir. The fact that no progress had been made with the proposed waterworks, which the townsmen had been debating for the past four years was, M.R.C.S reasoned, entirely due to their own misguided penny-pinching.[10]

'M.R.C.S' may well have been none other than Clark himself, since he was a qualified surgeon as well as an engineer and historian. If so, it was probably on his advice, and at Charlotte's instigation, that John Evans made an informal survey of the nearby watercourses from which he concluded that it would be possible to bring 'water down to Dowlais' from the Iron Company's own water supply 'for some three thousand pounds'.[11] It promised to be a large undertaking, but Charlotte immediately wrote to the local Board of Health, proposing that the Dowlais Company build the infrastructure necessary to supply Dowlais with water from Company property, and provide the necessary funds.[12] Unfortunately when the Board met to consider her suggestion, many of its influential members were missing. Dowlais surgeon Mr White, who might well have supported the proposition, chose to pay Charlotte a social call at just the time of the meeting; Crawshay's sister had recently died, so he, understandably was otherwise engaged, and Anthony Hill was absent, for reasons unexplained. It was not until 5 November that the matter featured on the Board of Health agenda and then, for their own reasons, the Board members postponed its discussion for a further three weeks.[13] Exasperated by their procrastination, Charlotte sent John Evans up to London to find how amenable Hill and Crawshay were to the prospect of her putting her plans into effect. In high excitement, the *Cardiff and Merthyr Guardian* rushed ahead of itself to cry up her triumph in an 'effusive editorial'.[14] But the jubilation was premature. Neither Hill nor Crawshay cared for her scheme at all. Hill required some £7,000 and Crawshay an immense £20,000 in compensation if the water were taken 'direct from the River without making the lower Reservoir' as Charlotte and Evans intended. Frustrated, Charlotte observed that their demands 'of course put such scheme out [of] the question'; in effect, they amounted to 'a refusal to grant it.'[15] Despite the energy and persuasive power that she brought to the venture, the vested interests of the other ironmasters proved invincible. In the event, it would not be until 1862 that the Merthyr Tydfil Waterworks opened and Clark secured for the town the supply of the clean water it so badly needed.[16]

Charlotte's relations with Charles changed subtly and almost imperceptibly. In her journal she was wary. To preserve its privacy in a house full of children and servants was not entirely easy, which may account for her tendency to couch her entries in enigmatic terms. Assuredly, she had no wish to encourage any speculation upon her growing intimacy with Ivor's tutor, and when she found her younger daughters playing at weddings with their dolls, she scornfully dismissed their game as 'extremely dull'.[17]

At about the same time that members of the Merthyr Board of Health were contriving their excuses to ignore the clear benefits of her Waterworks scheme, Charlotte was at Spring Gardens, expecting a visit from Ivor. When the door opened to admit Charles, who informed her son would not be coming because he had 'been taken with a slight attack of English cholera', she took the news with remarkable composure. Admittedly 'English cholera' was a mild strain of the disease and she was sorry not to see her son, but she was also very quick to invite Schreiber in to share her breakfast and chat by the fireside.[18] Two days later, the arrival of 'a letter from Mr Schreiber' gave her high pleasure, which abated rather when it turned out 'merely' to say that Ivor had recovered.[19] It begs the question of what, exactly, she had hoped for. Soon afterwards, youngest daughter Blanche had to undergo the surgical removal of a tumour on her eyelid. Recording the event, Charlotte said that she was 'desolate' all day and burst into tears in the evening.[20] Whether it was on Blanche's account – the experience must have been harrowing for a 6-year old – or her own, is impossible to say and, in the stress of the moment, Charlotte may not have known herself. But the day after, using some rinse or dye, she attempted to return her greying hair to its original black. Clearly self-conscious about the step she was taking – 'What a thing for a woman not very old to own in her journal', she mused – she added that she had acted on the advice of 'the only authority … whose opinion or feeling on the matter I care for', that is say, Charles.[21]

The first anniversary of John's death was upon her and she returned to Dowlais to pay her respects. At his grave, she confronted the confusion of her own thinking. Viewed in conjunction with the sharp sadness of his death and what she calls her 'present difficult position' – a reference, presumably, to her anomalous relationship with the other local ironmasters – the memory of 'the long happy years' of her marriage she found strangely 'trying'. She might endeavour to follow John's broad precepts of management, while introducing a few timely improvements in matters of work-practice and communication, but she could not experience the same informal ease of association with the managers and men that he had known. No wonder, if the recollection of the strike and the debacle over the waterworks should discomfit her; no wonder also that she should look to the future. 'Now I have but one hope,' she said, 'and to that I cling with a passionate tenacity.'[22] She was, in other words, ready to stake her future happiness on marriage to Charles.

At the end of November she lamented about 'being so much alone'. 'My thoughts will return to the difficulties of my position', she complained, her underlining emphasising the impossibility of banishing the sore subject from her mind. Indeed, the relevant journal passage bristles with detail of her latest plans for the works. John Evans was about to follow up the terms of an agreement with one Worthington for the supply of Black Band ore, the contract being 'not quite in order'; with William Menelaus, Charlotte discussed, not for the first time, the chance of ending the works' women's pattern of piling iron at night. Menelaus evidently shared her opinion that it was a 'dreadful' system and, perhaps with more optimism than conviction, promised that the practice should cease within two months. Late one afternoon, she made her way 'through the Old Furnaces' and went to inspect the forges and rolling mills where she found John Evans in earnest talk with Menelaus's assistant, Edward Williams, about the recent downturn in orders for rails, which were now so few that they had turned to using the Big Mill for production of bar iron. On her way back to Dowlais House, she went briefly into the new reading room. She also mentioned a project for a 'Model Lodging House' – presumably a works hostel, intended to afford better accommodation to her more far-flung employees than the rooms they could rent in the slums of the town – and said that if that, and the end to the women's night piling came about, she would have achieved enough in her visit to repay all the hardship it had brought her.[23] Yet it is hard to believe that, for all their merit, planning these projects afforded her much satisfaction. She pursued them as a matter of duty, but the true focus of her attention was upon her future.

Charles spent Christmas with the Guests at Canford, which may not have been entirely comfortable, since Maria and Katharine were openly critical about their mother's hair. Being somewhat self-conscious about the black dye, Charlotte tried to make light of it and assured them that 'something' should be done to render her appearance suitably 'old and venerable' once more. But the joke betrays the strain of her situation.

For the time being, she did not want the girls to grasp the direction of thinking. 'I can quite understand all their feelings about it', she wrote in a cryptic reference to her attempts at rejuvenating her appearance. 'They must be very far from entering into mine, and so for a while I hope they must continue…'.[24]

Having reviewed her finances, in the new year she decided to let out the splendid house in Spring Gardens and rent premises in the rather more modest Suffolk Street as her new London home. Around the same time, she consulted Francis Bircham about selling the works.[25] Even to contemplate such a measure, particularly after all the trouble that renewing the lease had brought to John and herself, shows how far her appetite for managerial responsibility had waned. But her sons were, in the main, too young and raw to take up any position in the concern, and she could not help but be aware of new competitors entering the iron-production field, both of which factors pointed to a need for strong leadership.[26] Respecting her reasoning, Bircham had the works valued and an inventory drawn up. But there was a flaw in her plans. The sheer size of the concern precluded any likelihood of finding a purchaser – it was valued at £400,000, exclusive of stocks of iron and other raw materials – and even the prospect of finding a tenant willing to lease it for a yearly rental seemed remote, particularly after the declaration of war with Russia.[27] Obliged to remain in her position as Head of the Works, Charlotte began to draw increasingly upon Clark's and Divett's advice and assistance.[28]

In February 1854 a visit to Ivor in Cambridge gave her the opportunity to spend some cherished time with Charles and, at home once more, she lived for his letters. 'I was very light hearted today,' she confided on 2 March, 'for the post was most propitious.' Two days later, deflated, she wrote, 'Hoped for a letter, but did not get the one I wanted, only disagreeable ones.' The next day was more promising. 'I have a letter,' she rejoiced, 'but it must remain unopened until after Breakfast when I can be quiet and alone. My hand shakes so I can hardly write…'.[29] Its content, when she digested it, was less pleasing than she had hoped. 'Alas,' she exclaimed,

> it was all couched in the most desponding, unhappy tone – and without one word of solace for me. I knew it must be illness. I trust not serious – but still – illness. I am not

alarmed, but grieved. Though future meetings are talked of, there is a bitter vein running through all that makes me <u>almost</u> doubt whether something I have done may not have annoyed, though I cannot guess what! the only consolatory point is that all the griefs, real & imaginary, are poured out to me thus without reserve – & indeed, the more I think it over, the more I feel convinced that health is at fault. But even this view of the case is very trying–. I must now be stouthearted in reality – for I think I foresee a good deal of anxiety–.[30]

The account of Charles's 'illness', and the 'bitter vein' in his writing which leads Charlotte to wonder whether she has unwittingly annoyed him raises some question about whether he was prone to depression. Even his readiness to confide in her does not speak of a love abounding in happiness. Yet love it clearly was, and Charlotte could not contemplate a future without him.

Nor could she continue to hide her feelings. At Dowlais, at the end of March, she and John Evans had a long discussion with one of the local sanitary commissioners about the constant fear of cholera and the lack of any progress with the waterworks. When William Kay, the sanitary man, took his leave, Evans who knew Charlotte well enough to speak his mind, told her straight out that she looked 'poorly'. Her activity on behalf of the ironworks together with her various social projects was, he thought, 'too much for any man [...] – much more a Lady!' She ought, he added, to have someone to help her.[31] Stung, Charlotte enquired whom, precisely, he had in mind. Realising that he had over-stepped some unspoken mark, Evans 'shifted his ground', and began to discuss a tenancy scheme. 'Well!' she exclaimed in response.

But the episode brought home to her the unremitting loneliness that she would face in managing John's works until their sons should inherit them. 'If I was happy,' she muses,

and had but the aid of a kind heart to commune with when my day's work was done, even though that dear one should take no share in my toil or my responsibility, I should do very well–. I feel within me such power & strength – & yet withal such weakness – & my heart so

overflowing–. This I suppose they would not consent – so
I must toil on till either I can transfer all the charge, or
till my spirit quite breaks.[32]

She does not specify who 'They' – the individuals who will not give
their consent to her remaining in her post, but with the support of a
husband – were but she presumably meant the trustees Clark and Divett,
with Bircham the lawyer. Yet she must have realised that they were
not empowered to alter the terms of the will as they touched upon her
remarriage. It was the provision which she had wished to incorporate,
and now it had trapped her.

If the language in which she explored her situation was febrile, she
nonetheless retained a hard-headed appreciation of the options open to
her. It is not clear what agreement – if any – she had made with Charles
by this time, but before long she took some decisive measures. Having
despatched Augustus, otherwise Geraint, to Harrow School under the
care of Mr Rendall, the 'mild, weak man' who was to be his housemaster,
she embarked on a round of consultations with the company clerks at
Lothbury as though to prepare them for a new regime. By a chance
of timing William Purnell who, she once complained, alarmed her
by 'always … predicting ruin', was about to leave the company.[33]
Installing Henry Austin Bruce as his successor at the London House
on John Evans's recommendation meant that, together with George
Kitson, he was able to exercise 'general directional supervision'
over the works, in a manner that ameliorated the effects of her own
withdrawal.[34] When Sir John's executors, Charlotte herself, Divett and
Clark, had a meeting with Bircham in mid-June 1854, although the
precise reasons underlying her decision remained secret, they seem to
have recognised that it was, in effect, her intention to retire. Having to
listen while the other trustees deliberated the extent of the allowance
to be made available to her 'for the maintenance, education &c of the
children', came as a shock.[35] She would, she foresaw, have to make
many economies in the future.

Her journal mentions no proposal of marriage, but on 1 October
1854, Charles showed her the letter he had just written to Ivor advising
him that when the new term opened at Cambridge, they would no longer
'read together'. Instead, like many of his friends, Ivor would 'read with
Girdlestone'. Beneath this outwardly dry and official notification of

a change of tutor was the tacit detail that Schreiber planned to marry Ivor's mother. Skimming the letter, Charlotte at first did not understand. Distressed, she did not go to church as she had planned, but remained at home in a ferment of uncertainty. 'For a moment,' she remembered,

> I really believed 'all over' & that henceforth my life was to be a blank! I went up to my room & knelt [in] fervent prayer. When I came down again, I found 'all serene' & that my alarm had been entirely groundless-. One "random word" had conjured up all this misery – Thank God it was so speedily & happily resolved![36]

They missed the second service of the day also, preferring to remain in Charlotte's room. In her journal she noted that the 'new arrangement' heralded a 'Great feeling of freedom & release from restraint'.

Even so, Charles and she continued to preserve considerable secrecy around their future plans. Another outbreak of cholera in Dowlais led Charlotte to abandon her proposed visit in the autumn and instead she went to Cambridge to explain to Ivor the consequences of her remarriage. He had not appreciated that she did not own the works outright, but on trust for her sons 'in such share or shares' as she might choose to allot. While she was there, she took the opportunity to 'read him a little lecture on economy'.[37] She and Charles told Mrs Schreiber about their plans and in due course, they received a letter back which gave the sense that she had considered it with great thoughtfulness. 'There is,' she wrote, 'nothing to be ashamed of, though there may be much to be said, for and against, on both sides....' Deliberate, Charlotte copied the statement into her journal entry for 23 November 1854, almost precisely two years to the date of John's death.

From about Christmas 1854 to her wedding day Charlotte's journal stayed bare. Not until 10 April 1855 did she resume her chronicle once more with the admission that it was 'very long now – more than three months' since she had last made any entry and the record was 'now all but irrecoverable,' but she expected, 'in a few hours to be the wife of Charles Schreiber.' The couple were married under special licence at St Martin in the Fields and Charlotte clearly saw the wedding as a chance to set aside various old quarrels. The celebrant was none other than Rev.

William Ponsonby, the Vicar of Canford Magna whose high church inclinations had once aroused all her wrath. John Guest's 'thoughtless' nephew Edward Hutchins gave the bride away, while his Catholic wife and sister-in-law were in the congregation along with George Thomas Clark, who would lead the Dowlais works into the future. 'I trust our marriage', prayed Charlotte,

> will be blest by that God without whom all we do is but vanity – and the bright sunshine that gleams around me while I write would, I will fain hope, give good omen of it.[38]

Perhaps the sunshine was not quite as steady as she might have wished. Although Maria, Katharine and Montague attended the wedding, together with Charles's brothers Henry and Brymer; his military uncles – two colonels – and Mr and Mrs Schreiber of Henhurst, neither Ivor nor Merthyr bach were present. Her friends viewed her second marriage with distinctly chilly eyes. Lady Llanover avoided the Schreibers' company; Henry Layard turned aloof and John Evans's granddaughter Phoebe went so far as to say that it had the result of leaving Lady Charlotte 'outcasted [*sic*] by everybody.'[39]

Like any married couple, Charles and Charlotte had to make many adjustments in their respective lives. Charles had to give up his Cambridge fellowship (the requirement that fellows be celibate did not disappear until the 1880s) and for Charlotte, it was the definitive end of her career as an industrialist. In time, they would turn their attention to ceramics, and the samples that they assembled would form the nucleus of the Victoria and Albert Museum's collection. Charlotte, with true collector's zeal, also developed an interest in fans and playing cards, and grew immensely knowledgeable about their decoration and history. When she revisited Dowlais, as she did at frequent intervals, it was usually to inspect the schools that she had established.

She was always touchingly keen to renew and maintain old friendships. In 1857, for instance, she and Charles traced Ivor's old tutor George Flamank to Stafford, where he was living in genteel poverty and 'struggling to publish a book'. Thinking him 'a sad specimen of a broken down gentleman', Charlotte sought some suitably judicious means of helping him.[40] It was a mission that required tactful handling, but it may not be entirely coincidental that when, with Ivor's goodwill, she and Charles had established a private press at Canford, one of the first publications to appear under the Canford Manor imprint was Flamank's tale of twelfth-century India, *The Golden Dragon of Golconda*.

Under the tenure of George Thomas Clark, the ironworks flourished, and by introducing the Bessemer process he drew Dowlais into the era of steel manufacture. As though to sever the links with the past, Clark dispensed with the services of George Kitson who became a banker. He also pensioned off John Evans, who died at Sully in March 1862.[41] William Menelaus became the works' general manager and not only adopted Charlotte's practice of taking regular walks through the works, but also shared on her insistence upon receiving regular reports from each department. While Charlotte requested the information at monthly intervals, Menelaus insisted upon being updated every week. If the old order changed, the works themselves lived on and while Plymouth, Penydarren and even the mighty Cyfarthfa ceased operations, Dowlais survived. But, in 1899 the old Dowlais Iron Company was renamed the Dowlais Iron, Steel and Coal Company and a year later, under Ivor's auspices, it merged with Birmingham man Arthur Keen's Patent Nut and Bolt Co. The new firm became known as 'Guest, Keen and Co' and in 1902, amalgamated with the Birmingham-based screw manufacturers Nettlefolds to form Guest, Keen and Nettlefolds Ltd., or GKN. At the time of writing, they are owned by Melrose Industries plc.[42]

Charles, in time, entered politics in the Tory interest, serving as Conservative MP for Cheltenham from 1865–8, and for Poole from 1880–4. Early in their marriage, Charlotte marked their difference of political affiliation, commenting that Charles had 'always been a Tory', while her own feelings 'took quite the other way'. Knowing that they disagreed, the couple thought it best 'never to speak on politicks to each other at all'.[43] As a general rule it served them well, although it did not stop Charles from blaming his wife when he failed to win the Cheltenham seat the first time that he contested it.[44] His relations with Charlotte's children were not always easy; they did not entirely care to have a stepfather, particularly one who arrived so soon after their actual father's death. Maria, in particular, found it difficult to adjust his presence in the family. The boys also had to live with the realisation that, for the future, they would not have the easy passage to the captaincy of industry which they had come to expect. Although they would inherit the Dowlais Iron Company, Clark, for sound reasons, refused to allow them to take any part in actually running the works. It was a point on which Charlotte gave him her full support. While she regretted their loss of any chance to learn about the business at first hand, she was quick to acknowledge that her sons' involvement in the day-to-day management of Dowlais could easily give him 'a great deal of trouble'.

It is a reflection whose wisdom is entirely consistent with her own courageous leadership of Dowlais. Her great initiatives, like organising the visit to the 1851 Exhibition; promoting schools and reading rooms for her workforce; and establishing excellent working relations with her deputies Evans, Truran, Wales and Menelaus speak of her humanity and the independence of thought that characterised her leadership. As a manager, she recognised the value of making herself approachable, preferring not to 'treat the people *de haut en bas*' [from the top to the bottom], but rather to seek, by 'a few firm, kind words' to set matters 'on a firm footing'.

If her second marriage took her away from Merthyr, an episode occurred at the end of 1877 which must have reawakened all her recollections. In the course of one of their china-collecting expeditions, Charles and she had taken the train from Poitiers to Bordeaux. 'At Angouleme' she wrote,

> we left the carriage to get a biscuit at the buffet, and were astonished at the appearance of two old Dowlais friends, Martin and Menelaus who were on their way to Bilbao to look after the iron mines there, which Ivor owns. We made Menelaus come in and talk with us the rest of our way to Bordeaux.[45]

Impulsive, like all her journal entries, in their minute compass, the lines distil all the power of memory. The chance encounter in the middle of France rolled back the years and for a fleeting instant Charlotte stood once more among her managers, the head of the works and an ironmaster to the end.

Appendix

In January 2017, reading Lady Charlotte's papers in the National Library of Wales, I found a loose sheet of paper on which there were two poems in her handwriting. One was an Italian sonnet; the other, an English translation of it in sonnet form which I take to be her work.

I have minimal knowledge of Italian, but by exploring online, I traced the Italian poem to the *Canzoniere* of Luigi Tansillo (1510–1568). At a guess, she first translated it because she liked it and the fact that she signed the page twice over, 'C.E. Bertie Feby 3 1832; C.E. Schreiber, Canford, 3 Jany 1877' suggests that her fondness for the piece never altered. Indeed, in her mid-sixties, she evidently re-visited and re-read her youthful translation before inserting it between the pages of her journal to keep it safe.

Here are the two poems:-

Bello s'il tentare le mananime improve

    Poichè spiegate hò l'ale al bel desio,
Quanto più sotto piè l'aria mi scorgo,
Più le superbe penne al vento porgo,
E spregio il Mondo, e verso'l Ciel m'invio.

    Nè del figliuol di Dedalo il fin rio
Fà, che giù pieghi; anzi via più risorgo.
Ch'io cadrò morto à terra ben m'accorgo;
Mà, qual vita pareggia il morir mio?

La voce del mio cor per l'aria sento:
Ove mi porti temerario? China:
Che raro è senza dual troppo ardimento.

Non temer, respond'io, l'alta ruina:
Fendi [sicur] le nubi, e muor' contento,
Se'l ciel sì illustre morte ne destina.

[Luigi Tansillo, 1510–1568, *Canzoniere*, Sonnetto XXV1]

Since I have spread my wings for bold surprise,
The more I've felt the air support my feet
The more I've spread my wings the air to meet.
I scorn the world, aspiring to the skies -.
　　　Nor does the fate of Icarus before me rise
To daunt me; ev'ry effort I repeat.
My certain fall with rapt'rous joy I greet.
Such death above ignoble life I prize.
　　　A voice proceeding from my heart enquires
Oh whence this rashness? Ere too late descend.
Too often grief attends such noble fires.
　　　I answer: should the course to ruin tend
Still fearless soar, 'twill crown all high desires
If heaven award thee such a glorious end.

It is a visionary expression of Charlotte's audacity, courage and warmth of heart.

Notes

Abbreviations

Bessborough (1950): *Lady Charlotte Guest – Extracts from her Journal 1833–1852,* ed. The Earl of Bessborough, P.C., G.C.M.G (John Murray: London, 1950)

Bessborough (1952): *Lady Charlotte Schreiber – Extracts from her Journal 1853–1891*, ed. The Earl of Bessborough, P.C., G.C.M.G. (John Murray: London, 1952)

Confidences of a Collector: *Lady Charlotte Schreiber's journals: confidences of a collector of ceramics and antiques throughout Britain, France, Holland, Belgium, Spain, Portugal, Turkey, Austria and Germany from the year 1869–1885*, edited by her son Montague J. Guest. Two volumes, (London: John Lane; The Bodley Head, 1911)

Guest and John: Revel Guest and Angela John, *Lady Charlotte: A Biography of the Nineteenth Century* (Weidenfeld and Nicolson: London, 1989), reissued as *Lady Charlotte Guest: An Extraordinary Life,* (Tempus: Stroud, 2007). Pages numbers are supplied for both editions.

LCJ: Lady Charlotte's Journals, held by the National Library of Wales, Aberystwyth. Roman numerals denote the volume number; the Bibliography gives the date-span of each volume.

Works Journal: Lady Charlotte Guest, Works Journal 1852–3, microfilmed December 1967. Glamorgan Record Office, location 2144S-446; Reel 129. (This item is the only part of Lady Charlotte's Works Journal that is known to survive).

Introduction

1. *Bristol Times and Mirror*, 21 February, 1852. The story was reprinted in the *Cardiff and Merthyr Guardian* 28 February 1852 and *Monmouthshire Merlin*, 19 March 1852. A slightly different version of the tale appears in John Randall's *The Severn Valley* (James Virtue: London, 1862) pp.144–45.

Chapter One

1. LCJ IX, 15 August 1833; Bessborough (1950), p.16.
2. *Gentleman's Magazine*, Vol 124, 1818, p.371.
3. Confidences of a Collector, Vol I., p.viii; Guest and John, (1989) p.15; (2008) p.34.
4. Bessborough, (1950) p.1.
5. Guest and John, (1989), p.12; (2007) p.31;
6. Guest and John (1989) pp.4-5; (2007) pp.25-26.
7. LCJ X, 19 July 1835.
8. Guest and John (1998) p.16; (2007) p.34. No primary source supplied.
9. Bessborough (1950), p.1.
10. Guest and John (1998) p.13; (2007), p.32.
11. LCJ VI 23 February 1827
12. Claire Rennie, 'The treatment of whooping cough in 18th century England,' https://humanities.exeter.ac.uk/media/universityofexeter/collegeofhumanities/history/exhistoria/volume8/Rennie_1-33.pdf),
13. LCJ VII, 22 April 1828.
14. *Alumni Oxonsienses*: the members of the University of Oxford, 1715-1886; their parentage, birthplace and year of birth, with a record of their degrees. Being the matriculation register of the University, Vol IV, (Oxford: Parker, 1888) pp.1576-7 (available online via archive.org).
15. Francis Willis, MD, *A Treatise on Mental Derangement*, (Longman et al; London, 1823) p.218.
16. LCJ VIII, 20 May 1830.
17. LCJ VII, found inside front cover.
18. The tales respectively of the Wife of Bath, Friar, Clerk and Squire appear together in vol III of John Bell's 1782 *Poetical Works*

of *Geoffrey Chaucer*, a popular edition, which may have been Charlotte's text.

19. LCJ IX, 12-13 December 1833. Travelling home from London to Wales with John, she read the 'Miller's Tale' commenting that 'it should be passed in silence', and the 'Merchant's Tale', which she pronounced 'wicked'. Given the disparity in their respective ages, it seems an unfortunate, not to say tactless choice.

20. Guest & John (1989) pp.37 and 249; (2007) pp.52; 238.

21. LCJ VIII, 9 July 1829. The lines adapt a passage from a sonnet by Vincenzo da Filicaia, 1642-1707 entitled 'Voto d'Eternita perle sue poesie'. The original runs 'Calma non chieggio a miei pensier, che alcuna/calma i miser non hanno; e gia veloce/Nel mar di Morte la turbata, e bruna/Onda va de miei giorni a metter foce.'

22. LCJ VIII 16 September, 1829.

23. Sally-Anne Shearn, 'An early description of Lady Charlotte Guest, translator of The Mabinogion' *Morgannwg*, Vol 62, 2018, pp.188-93, at p.192. (Given Source, Letter 7, Hon Henrietta Crewe to Hon Annabella Crewe (later Hungerford Milnes), 12 November [1830], Milnes Coates Archive, Borthwick Institute for Archives, York.)

24. Ibid.

25. LCJ VIII, 13 November 1830.

26. LCJ VIII, 19 March 1832.

27. Ibid.

28. Guest and John (1989) p.16; (2007) p.35.

29. Guest and John (1989) p.17; (2007) pp.35-6.

30. LCJ VIII, 29-31 July 1832.

31. Ibid.

32. Guest and John (1989) p.18; (2007) p.36.

33. *Morning Post*, 13 May 1833.

34. Diary of Mary [Maria Antoinetta] Pegus, later Lady Huntly, unnumbered volume beginning 15 November 1832, Northamptonshire Record Office, Wickham Box 12/2; 3116, 19 May 1833.

35. Ibid.

36. *The Atlas, 19 May 1833.*

37. *Morning Post*, 20 May 1833.

38. Bessborough (1950), p.2.

39. Guest and John (1989) pp.18 and xx; (2007), pp.36 and 19.

40. The full title is *Lady Charlotte Schreiber's journals: confidences of a collector of ceramics & antiques throughout Britain, France, Holland, Belgium, Spain, Portugal, Turkey, Austria & Germany from the year 1869 to 1885 in two volumes,* ed. Montague Guest, (John Lane; The Bodley Head: London, 1911).

41. The typescript remains in the hands of her descendants. (Email from Revel Guest to the author, 3 October 2016).

42. *Confidences of a Collector* (1911) p.xxi. Given source, Lady Charlotte Bertie, Journal entry for 20 May 1833. The relevant pages appear to have been removed from the manuscript.

43. *Lord Beaconsfield's Correspondence with his Sister,* 1832–1852 9 (John Murray: London, 1886) p.20.

44. B.R. Jerman, *The Young Disraeli* (Oxford University Press: London 1960). p.187.

45. Diaries of Mary [Maria Antoinetta] Pegus, later Lady Huntly, unnumbered volume beginning 15 November 1832 Northamptonshire Archives, Wickham Box 3116, item 2/12. 18 June; 28 June; 10 July 1833.

46. Daisy Hay, *Mr and Mrs Disraeli – A Strange Romance* (Penguin: London, 2015), p.52. Given source, letter from Mary Anne Disraeli to her brother John Evans, 27 July 1833, Bodleian Library Hughenden Deposit, 169/4, fols 34-5.

47. Guest and John (1998) p.283; (2008) p.262.

48. *Morning Post*, 30 July 1833.

49. LCJ IX, 29 July 1833; Bessborough (1950) p.15.

Chapter Two

1. Benjamin Heath Malkin *The Scenery, Antiquities and Biography of South Wales* (T.N. Longman and O. Rees: London, 1804), p.178.

2. Ibid., p.177.

3. T.E. Clarke, *A Guide to Merthyr Tydfil and the Traveller's Companion in visiting the iron works and the various interesting localities of the surrounding neighbourhood* (J.P. LEWIS, PRINTER; Merthyr Tydfil, 1848) p.14

4. Ibid, p.41.

5. LCJ XIV, 1 January 1849.

6. LCJ IX, 20 October 1834.

7. LCJ XI, 8 December 1838.

8. *Iron in the Making – Dowlais Iron Company Letters 1782-1860*, ed. Madeleine Elsas, (Glamorgan County Council et al: Cardiff, 1960), p.vii.

9. *Iron in the Making*, p.viii.

10. Edgar Jones, *A History of GKN*, Vol I, *Innovation and Enterprise, 1759-1918* (Macmillan: Basingstoke, 1987) p.84. Given source, Revd J. Hathren Davies, 'History of Dowlais' Merthyr Tydfil Library, (1891) p.9.

11. LCJ X, 26 October 1835.

12. William Taitt to Thomas Guest, 13 May 1799, *Iron in the Making* (1960) pp.19-20.

13. John A Owen, *A Short History of the Dowlais Ironworks* (Merthyr Tydfil Library Service: Merthyr Tydfil, 2001) p.13.

14. William Taitt to Josiah John Guest, 20 January 1809. *Iron in the Making* (1960) p.28.

15. Stephen K. Jones, *Brunel in South Wales* Vol I – *In Trevithick's Tracks* (History Press: Stroud, 2010) pp.45-61.

16. https://www.historyofparliamentonline.org/volume/1820-1832/constituencies/honiton

17. John Davies, *A History of Wales* (Penguin: Harmondsworth, 1994)

18. Gwyn A. Williams, *The Merthyr Rising* (Croom Helm: London, 1978) p.134.

19. Williams, p.226.

20. Guest and John 1998, pp.6-7; 2007 p.26.

21. The present Cardiff Castle owes its Gothic revival flamboyance to the Third Marquess of Bute and his architect William Burges.

22. LCJ IX, 15 August 1833.

23. Notice of John Guest's marriage to Maria Ranken appears in the *Gentleman's Magazine*, Vol LXXXVII, (Jan-Jun 1817), p.370. Robyn Bray provides an extensive Ranken family tree in her PhD thesis 'A Scholar, a Gentleman, and a Christian': John Josias Conybeare (1779–1824) and his 'Illustrations of Anglo-Saxon Poetry' (1826), University of Glasgow, 2013, p.407.

24. Woods, C.J. 'SAMUEL TURNER'S INFORMATION ON THE UNITED IRISHMEN, 1797–8.' *Analecta Hibernica*, no. 42, 2011, pp.181–227, at p.213. *JSTOR*, www.jstor.org/stable/23317233.

Information about the family's flight from Ireland from an online discussion about the Ranken family on www.rootschat.com/forum/.

25. Wilkins, *History of Merthyr Tydfil* (Harry Wood Southey: Merthyr Tydfil, 1867) pp.179-80

26. LCJ IX, 14 August 1833.

27. Ibid.

28. Guest and John (1989) pp.141-43; (2007) pp.134-5.

29. *Merthyr Guardian*, 22 August 1857.

30. LCJ IX, 26 December 1833.

31. Ibid.

32. LCJ X, 17 November 1836.

33. LCJ IX, 4 September 1833.

34. LCJ IX, 27 September 1833.

35. LCJ IX, 4 October 1833.

36. LCJ IX, 26 October 1833.

37. LCJ IX, 4 November 1833; Bessborough (1950), pp.18-19.

38. Ibid.

39. Ibid.

40. http://www.alangeorge.co.uk/Dowlais_Works_Locomotives_List. htm

41. Works Journal, 18 March 1853.

42. LCJ IX, 14 November 1833; Bessborough (1950) p.20.

43. LCJ IX, 9 December 1833. Henry Robert Addison, 1805-1876 was the author of *The Butterfly's Ball, or The Loves of the Plants: An Operatic Extravaganza* (London: J. Miller 1834), http://www. ricorso.net/rx/az-data/authors/a/Addison_HR/life.htm.

44. LCJ IX, 29 January 1834; Bessborough (1950) p.20.

45. LCJ IX, 1 February 1834; Bessborough, (1950) p.21.

46. LCJ X, 22 April 1836.

47. LCJ IX, 2 February 1834; Bessborough (1950), p.22. Strictly speaking, the verse reads, 'Better is a dinner of herbs where love is, than a stalled ox and hatred therewith,' (Proverbs ch.15, v.17, KJV.)

48. LCJ IX, 19 March 1834; Bessborough (1950), p.25.

49. LCJ IX, 28 June 1834.

50. LCJ IX, 8 May 1834; Bessborough (1950), p.28.

51. History of the County of York: the City of York (1961) – Victoria County Histories from British History Online, pp.268-9.

52. LCJ IX, 12 May 1834; Bessborough (1950) p.28.

53. LCJ IX, 13 June 1834; Bessborough (1950) p.30.
54. *Morning Post,* 16 June, 1834.
55. www.welshnot.com/scotch-cattle-wales-weirdest-terrorists/ gives possible sources of the nickname
56. *Cardiff and Merthyr Guardian*, 7, 14 and 28 June 1834.
57. LCJ IX, 19 June 1834; Bessborough (1950) p.30.

Chapter Three

1. LCJ IX, 18 August 1834; Mary Pegus, MS Diary 10 July 1834.
2. Mary Pegus, MS Diary, 18 August 1834.
3. LCJ IX, 18 August 1834.
4. Ibid.
5. Mary Pegus, MS Diary, 26 August 1834
6. Mary Pegus, MS Diary, 4 September 1834.
7. LCJ IX, 20 August 1834; Bessborough (1950) p.33.
8. Mary Pegus, MS Diary, 22 August 1834.
9. LCJ IX, 14 September 1834.
10. LCJ XI, 16 November 1834; Bessborough (1950) p.36.
11. Llewellyn Woodward, *The Age of Reform* (Oxford: Clarendon Press, 1962, pp.101-2; Ted Rowlands, 'The Merthyr Tydfil 1835 Election Revisited – Lady Charlotte Guest's Account', *Merthyr Historian* vol 25, 2013, pp.7-22, at pp.8-9.
12. *Saunders's News-Letter*, 9 December 1817 and Edgar Jones, *A History of GKN* Vol One (Macmillan: London 1987), p.xxx
13. *Charterhouse Register 1769-1872.*
14. LCJ IX, 15 August 1833; Bessborough (1950) p.17.
15. Pierre Armand Dufrénoy, 'Rapport a Monsieur le Directeur general des ponts et chaussées et des mines, sur l'emploie de l'air chaud dans les usines à fer de l'Ecosse et de l'Angleterre' *Annales des Mines,* troisième série, tome IV, 1833, pp.431–508.
16. For a succinct account of the science behind the hot blast see http://iainthepict.blogspot.com/2011/06/james-beaumont-neilson.html.
17. Neilson et al v Harford Co, 1841; Neilson and Others v. Househill Coal Co., 1842; Neilson and Others v. W. Baird & Co (1843). David Philip Miller (see note 18) analyses the litigation to which the Hot Blast gave rise.

18. David Philip Miller, 'Of Patents, Principles and the Construction of Heroic Invention: The Case of Neilson's Hot Blast' *Proceedings of the American Philosophical Society*, Vol. 160, Dec 2016, pp.361–422.

19. David Mushet, 'On the Various Effects Produced by the Nature, Compression and Velocity of the Air Used in the Blast Furnace,' (written c.1810), *Papers on Iron and Steel*, 1840 p.329)

20. Samuel Smiles, *Industrial Biography – Ironworkers and Toolmakers* (London: John Murray, 1876) p.154.

21. LCJ IX, 3 December 1834.

22. https://theclergydatabase.org.uk/

23. LCJ IX, 28 November 1834.

24. LCJ IX, 2 December 1834.

25. *Newcastle Journal*, 24 January 1862; *Lincolnshire Chronicle*, 16 December 1864.

26. *Western Times*, 10 July & 7 August, 1830.

27. LCJ IX, 30 December 1834; Rowlands (2013) p.9.

28. LCJ IX, 1 December 1834; Bessborough (1950) p.37.

29. LCJ IX, 28 November 1834.

30. LCJ IX, 5 December 1834.

31. LCJ IX, 3 December 1834.

32. Ibid.

33. LCJ, IX, 9 December 1834.

34. LCJ IX, 18 December 1834.

35. Armand Dufrénoy, *Rapport a M le Directeur General des ponts et chaussees et des mines, sur l'Emploi de l'air chaud dans les usine a fer de l'Ecosse et de l'Angleterre* (Chez Carilian-Goeury, Libraire: Paris, 1834.) pp.6-7.

36. *On the Use of Hot Air in the Iron Works of England and Scotland, translated form a report made to the Director-General of mines in France by M. Dufrénoy,* (John Murray: London, 1836) p.6.

37. LCJ IX, 16 December 1834.

38. Caroline Bowles Southey, *Olympia Morata: Her Times, Life and Writing* (Smith, Elder & Co: London, 1834) and *Memoirs of Mrs Inchbald, Including her Familiar Correspondence with the most Distinguished Persons of her Time*, ed. James Boaden (Richard Bentley: London, 1833)

39. Southey (1834) p.109, quoting Nolten, *Vita Olympiae Moratae* (Frankfurt, 1775). Jane Austen depicts some dismayingly revealing

rehearsals for a country house production of *Lovers'Vows*, Elizabeth Inchbald's English version of August von Kotzebue's *Das Kind der Liebe* in *Mansfield Park* (1814).

40. LCJ IX, 6 December 1834.
41. LCJ IX, 19 December 1834
42. LCJ IX, 3 December 1834.
43. Ibid.
44. LCJ IX, 9 December 1834.
45. LCJ IX, 8 and 14 December 1834; https://www.gracesguide.co.uk entry for William Thompson.
46. LCJ IX, 11 December 1834.
47. LCJ 19, December 1834.
48. LCJ IX, 22 December 1834.
49. Rowlands (2013) p.15.
50. *The Cambrian*, 17 January 1835.
51. LCJ IX, 18 December 1834.
52. LCJ IX, 19 December 1834.
53. LCJ IX, 23 December 1834.
54. *Hereford Times*, 10 January 1835.
55. *Monmouthshire Merlin* and *Cardiff and Merthyr Guardian* 24 January 1835.
56. *Cardiff and Merthyr Guardian*, 24 January, 1835.
57. LCJ X, 13 February, 1835.
58. LCJ IX, 10 December 1834.
59. Blunt Roy Blunt & Duncan to Guest, Lewis & Co., 12 March 1836, *Iron in the Making* (1960) p.94.
60. *On the Use of Hot Air in the Iron Works of England and Scotland*, pp.16, 49 and 54.
61. (Edgar Jones (1987) p.69).
62. LCJ X, I October 1836.
63. *Cardiff and Merthyr Guardian,* 10 December 1836
64. LCJ X, 26 September 1836.

Chapter Four

1. LCJ X, 29 May 1835.
2. LCJ X, 4 June 1835; Bessborough (1950), p.39.

3. LCJ X, 6 June 1835; Bessborough (1950) p.40
4. LCJ X, 4 and 6 June 1835.
5. *Morning Post*, 5 and 19 June 1835.
6. LCJ X, 16 June 1835; Bessborough (1950) p.40.
7. LCJ XII, 7 May 1842; Bessborough (1950) p.133.
8. LCJ X, 30 June 1835.
9. LCJ X, 13 July 1835.
10. LCJ X, 17 July 1835.
11. LCJ X, 18 July 1835.
12. LCJ X, 20 July 1835.
13. LCJ X, 22 July 1835.
14. LCJ X, 24 October 1835.
15. LCJ X, 29 August 1835.
16. Ibid. 'I was taken ill,' Charlotte explains.
17. Thomas Vaughan to Robert Thompson, 8 December 1794, *Iron in the Making* (1960) pp.152-53.
18. William Hood to Dowlais Works, 25 January 1817. I *Iron in the Making* (1960) p.153.
19. Thomas Reece to Dowlais Works, 2 August 1817, *Iron in the Making* (1960) p.153. The cill is a horizontal ledge which protrudes a short way into the lock chamber below the upper gates. Arguably the consequences of hitting a lock cill are worse for the boat than they are for the lock structure.
20. Edgar Jones (1987) p.49.
21. Stephen K. Jones, (2010) p.94.
22. Ibid, p.105.
23. *Cardiff and Merthyr Guardian*, 17 October, 1835.
24. Stephen K Jones (2010) p.107.
25. www.historyofparliamentonline.org/volume/1832-1868/member/hutchins-edward-john-1809-1876
26. LCJ X, 26 February 1836.
27. www.historyofparliamentonline.org/volume/1832-1868/member/hutchins-edward-john-1809-1876.
28. LCJ X, 25 February 1836.
29. LCJ X, 29 February 1836.
30. LCJ X, 13 April 1836.
31. Guest and John (1998) p.36; (2007) p.50.
32. LCJ X, 12 April 1836.

33. Ibid.

34. Ibid.

35. LCJ X, 21 October 1836.

36. Beaumont and Fletcher, *The Maid's Tragedy*, Act IV, Sc 1.

37. LCJ X, 21 October 1836.

38. Daniel Defoe, *The Complete English Tradesman* 1st pub 1726. (This edition D.A. Tallboys: Oxford, 1841) pp.220-221).

39. LCJ X, 9 September 1836.

40. LCJ X, 10 September 1836.

41. Ibid. The Wikipedia entry for the Bude Canal describes its unusual system of operation.

42. LCJ X, 13 September 1836.

43. LCJ X, 17 September 1836.

44. www.findagrave.com/memorial/171139381/samuel-biddick-truran

45. LCJ X, 8 November 1835.

46. LCJ X, 19 October 1836; Bessborough I p.41.

47. https://biography.wales/article/s-HILL-PLY-1786

48. Wikipedia entry for Crawshay Bailey.

49. www.historyofparliamentonline.org/volume/1820-1832/member/thompson-william-1792-1854

50. www.bioeddie.co.uk/ebbw-vale/tinplateiron.html

51. www.alangeorge.co.uk/Cyfarthfa,TheCrawshays.htm

52. LCJ X, 14 November 1836.

53. *Cardiff and Merthyr Guardian*, 19 November 1836.

54. www.irsociety.co.uk/Archives/59/Locos.htm. *John Watt* was built at Neath Abbey in 1838.

55. Charles E. Lee, 'Adrian Stephens: Inventor of the Steam Whistle,' *Transactions of the Newcomen Society* (1949), Vol 27, pp.163-173. Lee quotes Stephens' son as giving the year of his father's invention as 1835 (p.169) but his assertion that it followed a boiler explosion suggests that he may have been a year adrift.

56. LCJ X, 27 December 1836.

Chapter Five

1. LCJ X, 3 January 1837; Bessborough (1950), p.42.

2. LCJ X, 26 January 1837.

3. LCJ X, 28 January 1837.
4. LCJ X, 26 February 1837.
5. LCJ X, 2 February 1837.
6. Williams(1978), p.213.
7. www.bandon-genealogy.com/newspapers_bandon.htm, entry for 'Biggs', given source, *Freeman's Journal*, 3 October, 1820.
8. *Southern Reporter and Cork Commercial Courier*, 24 April 1825.
9. *Cork Constitution*, 29 November 1827
10. *Southern Reporter and Cork Commercial Courier*, 5 August 1828.
11. Williams, (1978) p.220; given source, *Cambrian*, 26 November 1831; *Cardiff and Merthyr Guardian*, 30 March 1833
12. Will of Thomas Revel Guest, National Archives ref PROB 11/1874/232.
13. For Thomas Revel Johnson's obituary, see *Bell's Life in Sydney and Sporting Chronicle*, 1 August, 1863.
14. LCJ X, 26 February 1837.
15. LCJ X, 14 February 1837.
16. LCJ X, 16 February 1837.
17. LCJ X, 23 April 1837.
18. LCJ X, 7 June 1837.
19. LCJ X, 8 June 1837.
20. Ibid.
21. LCJ X, 21 June 1837
22. *Journal of the House of Commons*, Vol 92, 1837, p.630.
23. 1837 was the last occasion on which the demise of the crown necessitated parliament's dissolution.
24. LCJ X, 24 June 1837.
25. Bessborough (1950) p.49.
26. www.historyofparliamentonline.org/volume/1832-1868/member/wyndham-quin-edwin-richard-windham-visct-adare-1812-1871
27. *Morning Chronicle*, 11 July; 3 August 1837.
28. *Cardiff and Merthyr Guardian*, 8 July 1837.
29. *Cardiff and Merthyr Guardian*, 22 July 1837.
30. *Cardiff and Merthyr Guardian*, 5 August 1837.
31. *Cardiff and Merthyr Guardian*, 29 July 1837.
32. LCJ X, 18 July 1837; Bessborough (1950) p.51. On 26 July 1837, she and John had indeed been 'drawn into the town [Cardiff] by

men instead of horses'; Charlotte described the experience as 'very complimentary but not perfectly agreeable'. (Bessborough, p.53)

33. *Cardiff and Merthyr Guardian*, 22 July 1837.
34. LCJ X, 22 July 1837; Bessborough (1950) p.51.
35. *Cardiff and Merthyr Guardian* 22 July 1837.
36. www.lantrissant.net/.../dr-william-price
37. Hansard, House of Commons, Corn Laws Debate, 16 March 1837.
38. LCJ X, 1 August 1837; Bessborough (1950), p.54.
39. *Cardiff and Merthyr Guardian*, 29 July 1837.
40. LCJ X, 16 August 1837; Bessborough (1950) p.56.
41. *Cardiff and Merthyr Guardian*, 19 August 1837.
42. LCJ X, 10 September, 1837; Bessborough I pp.58-59.
43. Report of the Seventh Meeting of the British Association for the Advancement of Science, Vol VI (London: John Murray, 1838), pp.117–126.
44. *Liverpool Mercury*, 22 September 1837
45. LCJ X, 12 September 1837; Bessborough (1950) p.59; *Leeds Mercury*, 16 September 1837.
46. *The Life of Sir William Fairbairn, Bart., partly written by himself,* edited and completed by William Pole (1st publ. London: Longman Green & Co, 1877; repr. David & Charles, 1970) pp.161-2.
47. LCJ X, 12 September 1837; Bessborough (1950) p.59.
48. LCJ X, 29 November 1837; Bessborough (1950) p.63. Bessborough gives the name of the lecturer as 'Dr Aukin' which looks like a misreading for Dr Arthur Aikin whose interests included mineralogy and who was active in the lecturing sphere in the 1830s.
49. Arthur Aikin, *Journal of a tour through North Wales and part of Shropshire; with observations in mineralogy, and other branches of natural history* (1797).
50. LCJ X, 26 November 1837.
51. https://museum.wales/media/7589/census.en.pdf recounts Scrivenor's connection with Blaenavon.
52. LCJ X, 24 September 1837
53. LCJ X, 12 November 1837; Bessborough (1950) p.62.
54. LCJ X, 16 June 1837.
55. Guest and John (1989) p.42; (2007) p.56.
56. LCJ X, 12 November 1837; Bessborough (1950) p.63.

Chapter Six

1. LCJ XI, 27 April 1839; Bessborough (1950) p.89.
2. The *Cambrian Register* is available online at https://journals.library. wales/view/2867877/ and the *Myvyrian Archaiology* at https:// archive.org/details/myvyrianarchaio00jone/page/n6
3. *Cambrian Register*, Vol I (1795) p.177 ff.
4. The original remains in the library of Jesus College. A digitised version is available online at https://digital.bodleian.ox.ac.uk
5. *Cambrian Register*, Vol I (1795) p.177.
6. Guest and John (1989) p.90; (2007) p.101.
7. *Cambrian Register* vol II (1796) p.327.
8. http://mabinogistudy.com/library/william-pughe/ and https://biography. wales/article/s-PUGH-OWEN
9. *Morning Post*, 7 December 1826.
10. *Chester Chronicle*, 6 February 1829.
11. *Hereford Times*, 26 November 1836.
12. *Cardiff and Merthyr Guardian* 21 January 1837.
13. *Monmouthshire Merlin*, 28 January 1837.
14. *Cardiff and Merthyr Guardian*, 17 June 1837.
15. *Monmouthshire Beacon*, 21 October 1837.
16. *Monmouthshire Beacon*, 21 October 1837, et al.
17. *Chester Chronicle*, 23 November 1838.
18. LCJ, XI, 30 November 1837; Bessborough (1950) pp.63-4.
19. LCJ XI, 8 December 1837; Bessborough (1950) p.64.
20. LCJ XI, 6 January 1838.
21. LCJ XI, 8 December 1837; Bessborough (1950) p.64.
22. Rev. T. Price to Lady Charlotte Guest, 13 March 1843, National Library of Wales, Lady Charlotte Guest's Deedbox papers.
23. Ibid.
24. *The Mabinogion. From the Llyfr Coch o Hergest, and other ancient Welsh manuscripts*, with an English translation and notes, by Lady Charlotte E. Guest, (Longman, Brown, Green and Longmans and W. Rees: London and Llandovery 1849) Vol III, p.308. *The Mabinogion* [...] Translated with notes by Lady Charlotte Guest (Bernard Quaritch: London, 1877) p.460.
25. LCJ XI, 4 December 1837; Bessborough (1950) p.64

26. Lady Charlotte Guest, *The Mabinogion* (1849) Vol II, p.362; (1877) p.291.
27. Ibid. Vol III (1849) pp.135-6; (1877) p.389.
28. Ibid, Vol II (1849) pp.157–161; (1877) pp.198-201.
29. Ibid, Vol II (1849) p.175; (1877) p.212.
30. Obey, 2007, p.114.
31. Lady Charlotte Guest, *The Mabinogion* (1849) Vol I, p.xxiii; (1877) p.xx.
32. William Rees to Taliesin Williams, 15 December 1837, (Letters to Taliesin ab Iolo, ref 629, National Library of Wales)
33. LCJ XI, 21 July 1838.
34. LCJ XI, 21 July 1838; Bessborough (1950) p.74.
35. LCJ XI, 1-2 November 1838.
36. LCJ XI, 6 October 1838.
37. Now displayed in Cyfarthfa Castle.
38. *Cardiff and Merthyr Guardian*, 6 October, 1838.
39. LCJ XI, 8 November 1838.
40. www.findagrave.com/memorial/83857842/bathsheba-bernabeu
41. *Cardiff and Merthyr Guardian*, 27 October 1838.
42. LCJ IX, 6 December 1838; D. Rhys Phillips, *Lady Charlotte Guest and the Mabinogion: some notes on the work and its translator* (W. Spurrell & Son: Carmarthen, 1921)
43. www.ancienttexts.org/library/celtic/jce/villemarque.html and http://www.berose.fr/?La-Villemarque-Theodore-Hersart
44. LCJ XI, 17 December 1838,
45. Ibid.
46. LCJ XI, 31 January 1839; Bessborough I p.87; Phillips (1921) p.22.
47. LCJ, XI, 13 March 1839; Phillips (1921) p.24.
48. LCJ XI, 28 (actually 29) March 1839.
49. The 'Peredur' illustrations bear the name 'B. Williams', whom Charlotte mentions at LCJ XII, 21 March 1844.
50. LCJ XI, 11 May 1839.
51. LCJ XI, 15 May 1839; Phillips (1921) p.25.
52. LCJ XI, 22 August 1839.
53. LCJ XI, 25 October 1839.
54. John Ross Dix [attrib] *Pen and Ink Sketches by a Cosmopolitan* (William Hayden & Thos M. Brewer: Atlas Office, Boston, 1845)

pp.71-96. I am grateful to Mr Michael Freeman for drawing my attention to this publication.

55. For Charlotte's reading of *Martin Chuzzlewit* see LCJ XII, 10 March 1843; 4 June 1844; *Jane Eyre* LCJ XIV, 28 December 1850; Bessborough (1950) p.255, and *Pride and Prejudice* et al, LCJ XXIII 1 July 1876; Bessborough (1952) p.134.

56. LCJ XIV, 28 Dec 1850; Bessborough (1950) p.253; LCJ XXIII, 1 July 1876; Bessborough (1952) p.134; LCJ X,27 April 1835.

57. LCJ XI, 12 October 1840.

58. LCJ XII, 22 July 1843; Phillips (1921) p.37.

59. Phillips (1921), pp.29, 31. Given source LCJ XI, 16 January 1841; 18 January 1842.

60. Phillips (1921), p.30, given source, LCJ XII, 26 October 1841.

61. Lady Charlotte's deed box papers, B11, item 7. Rev. T. Price to Lady Charlotte Guest, 6 May, 1843.

62. *Morning Chronicle,* 4 September 1850.

63. *The Mabinogion – A new translation* by Sioned Davies (Oxford World's Classics: Oxford, 2007) 'The Lady of the Well', pp.116-138, at p.123.

64. *Silurian*, 9 April 1853.

65. For Lanier's life and work, see Obey (2007) pp.168-183.

66. *Western Mail*, 25 April 1921.

67. D. Rhys Phillips *Lady Charlotte Guest and the Mabinogion: some notes on the work and its translator* (W.Spurrell & Son: Carmarthen, 1921)

Chapter Seven

1. John Davies, *Cardiff and the Marquesses of Bute* (University of Wales Press: Cardiff, 1981), p.14.

2. LCJ IX, 15 October 1834.

3. Norena Shopland, 'What Lies Before....' www.savethecoalexchange. com, blog entry dated 11 February, 2016.

4. The premises were sold off after John's death. (*Silurian Cardiff, Merthyr and Brecon Mercury, and South Wales General Advertiser*, 26 March 1853.)

5. Davies (1981), p.93.

6. Davies (1981) p.252.
7. LCJ XI, 8 October 1839.
8. *Monmouthshire Merlin*, 12 October 1839.
9. Stephen K. Jones (2010), Vol 1 pp.162-3, given source, *The Cambrian*, 17 October, 1840.
10. LCJ XI, 8 October 1840; Bessborough (1950) p.116.
11. *Monmouthshire Merlin*, 10 October 1840; *The Cambrian*, 17 October, 1840.
12. LCJ XI, 8 October 1840; Bessborough (1950) p.116-7. Bessborough's text refers to 'Inchin plane'; a spelling error resulting from the difficulties which Montague Guest's typist experienced both in reading Lady Charlotte's handwriting and with the unfamiliar terminology.
13. *Monmouthshire Merlin*, 10 October 1840; LCJ XI, 8 October 1840; Bessborough (1950) pp.116-7.
14. *Monmouthshire Merlin* 10 October 1840.
15. The www.wikipedia.org/ entry for 'History of Rail Transport in the Netherlands' gives an overview of William A Bake's railway plans.
16. LCJ XII, 7 April 1841.
17. Lord Bute to Richard Roy, 30 March 1839 and 18 March 1842. Letter book to Coutts, Farrer and Roy in Bute Papers; National Library of Wales, Aberystwyth.
18. Edgar Jones, (1987), pp.76-77.
19. LCG XII, 9 July 1842; Bessborough (1950) p.135.
20. LCJ XII, 29 April 1843; Bessborough (1950) p.149.
21. LCJ XII, 13 June 1843; Bessborough (1950) p.152.
22. LCJ XII, 26 June 1843; Bessborough (1950) p.153.
23. Ibid.
24. Although Guest and John in their Appendix 2 give Enid's birthday as 11 July 1843, it appears to be an error. Charlotte's ms journals and Bessborough (1850) pp.153-4 indicate that she was actually born on 1 July 1843.
25. LCJ XII, 1 July 1843.
26. LCJ XII, 14 January 1844.
27. LCJ XII, 30 January 1844.
28. LCJ XII, 16 February 1844.
29. LCJ XII, 18 February 1844. Mary Pegus had recently become engaged to Charles Gordon, 10th Marquess of Huntly and Earl of Aboyne.
30. LCJ XIII, 26 August, 1844.

31. LCJ XIII, 18 December 1844.
32. LCJ XIII, 17 October 1844.
33. LCJ XIII, 24 December 1844.
34. LCJ XIII, 22 July 1845.
35. *Iron in the Making* (1960) 'Table of 'Railways Supplied by Dowlais Iron Company', pp.xviii – xix.
36. LCJ XIII, 19 November 1845.
37. Owen (2001), p.24.
38. Edgar Jones (1987), p.xxvi.
39. LCJ XII, 19 May 1844; LCJ XIII, 23 January 1845.
40. Guest and John (1989) p.145; (2007) p.137.
41. Mark Rathbone, *Canford Manor – a concise history* (Canford School History Department: Canford, 1994, revised 2006) p.8.
42. Obey (2007) pp.50-51.
43. *Monmouthshire Merlin* 23 May 1846 and *Cardiff and Merthyr Guardian*, 30 May 1846, both of which mistakenly assumed that Canford was in Devon.
44. Edgar Jones (1987), pp.240-42; Calendar of Dowlais Iron Company Correspondence, Glamorgan Archives, ref GRO 50.
45. LCJ XIII, 27 February 1845.
46. LCJ XIII, 9 and 31 December 1846.
47. LCJ XIII, 18 March 1847.
48. It is attributed to Professor Gwyn A Williams.
49. *Morning Advertiser*, 22 June 1847.
50. LCJ XIII, 12 June 1847,
51. LCJ XIII, 23 June, 1847.
52. LCJ XIII, 22 July 1847; Bessborough (1950), p.193.
53. LCJ 26-27 February 1850; Bessborough (1950) p.236.
54. LCJ XIV, 10 August 1849.
55. LCJ 27 November 1847; Bessborough (1950) p.199.
56. Ibid.
57. *London Daily News*, 12 January 1848.
58. *Bristol Mercury*, 15 January, 1848.
59. *Cardiff and Merthyr Guardian*, 22 January 1848.
60. *Cardiff and Merthyr Guardian*, 25 March 1848.
61. LCJ XIV, 20 March 1848; Bessborough (1950) pp.205-6.
62. Davies (1981) p.21.
63. *Cardiff and Merthyr Guardian* 1 April 1848.

Chapter Eight

1. John Malcolm Russell, 'Stolen Stones' https://archive.archaeology. org/online/features/nineveh/
2. LCJ XIV, 7 April 1848; Bessborough (1950) p.209.
3. LCJ XIV, 30 April 1848.
4. *Cardiff and Merthyr Guardian*, 15 July 1848; LCJ XIV, 12 July 1848.
5. *London Daily News*, 12 September 1846.
6. LCJ XIV, 5 August 1848.
7. Leslie Wynne Evans, 'Sir John and Lady Charlotte Guest's Educational Scheme at Dowlais in the mid-nineteenth century', *National Library of Wales Journal*, IX, no 3, Summer 1956, p.281.
8. Ibid, p.267.
9. *Reports of the commissioners of enquiry into the state of education in Wales* (1847) pt 2, no 9, p.66.
10. Ibid. Symons' note refers to Price's *Hanes Cymru* [...] (1836-42).
11. LCJ XIV, 27 September 1848.
12. Ibid.
13. LCJ XIV, 6 October 1848.
14. LCJ XIV, 9 October 1848.
15. LCJ XIV, 25 December 1848.
16. LCJ XIV, 10 February 1849.
17. Glamorgan Archives, Calendar of DIC Correspondence, GRO/50, Folio 210, 11 April, 1846.
18. Ibid, Folio 211, 13 April 1846.
19. Ibid, Folio 214, 15 April 1846
20. Ibid, Folio 222, 23 April 1846.
21. Ibid, Folio 224, 24 April 1846
22. Ibid, Folio 226, 28 April 1846.
23. Ibid, Folio 228, 6 May 1846.
24. Ibid, Folio 231, 8 May 1846.
25. Ibid, Folio 338, 6 November 1846.
26. Ibid, Folio 340, 11 November 1846.
27. Ibid, Folio 341, 12 November 1846.
28. Ibid, Folio 348, 19 November 1846.
29. Ibid, Folio 358, 30 November 1846.
30. Ibid, Folio 574, 1 January 1848,
31. Ibid, Folio 594, 1 February 1848.

32. Ibid, Folio 594, 1 February 1848.
33. Ibid, Folio 600, 12 February 1848.
34. LCJ XIV, 24 January 1849.
35. Journal of the House of Commons, vol 104, 1 Feb 1849 – 31 Jan 1850, p.27.
36. Strictly speaking the 1836 powers had been inadequate, allowing only for a branch to communicate with the tram road. For a full account of the various attempts to make the Dowlais Branch see Stephen K Jones, *Brunel in South Wales*; Vol I, *In Trevithick's Tracks* (History Press: Stroud, 2005), p.168.
37. LCJ XIII, 11 June 1849.
38. A.N.Wilson, *The Victorians*, (Hutchinson: London, 2002) p.139-42.
39. LCJ XV, 17 January 1851; Bessborough (1950) p.254.
40. LCJ XV, 20 January 1851; Bessborough (1950) p.259.
41. LCJ XV, 13 February 1851; Bessborough (1950) p.259.
42. LCJ XV, 15 Feb 1851; Bessborough (1950) pp.260-1.
43. 'Mr Locke' may have been Joseph Locke, engineer and MP for Honiton, no great distance from Exeter, the constituency of Guest's friend Edward Divett.
44. LCJ XV, 12 June 1851.
45. LCJ XV, 4 July 1851.
46. LCJ XIII, 22 July 1847; Bessborough p.193.

Chapter Nine

1. Roughly speaking, a Cornish boiler is a long horizontal cylinder with a single large flue containing the fire. Because the boiler furnace required a natural draught to draw, there would be a tall chimney – stack –at the far end of the flue to encourage a good supply of air (oxygen) to the fire. The Lancashire boiler had a somewhat more sophisticated design, with two large flues containing the fire, instead of one. (Detail from Wikipedia.)
2. LCJ XIV, 16 July 1849.
3. LCJ XIV, 30 December 1850; Bessborough (1950) p.253.
4. *Cardiff and Merthyr Guardian*, 22 February 1851.
5. John Burnett, *England Eats Out: A Social History of Eating Out in England,* 1830 to the Present, (Routledge, 2004) p.61.

6. LCJ XV, 21 July 1851.
7. LCJ XV, 22 July 1851.
8. *Cardiff and Merthyr Guardian*, 2 August 1851.
9. LCJ XV, 23 July 1851.
10. https://www.parliament.uk/about/living-heritage/ The House of Commons would not be finished until 1852.
11. LCJ XV, 24 July 1851.
12. Ibid.
13. LCJ XV, 25 July 1851.
14. *Cardiff and Merthyr Guardian*, 15 March 1851.
15. Unattributed article, 'The Dowlais Railway', *The Railway Magazine*, Vol LXXXI, October 1937, pp.291-93.
16. Spellings of the Nawab's name vary. This version appears in Sir A. Henry Layard, G.C.B., D.C.L., *Autobiography and letters from his childhood until his appointment as H.M. ambassador at Madrid,* (London: John Murray, 1903), pp.337-8.
17. *Cardiff and Merthyr Guardian*, 23 August 1851; *Silurian,* 30 August 1851.
18. LCJ XV, 21 August 1851.
19. *Silurian,* 30 August 1851.
20. LCJ XV, 10 September 1851.
21. LCJ XIV, 30 March 1849.
22. LCJ XIV, 3 April 1849.
23. http://www.tenbyhistoricalsociety.org.uk/downloads/Menelaus_Williams.pdf
24. LCJ XV, 8 December 1851.
25. LCJ XV, 11 December 1851.
26. LCJ XV, 13 December 1851.
27. LCJ XV, 13 December 1851; Bessborough (1950) p.284
28. LCJ XV, 16 December 1851; Bessborough (1950) p.284.
29. LCJ XV, 1 January 1852; Bessborough (1950) pp.286-7.
30. LCJ XV, 9 January 1852; Bessborough (1950) p.287
31. LCJ XV, 13 January 1852; Bessborough (1950) p.287.
32. LCJ XV, 8 December 1851.
33. LCJ XV, 23 March 1852.
34. www.historyofparliamentonline.org/volume/1832-1868/constituencies/poole

35. www.historyofparliamentonline.org/volume/1832-1868/member/
    seymour-henry-danby
36. LCJ XV, 3 February 1852; Bessborough,(1950) p289.
37. *Poole and Dorset Herald*, 28 October 1852.
38. *Sherborne Mercury* 15 June 1852; *Southern Times & Dorset County Herald*, 19 June 1852; *Dorset County Chronicle*, 16 June 1852.
39. Bessborough (1952), pp.82-87. An obituary for Georgina Weldon, aka Georgina Treherne (1837–1914) appears in the *Musical Times*, 1 February 1914.
40. LCJ XV, 5 and 9 July 1852; Bessborough (1950) p.298.
41. LCJ XV, 16 September 1852.
42. LCJ XV, 24 September 1852.
43. LCJ XV, 10 October 1852. John Evans complained that Cartwright was 'a disreputable man' who 'used to go with his daughters at night to a penny dancing house in Merthyr.' (*Iron in the Making* (1960), pp.47-48).
44. Edgar Jones (1987) p.121.
45. LCJ XV, 26 September 1852.
46. LCJ XV, 18 November 1852; Bessborough (1950) p.300.
47. LCJ XV, 22 November 1852.
48. LCJ XV, 24 November 1852.
49. LCJ XV, 24 (actually 25) November 1852.

Chapter Ten

1. *Cardiff and Merthyr Guardian*, 11 December, 1852.
2. *A Sermon Preached In Dowlais Church on the occasion of the death of Sir J. John Guest, Bart., MP., by the Rev. Canon Jenkins, Rector of Dowlais,* (London: Longman and Co, et al, 2nd Edition, [1853]).
3. LCJ XV, 11 December 1852.
4. Ibid.
5. LCJ XV, 12 December 1852.
6. LCJ XV, 14 December 1852.
7. LCJ XV, 20 December 1852.
8. Letter photographed in Guest and John (1989) at pp.184-5; (2007) pp.186-7. Given source, Glamorgan Archives.

9. LCJ IV, 14 December 1852.
10. The first Merthyr Stipendiary Magistrates' Act came into force in 1829. It lapsed after seven years, but had been renewed in 1843. (*Iron in the Making* (1960) p.211, n. to Lady Charlotte's letter of 13 February 1841.). For the levy made upon the ironmasters, see Wilkins, *History of Merthyr Tydfil*, (1908 edn.) p.366.
11. Lady Charlotte Guest to Henry Temple, Viscount Palmerston, 30 December 1852, *Iron in the Making* (1960) pp.236-7.
12. Elizabeth Havill, 'The Respectful Strike', *Morgannwg – the Journal of Glamorgan History*, Vol XXIV, (1980) pp.61-81, fn 1.
13. LCJ XV, 21 December 1852.
14. Lady Charlotte Guest, Works Journal 1852–3, microfilmed December 1967 for Glamorgan Record Office, location 2144S-446; Reel 129. Entry for 21 December 1852.
15. Works Journal, 14 March 1853.
16. Works Journal, 18 December 1852.
17. LCJ XV, 16 February 1853.
18. Works Journal, 14-16 February 1853.
19. Works Journal 18 December 1852.
20. Works Journal, 9 March 1853. Exactly whom she means by 'Wrights' is unknown.
21. LCJ XV, 9 March 1853.
22. Works Journal 19 March 1853.
23. Edgar Jones (1987), p.243, citing LCJ XV, 8 November 1852.
24. Ibid, although Jones' statement that John Guest commissioned Wales' Report 'in 1857' is an error.
25. www.gracesguide.co.uk/Great_Indian_Peninsula_Railway; *Illustrated London News,* 4 June 1853.
26. LCJ XV, 14 February 1853; Bessborough II, p.4.
27. LCJ XV, 15 February 1853.
28. Lady Charlotte Guest, Papers, National Library of Wales. Coal Reports, 1851-53, p.10.
29. Edgar Jones (1987), p.244.
30. Ibid and Works Journal 28 December 1852 and 13 January 1852.
31. Coal Reports, 1851 – 53, p.17.
32. Works Journal, 10 February 1853.
33. Works Journal, 10 and 17 February 1853.

34. Works Journal, 28 December 1852.
35. Works Journal, 27 Feb 1853.
36. Works Journal, 11 March 1853.
37. Works Journal, 19 July 1853.
38. T.F. Sibly, *Iron ores: the haematites of the Forest of Dean and South Wales* (2nd edition revised by W Lloyd) (HMSO: London, 1927) p.32.
39. Works Journal, 1852-3; 18 December 1852.
40. Ibid.
41. LCJ XV, 2 June 1853.
42. Glamorgan Archives Ref DG/P/3 is, suggestively, a 'Sketch of engine House for Pumping Engine for the Forest of Dean' dated September 1855.
43. Works Journal, 21 February 1853.
44. Works Journal 11 March 1853.
45. www.findagrave.com/memorial/171139381/samuel-biddick-truran
46. Works Journal 17 February 1853.
47. Durham Mining Museum, Mining Who's Who. www.dmm.org.uk/whoswho/
48. Works Journal 5 and 23 July 1853.
49. Durham Mining Museum, Mining Who's Who. www.dmm.org.uk/whoswho/
50. Works Journal 8 January 1853; LCJ XV, 5 March 1853; Bessborough (1952), p.4.
51. Angela John, 'The Iron-master's wife in the industrial community', from *Our Mothers' Land – Chapters in Welsh Women's History, 1830-1939 (University of Wales Press*: Cardiff, 1991) p.52.
52. LCJ XV, 28 September 1851.
53. A *Prospectus for Merthyr Tydfil Water Works* appeared in 1851.
54. LCJ XV, 13 October 1851.
55. LCJ XV, 17 November 1851.
56. *Cardiff and Merthyr Guardian*, 24 July 1852; Angela John (1991), p.52.
57. LCJ XV, 16 May 1853; Bessborough (1952) p.6.
58. Works Journal, 18 May 1853.
59. LCJ XV, 21 May 1853; Bessborough (1952) p.7.
60. Works Journal, 14 May 1853.

Chapter Eleven

1. *Cardiff and Merthyr Guardian*, 8 January 1853
2. Elizabeth Havill, 'The Respectful Strike', *Morgannwg*, XXIV (1980) pp.61-81, pp.63-4.
3. Works Journal, 20 February 1853.
4. Works Journal, 24 May 1853; Havill (1980) p.65.
5. Havill (1980) p.63; Guest and John (1989) p.178; (2007) p.182.
6. Works Journal, 25 May 1853.
7. Works Journal, 2 June 1853.
8. Works Journal 14 June 1853.
9. Works Journal, 24 June 1853.
10. LCJ XV, 23 June 1853; Bessborough (1952) p.9; Works Journal, 24-25 June1853.
11. LCJ XV, 23 June 1853; Bessborough (1952) p.10.
12. LCJ XV, 27 June 1853; Bessborough (1952) p.11.
13. Works Journal, 28 June 1853.
14. Works Journal, 1 July 1853.
15. LCJ XV, 1 July 1853; Bessborough (1952) p.13.
16. (www.gracesguide.co.uk/Edward_Riley)
17. Works Journal, 1 July 1853; LCJ XV, I July 1853.
18. LCJ XV, 5 July 1853; Bessborough (1952) p.16.
19. LCJ XV, 2 July 1853.
20. LCJ XV, 6 July 1853; Bessborough (1952) p.16.
21. Works Journal 6 July 1853.
22. Ibid.
23. LCJ XV, 15 July 1853.
24. Works Journal 14 July 1853; LCJ XV, 14 July 1853; Bessborough (1952) p.18.
25. LCJ XV, 11 July 1853; Bessborough (1952) p.17.
26. LCJ XV, 9 July 1853.
27. LCJ XV, 13 July 1853.
28. LCJ XV, 18 July 1853.
29. Works Journal 18 July 1853; LCJ XV, 18 July 1853; Bessborough (1952) p.19.
30. LCJ XV, 18 July 1853.
31. Works Journal, 18 July 1853.
32. LCJ XV, 18 July 1853.

33. Works Journal and LCJ XV, 19 July 1853. A 'drift mine' is one which is accessed through a horizontal adit driven into the side of a hill.
34. LCJ XV, 20 July 1853.
35. Works Journal and LCJ XV, 20 July 1853; Bessborough (1952) pp.20-21 and see illustration 18.
36. LCJ XV, 20 July 1853;
37. Elizabeth Havill (1980) p.67
38. LCJ XV, and Works Journal, 20 July 1853.
39. Works Journal, 21 July 1853.
40. Works Journal, 22 July 1853.
41. LCJ XV, 23 July 1853.
42. LCJ XV, and Works Journal 22 July 1853.
43. Ibid.
44. LCJ XV, 23 July 1853.
45. LCJ XV, 22 July 1853.
46. LCJ XV, 26 July 1853.
47. Havill (1980) p.68.
48. Works Journal, 4 August 1853.
49. LCJ XV, 27 July 1853.
50. LCJ XV, 22 July 1853.
51. Havill (1980), p.70.
52. *Monmouthshire Merlin*, 5 August 1853.
53. Online Welsh Dictionary of Biography, entry for Morgan Lloyd. https://biography.wales/article/s-LLOY-MOR-1820
54. LCJ XV, 7 August 1853.
55. LCJ XV, 2 August 1853.
56. G.T. Clark, letter to Lady Huntly 12 December 1857. George Thomas Clark papers, NLW 57/323-324.
57. *Silurian*, 20 August 1853.
58. *Cardiff and Merthyr Guardian,* 7 January 1854.

Chapter Twelve

1. LCJ XVI, 3 September 1853.
2. Ibid.
3. LCJ XVI, 5 September 1853.

4. LCJ XVI, 5 and 9 September 1853.
5. LCJ XVI, 9 September 1853. Charlotte's emphasis.
6. LCJ XVI, 14 September 1853.
7. LCJ XVI, 19 September, 1853.
8. Ibid.
9. LCJ XVI, 8 October 1853
10. *Cardiff and Merthyr Guardian*, 1 October 1853.
11. LCJ XVI, 17 October 1853.
12. Ibid.
13. *Silurian*, 5 November 1853.
14. Angela V. John (1991), pp.52-53 citing *Cardiff and Merthyr Guardian*, 26 November 1853.
15. LCJ 16 November 1853.
16. Edgar Jones, (1987), p.120.
17. LCJ XVI, 12 August 1853.
18. LCJ XVI, 17 November 1853.
19. LCJ XVI, 19 November 1853.
20. LCJ XVI, 22 November 1853.
21. LCJ XVI, 23 November 1853; Bessborough (1952) p.28.
22. LCJ XVI, 26 November 1853.
23. LCJ XVI, 30 November, 1853.
24. LCJ XVI, 17 December 1853; Bessborough (1952) p.29.
25. LCJ XVI, 10 and 20 Jan 1854; Edgar Jones, (1987) p.259 (and note 103)
26. Edgar Jones (1987) pp.259-60, also Bessborough (1952), p.33.
27. Edgar Jones (1987) p.260.
28. Ibid.
29. LCJ XVI, 2, 5 and 6 March 1854.
30. LCJ XVI, 6 March 1854.
31. LCJ XVI, 28 March, 1854.
32. Ibid.
33. LCJ XVI, 16 Nov 1853
34. LCJ XVI, 6 and 8 May 1854; Bessborough (1952) pp.34-35; Edgar Jones (1987), pp.261-2.
35. LCJ XVI, 15 June 1854; Bessborough (1952) p.38.
36. LCJ XVI, 1 October 1854.
37. LCJ XVI, 16 October 1854; Bessborough (1952) p.42.
38. LCJ XVI, 10 April 1855.

39. Guest and John (1989) p.199; (2007) p.197.
40. LCJ XVII, 19 October 1857.
41. *Cardiff and Merthyr Guardian*, 9 March 1862.
42. Edgar Jones (1987) p.321; John A. Owen (2001) pp.52-3; www.engineering-timelines.com/ entry for 'Dowlais Ironworks'
43. LCJ XVII, 8 March 1857; Bessborough (1952) p.67 --
44. LCJ XVIII, 2 May 1859; Bessborough (1952) p.105; Obey (2007) pp.81-82.
45. *Confessions of a Collector* Vol II, 16 Nov 1877, p.61. The 'Martin' whom she mentions was Edward Pritchard Martin, (1844-1910), Menelaus's sometime deputy and assistant.

Bibliography

Manuscript Sources
In the National Library of Wales, Aberystwyth.

Lady Charlotte Bertie, Vol VI, 1 January 1827 – 20 April 1828
        Vol VII, 22 April 1828 – 30 April 1829
        Vol VIII, 30 April 1829 – 23 September 1832
        [lacking end pages]

Lady Charlotte Guest, Vol IX, 29 July 1833 – 1 Feb 1835
        Vol X, 31 January 1835 – 20 November 1837
        Vol XI, 21 November 1837 – 28 March 1841
        Vol XII, 29 March 1841 – 23 June 1844
        Vol XIII, 24 June 1844 – 7 March 1848
        Vol XIV, 8 March 1848 – 26 Feb 1851
        Vol XV, 27 Feb 1851 – 1 Sept 1853
        Vol XVI, 1 Sept 1853 – 28 Dec 1854; 10 April –
        3 June 1855

Lady Charlotte Schreiber, Vol XVII, 1 Jan 1856 – 20 Oct 1857
        Vol XVIII, 20 Oct 1857 – 23 Sept 1859;
        Jan 1863.
        Vol XXIV, Nov 1877 – Sept 1878.

Guest, Lady Charlotte, Collected Papers, National Library of Wales, Aberystwyth

Bute Estate Records, Papers of Crichton Stuart Family, Marquesses of Bute (accumulated 1547-1936), National Library of Wales, Aberystwyth

In Glamorgan Record Office, Cardiff

Guest, Lady Charlotte, Works Journal 1852-3, microfilmed December 1967 for Glamorgan Record Office, location 2144S-446; Reel 129

Calendar of Dowlais Iron Company Correspondence, Glamorgan Record Office, ref GRO/50.

*   *   *   *   *   *   *

Mary [Maria Antoinetta] Pegus, later Lady Huntly, MS Diaries, unnumbered sequence, Northamptonshire Record Office, Wickham Box 12/2; 3116.

Will of Thomas Revel Guest, National Archives ref. PROB 11/1874/232.

Will of Josiah John Guest, National Archives, ref. PROB 11/2165/63

Books

Lady Charlotte Schreiber's journals: confidences of a collector of ceramics & antiques throughout Britain, France, Holland, Belgium, Spain, Portugal, Turkey, Austria & Germany from the year 1869 to 1885 in two volumes, ed. Montague Guest, (John Lane; The Bodley Head: London, 1911). Available online at https://archive.org.

Lady Charlotte Guest: Extracts from her Journal, 1833-1852, ed. the Earl of Bessborough, P.C., G.C.M.G. (John Murray; London, 1950).

Lady Charlotte Schreiber: Extracts from her Journal, 1853–1891, ed. the Earl of Bessborough, P.C., G.C.M.G. (John Murray; London, 1952).

Aikin, Arthur, *Journal of a tour through North Wales and part of Shropshire; with observations in mineralogy, and other branches of natural history* (1797).

Boaden, James, (ed.) *Memoirs of Mrs Inchbald, Including her Familiar Correspondence with the most Distinguished Persons of her Time* (Richard Bentley: London, 1833)

Burton, Anthony, *The Locomotive Pioneers* (Pen and Sword: Barnsley, 2017)

Charterhouse Register 1769-1872.

Clarke, T.E., *A Guide to Merthyr Tydfil and the Traveller's Companion in visiting the iron works and the various interesting localities of the surrounding neighbourhood* (J.P.LEWIS, PRINTER; Merthyr Tydfil, 1848)

Davies, John, *Cardiff and the Marquesses of Bute* (University of Wales Press: Cardiff, 1981)

Defoe, Daniel, *The Complete English Tradesman* 1st pub 1726.

Dix, John Ross, [attrib] *Pen and Ink Sketches by a Cosmopolitan* (William Hayden & Thos M Brewer: Atlas Office, Boston, 1845)

Dufrénoy, Armand, *Rapport a M le Directeur General des ponts et chaussees et des mines, sur l'Emploi de l'air chaud dans les usine a fer de l'Ecosse et de l'Angleterre* (Chez Carilian-Goeury, Libraire: Paris, 1834.)

Elsas, Madeleine, (ed.) *Iron in the Making – Dowlais Iron Company Letters 1782-1860*, (Glamorgan County Council et al: Cardiff, 1960)

Fairbairn, William, *The Life of Sir William Fairbairn, Bart., partly written by himself*, edited and completed by William Pole (1st publ. London: Longman Green & Co, 1877; repr. David & Charles, 1970)

Guest, Revel and Angela V. John, *Lady Charlotte – a biography of the nineteenth century* (Weidenfeld &Nicolson: London, 1989); Revised edition *Lady Charlotte Guest – An Extraordinary Life* (Tempus: Stroud, 2007).

Hay, Daisy, *Mr and Mrs Disraeli – A Strange Romance* (Penguin: London, 2015)

James, Brian Ll., (ed.) *G.T.Clark, Scholar Ironmaster of the Victorian Age*, (University of Wales Press: Cardiff, 1998)

Jerman, B.R., *The Young Disraeli* (Oxford University Press: London 1960, repr, 2015)

Jenkins, Rev. Canon Evan, *A Sermon Preached In Dowlais Church on the occasion of the death of Sir J. John Guest, Bart., MP., by the Rev. Canon Jenkins, Rector of Dowlais,* (London: Longman and Co, et al, 2nd Edition, [1853])

Jones, Edgar, *A History of GKN: Innovation and Enterprise, 1759-1918* (Macmillan: Basingstoke, 1987)

Jones, Stephen, K., *Brunel in South Wales: In Trevithick's Tracks* (Vol I); *Communications and Coal* (Vol II); *Links with the Leviathans* (Vol III) (History Press; Stroud, 2005–2009).

Kay, William, *Report on the Sanitary Condition of Merthyr Tydfil*, (Rees Lewis: Merthyr Tydfil, 1854)

Lord Beaconsfield's Correspondence with his Sister, 1832-1852 (John Murray: London, 1886) Available online at https://archive.org.

The Mabinogion translated with an introduction and notes by Sioned Davies (Oxford World's Classics: Oxford, 2007)

The Mabinogion, translated with an introduction by Jeffrey Gantz (Harmondsworth: Penguin, 1976)

The Mabinogion, from the Llyfr Coch o Hergest, and other ancient Welsh manuscripts, with an English translation and notes in 7 parts by Lady Charlotte E. Guest, (Longman, Brown, Green and Longmans: London and W.Rees, Llandovery: 1838-1849)

The Mabinogion, from the Llyfr Coch o Hergest, and other ancient Welsh manuscripts, with an English translation and notes in 3 vols by Lady Charlotte E. Guest, (Longman, Brown, Green and Longmans: London and W. Rees, Llandovery: 1849)

The Mabinogion […] Translated with Notes by Lady Charlotte Guest (London: Bernard Quaritch, 1877)

Malkin, Benjamin Heath *The Scenery, Antiquities and Biography of South Wales* (T.N. Longman and O. Rees: London, 1804).

Obey, Erica, *The* Wunderkammer *of Lady Charlotte Guest (*LeHigh University Press: Bethlehem, Pennsylvania, 2007)

On the Use of Hot Air in the Iron Works of England and Scotland, translated form a report made to the Director-General of mines in France by M. Dufrénoy, (John Murray: London, 1836)

Owen, John, A., *A Short History of the Dowlais Ironworks* (Merthyr Tydfil Library Service: Merthyr Tydfil, 2001)

Owen, Mary, *Enid Guest – Daughter of an Ironmaster* (Private publication: Merthyr Tydfil, 2009)

Rammell, T.W., *Report to the General Board of Health on a preliminary inquiry into the Sewerage [...] and sanitary conditions [...] of Merthyr Tydfil* (HMSO: London, 1850)

Rathbone, Mark, *Canford Manor – a concise history* (Canford School History Department: Canford, 1994, revised 2006)

Reports of the commissioners of enquiry into the state of education in Wales, appointed by the Committee of Council on Education. 3 parts. (1847)

Rhys Phillips, David, *Lady Charlotte Guest and the Mabinogion: some notes on the work and its translator* (W. Spurrell & Son: Carmarthen, 1921),

Smiles, Samuel, *Industrial Biography – Ironworkers and Toolmakers* (London: John Murray, 1876)

Southey, Caroline Bowles, *Olympia Morata: Her Times, Life and Writing* (Smith, Elder & Co: London, 1834)

Williams, Gwyn. A, *The Merthyr Rising* (Croom Helm: London, 1978), p.213.

Wilson, A.N., *The Victorians* (Hutchinson: London, 2002)

Woodward, Llewellyn, *The Age of Reform* (Oxford: Clarendon Press, 1962)

Y Mabinogion diweddariad Dafydd a Rhiannon Ifans (Gomer: Llandysul, 2007)

Articles, Theses, etc.

Anonymous, 'The Dowlais Railway', *The Railway Magazine*, Vol LXXXI, October 1837, pp.291-93

Bray, Robyn, '"A Scholar, a Gentleman, and a Christian": John Josias Conybeare (1779–1824) and his "Illustrations of Anglo-Saxon Poetry"' (1826), PhD thesis, University of Glasgow, 2013

Davies, Leo, 'The Dowlais Railway or Incline' *Merthyr Historian*, Vol 8, pp.153-7.

Davies, Sioned, 'A Charming Guest: Translating the Mabinogion', *Studia Celtica* XXXVIII (2004) pp157-178.

Havill, Elizabeth, 'The Respectful Strike', *Morgannwg – the Journal of Glamorgan History*, Vol XXIV (1980) pp.61-81

Lee, Charles, E., 'Adrian Stephens: Inventor of the Steam Whistle,' *Transactions of the Newcomen Society* (1949), Vol 27, pp.163-173.

John, Angela, 'The Iron-master's wife in the industrial community', *Our Mothers' Land – Chapters in Welsh Women's History, 1830-1939 (University of Wales Press*: Cardiff, 1991) pp.43-68.

Johnstone, Judith, 'Victorian Appropriations: Lady Charlotte Guest translates the Mabinogion,' *Appropriating the Middle Ages: Scholarship, Politics, Fraud – Studies in Medievalism XI,* 2001 (D.S. Brewer: Cambridge 2001) pp.145-166.

Miller, David Philip, 'Of Patents, Principles and the Construction of Heroic Invention: The Case of Neilson's Hot Blast' in *Proceedings of the American Philosophical Society*, Vol. 160, Dec 2016, pp.361–422.

Mushet, David 'On the Various Effects Produced by the Nature, Compression and Velocity of the Air Used in the Blast Furnace,' (written c.1810), *Papers on Iron and Steel*, 1840 p.329)

Rowlands, Ted, 'The Merthyr Tydfil 1835 Election Revisited – Lady Charlotte Guest's Account', *Merthyr Historian* Vol 25, 2013, pp.7 -22

Shearn, Sally-Anne, 'An early description of Lady Charlotte Guest, translator of The Mabinogion' *Morgannwg*, Vol 62, 2018, pp.188-93

Thomas, Claire Louise, The Public Life and Image of Lady Charlotte Guest and the Society in which she lived: 1833-1852 *Merthyr Historian*, Vol 8, pp.174- 88.

Wynne Evans, Leslie, 'Sir John and Lady Charlotte Guest's Educational Scheme at Dowlais in the mid-nineteenth century', *National Library of Wales Journal*, IX, no 3, Summer 1956, pp.265–286.

Selected Online Sources

www.alangeorge.co.uk/
https://archive.archaeology.org/online/features/nineveh/
https://archive.org/
www.british-history.ac.uk/ https://biography.wales/
http://www.engineering-timelines.com/
www.findagrave.com/
www.gracesguide.co.uk/
https://hansard.parliament.uk/
www.hathitrust.org/
www.historyofparliamentonline.org/
www.parliament.uk/about/living-heritage
https://theclergydatabase.org.uk/
www.savethecoalexchange.com
www.welshnot.com/
www.wikipedia.org/

Index

Abercynon 46-7, 80, 89, 120

Aberdare 129, 135

Aberdare, Lord. See Henry Austen Bruce

Aberteifi, Mari 16

Abergavenny (see also *Cymdeithas Cymreigyddion Y Fenni*) 71, 78-9, 97

Abersychan Ironworks 121, 138

Adare, Viscount 63-6

Aikin, Arthur 69

Almack's Assembly Rooms 10, 12, 42-3

Althorp, Lord 30

Antwerp 76

'Ap Dowlais' 85

Arabian Nights 6

Ariosto 25

Armstrong, Mr 160-1

Arthur, legendary king 52, 75, 85

Austen, Benjamin 70

Austen, Jane 81, 181 (n)

Babbage, Charles 67

Bailey, Crawshay and Joseph 54, 123-4, 129

Bake, William A., aka 'Captain Back' 90

Bandon, Co. Cork 59-60, 109

Barry, Charles 96, 103, 108, 117-8

Bartolini, Lorenzo 77

Beaumont, Francis 50

Bell's Life in Sydney and Sporting Reviewer 60, 185 (n)

de Bernabeu family 78

Bertie, Albemarle, Lt- General and 9th Earl of Lindsey (Charlotte's father) 2

Bertie, Albemarle George Augustus Frederick, 10th Earl of Lindsey, known as 'Lindsey,' (Charlotte's brother) 3, 4, 6-10, 29, 48, 50, 56, 70, 94

Bertie, Lady Charlotte Susanna, Dowager Countess of Lindsey (Charlotte's mother) viii, 2-3, 6, 8, 9-10, 12-13, 23, 28-9, 39, 44, 118, 58, 147

Bertie, Montague Peregrine, known as 'Bertie' (Charlotte's brother) 2, 4, 25, 60, 94, 118

Bessborough, 9th Earl of, (Compiler of published 'Extracts' from Lady Charlotte's Journals) vi, x, 2, 3, 7

Bircham, Francis 113-15, 127, 129, 165, 167

Bird, John 156

Birmingham 23-4, 58, 67, 170

Blaina Iron Company 48, 55, 61

Blore, Edward 96, 105

'Blue Books,' see Education in Wales

Boiler explosion 55-6

Bosanquet, Judge John 73-5

Boyle, Mary, Countess of Cork 27

'Branwen daughter of Llyr' 72, 75, 82

Brecon 18, 78, 141, 160

Bridgnorth Grammar School 16
Bridgewater Canal 105
Brighton 9-10, 116, 143, 148
Bristol 1, 31, 47, 54, 81, 88-9, 108
British Association for the
  Advancement of Science 67, 81
Brodie, Benjamin 93, 99, 115-16, 170
Bronte, Charlotte 81
Broseley 15
Brougham, Henry, 1st Baron
  Brougham and Vaux, Lord
  Chancellor 9
Brown, Rev Joseph, O.S.B., 111-13
Bruce, Henry Austen 131, 138, 151,
  153, 167
Brunel, Isambard Kingdom 47-8,
  80, 89
Brunel, Marc 48
von Brunnow, Phillip, 98, 110, 123
Bull Run, see Stamford.
Bute, 2nd Marquess of 33, 36, 43,
  87-92, 95-102
Bute Docks 88, 91, 94, 101

Cambrian Register, The (Journal
  founded by William Owen Pughe)
  71-2
Cambridge 4, 66, 130, 159, 165, 167-9
Canford Magna 99, 169
Canford Manor 96-7, 99-101,
  103-105, 117-18, 154-55, 159-60,
  164, 170, 172
Canning, Sir Stratford 134
Cardiff 1, 29, 39, 46-7, 59, 65, 75, 87-
  91, 94-5, 102, 104, 108, 110, 119,
  133, 137, 145, 154
  Castle 19, 91, 101
  Crockherbtown Station 89
  Glass Bottle Company 88
Carnhuanawc 73-4, 78-9, 82, 106
Chalon, Alfred Edward 1, 93

Charterhouse School 31
Chaucer, Geoffrey 5, 25
'Chevalier au Lion' 79
Cholera 14, 39, 42, 96, 140, 149, 161,
  163, 166, 170
Clark, George Thomas 134, 141, 145,
  157, 161-2, 167, 169-70
Clarke, T.E. 14
Clive, Hon Robert Henry 36-8
Colliers' strike Ch 11 *passim*
Collieries 134, 136, 138, 145, 149
Coffin, Walter 89
Constantine, Grand Duke of Russia,
  See Konstantin
Conybeare, Rev Daniel William 20
Cork 59-60, 109
Corn Laws 17, 64, 66
Cornwall 52-3
Countess of Cork, see Boyle, Mary
'Court of Requests' 17
Crawshay, Francis of Hirwaun 102
  Richard of Cyfarthfa 46, 54
  Robert of Cyfarthfa 129, 143, 146-7,
    150, 154, 162
  William II of Cyfarthfa 17, 33, 36-7,
    39, 47, 54, 140, 148
Crewe, Henrietta 6
Crichton-Stuart, John, see Bute
Crystal Palace 116-17
'Culhwch ac Olwen', see 'Kilhwch and
  Olwen'
Cyfarthfa Castle 54
Cyfarthfa Ironworks 33, 46, 54, 71,
  120, 139, 143, 146-8, 151, 170
Cymdeithas Cymreigyddion y Fenni 71,
  73, 82, 106

Davies, John 88
Davies, Professor Sioned 84
Davis, R.P. 69, 108-110
Defoe, Daniel 52

Dic Penderyn 18

Dickens, Charles 81

Disraeli, Benjamin 11-12

Disraeli, Sarah 12

Divett, Edward 49, 76, 80, 94, 100, 114, 118-19, 125, 129, 140, 167

Divett, Anne 49, 76, 80, 118-19

Dix, John Ross 80

Dowlais House 13-14, 20-21, 28, 41, 50, 55-6, 78, 96-8, 107, 111-13, 119, 122, 127, 130, 153, 160-61, 164

   Iron Company viii, 11, 31, 37, 40, 45, 56, 59, 61, 69, 71, 90-2, 94-5, 97, 100, 108-10, 113-15, 122-3, 131, 138, 140, 157, 161, 170-71

   Village viii, 1, 22-3, 27, 29, 31, 37, 44, 52-3, 58, 62, 65, 76, 85, 90, 97, 99, 104-8, 111, 116, 119-20, 125-6, 129, 130, 139-41, 157, 159-60, 163, 166, 168-69

   Works 1, 15, 17, 19, 24-5, 30, 39-40, 46, 53, 60, 68, 87-90, 98-9, 101, 104, 111, 115, 121, 129, 132-7, 141, 143-58, 161, 169, 170-71

'Dream of Rhonabwy, The' 77, 82, 84

Dublin 58-60, 63

Dufrénoy, Pierre-Armand 31-2, 34-5, 38, 40-41, 44, 103

Ecclesiastical Titles Act 112, 124

Education in Wales, Report of the Commissioners 106

Eisteddfod, Cardiff 29-30, 38

Eliot, George 50

Ellesmere, Earl and Countess of, 104-5, 139

Eton College 3-4

European Travel, 76-7, 94

Evans, John viii, 91, 112, 119, 121-3, 127, 129, 133, 137-9, 146-8, 150-5, 157-62, 164, 166, 169-71

Evans, Thomas 89, 91-2, 94-5, 121

Evans, William 161

Fairbairn, Sir William 68-9

Faraday, Michael 68

Feminism 51

Flamank, George 124, 130, 169-70

Fletcher, John 50

Forest of Dean 21, 137, 141

Forman, William of Penydarren 47, 97, 144, 148, 152-3

Fothergill, Rowland of Abernant and Llwydcoed 37, 102, 121

Fowler, John Coke 131, 156

Geddes, John 91, 97

General Elections 17 (1831); 18 (1832); 31, 34-9 (1835); 62-9 (1837); 99-100 (1847); 124-5 (1852)

'Geraint the Son of Erbin' 76-82

Glamorganshire Canal 46-7, 88, 140, 148, 154

Glamorgan, County 34-9

Goitre Coed Viaduct 47, 80, 89

Great Exhibition 114, 116-7, 121, 171

G.K.N, see Guest, Keen & Nettlefold

Guest, Keen & Nettlefold 40, 170

Guest, Anne (wife of Thomas Revel) 31, 59, 60

Guest, Arthur (JJG and LC's 5th son) 120, 127, 157, 159

Guest, Augustus, known as 'Geraint' (JJG and LC's 4th son) 82, 120, 127, 167

Guest, Blanche Vere (JJG and LC's 5th daughter) 86, 100, 120, 163

Guest, Lady Charlotte (LC) née Bertie, later Schreiber *Passim*

Guest, Constance Rhiannon (JJG and LC's 4th daughter) 95, 120

Guest, Ivor Bertie (JJG and LC's 1st son) 15, 45, 47, 49, 55, 60, 70, 76, 81, 94, 120, 124, 130, 159, 161, 163, 165, 167-9, 171

Guest, Jemima (JJG's mother) 15-16

Guest, John (JJG's grandfather) 15

Guest, Sir Josiah John (Bart) (JJG) known to Charlotte as 'Merthyr', Ch 1-9, *passim*

Guest, Katharine Gwladys (Cattws) (JJG and LC's 2nd daughter) 15, 58, 60, 81, 120, 127, 130, 164, 169

Guest, Maria, John's first wife, see Ranken

Guest, [Charlotte] Maria, (JJG and LC's 1st daughter) 28-30, 38-9, 49, 55, 60, 94-5, 100, 120, 130, 164, 169, 170

Guest, [Mary] Enid Evelyn (JJG and LC's 3rd daughter) vii, 92, 120

Guest, [Thomas] Merthyr (JJG and LC's 2nd son) 15, 95, 120, 125, 129-30, 169

Guest, Montague John ('Monty') (JJG and LC's 3rd son) ix-x, 11, 79, 120, 127, 169

Guest, Revel (LC's descendant and biographer) ix, 2, 11

Guest, Sarah (JJG's aunt) 16

Guest, Thomas (JJG's father) 15-16

Guest, Thomas Revel (JJG's brother) 16, 47, 59

Guest family tutors, see Milton, Newton, Flamank, Schreiber

Guest family governess, see Kemble

Gunters of Mayfair 98

Hall, Augusta, see Llanover

Hall, Benjamin see Llanover

'Hanes Cymry' (Publication by Carnhuanawc) 54

'Hanes Taliesin' 82

Harford family 54, 161

Harrow School 124, 167

Hawkins, Charles 120

Hawthorn, R and A of Newcastle, 119

Hengwrt Manuscripts 83

Hill, Anthony, of Plymouth 17, 33, 36, 46-7, 54, 129, 144, 146-8, 152, 154, 162

Hillyard, Anne 126, 128

Homfray, Amelia 54

Homfray, Samuel, of Penydarren 17, 40

Honiton 17, 33

Hot Blast 31-2, 35, 39-42, 68-9

Houses of Parliament 22, 116-18

Hudson, George and Elizabeth 27

Huntly, Lady, see Pegus, Mary

Hutchins, Edward 31, 33-4, 38-9, 47-8, 60-2, 77-8, 90, 96-7, 101, 108-15, 129, 155, 169

Hutchins, Eliza 20

Hutchins, Isabella 78, 89, 97-8, 111, 113

Hutchins, Sarah-Anne 20

Inchbald, Elizabeth 36

Ioan Tegid also known as Rev John Jones 73-4, 78-9

Iolo Morgannwg also known as Edward Williams 22, 82

Iron ore 15, 19, 69, 87, 90, 97, 136-7, 146, 150, 164

Ivor Works 120, 122, 152, 160

James, John 155-6

Jenkins, Rev. Evan 22, 66, 99, 104, 126-7, 129, 159

Jesus College, Oxford 71, 78

John Murray, (Publisher) 40, 103

John, Professor Angela V ix, 2, 11

Johnes, Rev Arthur 73

Johnson, Sarah, aka 'Sarah Guest' 59-60

Johnson, Thomas Revel aka 'Thomas Guest' 59-60

Jones, Edgar 40

Jones, Rev John see Ioan Tegid

Jones, Owen (compiler of *Myvyrian Archaiology of Wales*) 71

Kay, William 139, 166

Kemble, Emily 107, 119

'Kilhwc and Olwen' 75, 82

Kirkwood, Alexander 16

Kitson, George 110, 123, 126, 129, 145, 155, 167, 170

Kleinmichel, Count Pyotr Andreevitch 123-4

Konstantin Nikolayevich of Russia 98

Lady Charlotte (locomotive) 24-5 (steam ship) 88

Lanier, Sidney 85

Llanover, Lady Augusta 22, 169

Llanover, Benjamin, 1st Baron 22

Layard, Rev. Brownlow 2, 7-8, 25-6, 56, 94

Layard, Austen Henry 11, 103, 117-20, 124, 129, 134, 145, 147, 153, 155, 157, 169

Lewis Lewis (Lewsyn yr Heliwr) 18

Lewis, Mary-Anne, later Disraeli 12-13, 26, 44, 49

Lewis, Richard, see Dic Penderyn

Lewis, Wyndham 10, 12, 26, 61-2

Lincoln Cathedral 33

Lindsey, Dowager Countess of, see Bertie

Lindsey, 9th and 10th Earl of, see Bertie

Lithotrity 94

Lloyd, Morgan 156

Llyfr Coch o Hergest 71-4, 78, 82

Lococke, Dr. 27-8, 44

Locomotives 24-5, 47, 56, 132-3, 135, 141-2, 146, 160

Longmans (Publisher) 78

Luff, John 117-18, 126

Mabinogion, The 69, 71-86, 103, 106

Makin, Richard 132

Malkin, Benjamin 14

Martin, Ben (Penydarren agent) 144, 147, 154

Martin, Frederick (Lindsey's tutor) 4-5, 7-10, 33-4, 49

Measles 95

Mechanics' Home, see Ranelagh Club

Melbourne, Lord 30

Mellish, Mr and Miss 9-10

Menelaus, William 25, 121-2, 126, 151-2, 160, 164, 170-71

Merthyr Rising (1831) 18, 54, 129

Merthyr Tydfil ix, 1, 14-15, 17-19, 27, 29, 31, 33, 37-8, 46-7, 59, 63, 67, 69, 85, 95, 99-100, 107, 111, 125, 131, 141

Merthyr Waterworks, plans for 140, 148, 161-4, 166

Meyrick, William 33-4, 36-8

Milton, Mr 126

Morata, Olympia 136

Morlais Castle 45, 161

Mushet, David 32

Myvyrian Archaiology of Wales 71, 82

Navigation House, see Abercynon

Nawab Ekbal ed Dowleh, sometime King of Oudh 119-20

Neath, Vale of 22-3

Neath Abbey Iron Company 24, 52

Neilson & Co of Glasgow (locomotive manufacturers) 133, 160

Neilson, James Beaumont 31-2, 35, 39-40, 42

Netherclift, Joseph (illustrator of the *Mabinogion*) 75, 79, 83

Newbridge, see Pontypridd

Newnham on Severn 21-2

Newton, Mr 119

On the Use of Hot Air 29-41, 57, 103

Ouseley, Sir Gore 27

Orleans, Ferdinand Philippe, Duke of 10

Partington, Charles 45

Peel, Sir Robert 30-1

Pegus, Elizabeth 29

Pegus, Mary (Maria Antoinetta, later Marchioness of Huntly) 12, 29, 60

Pegus, Rev Peter (Charlotte's stepfather) 2-4, 6-10, 13, 25-6, 29, 39, 48, 56, 58, 70, 94, 129-30

Penydarren Ironworks 17, 27, 40, 46-7, 54, 97, 111, 143-8, 151-4, 170

Phillips, David Rhys 86

Plymouth Ironworks 17, 33, 46-7, 54, 97, 111, 143-8, 151, 170

Poole 99, 124-5, 170

'Popery', Charlotte's dislike of 78, 112

Posnett, Miss 8

Ponsonby, Vere, see Bessborough, 9th Earl of

Ponsonby, Rev Walter 99

Pontypridd 46-7, 67, 80, 89

Price, Joseph Tregelles 52

Price, Rev Thomas, See Carnhuanawc

Price, William of Llantrissant 66

Prout, Dr 93

Puddlers' strike 156-7

Pughe, William Owen 71-2

Purnell, William 109, 123-4, 129, 155, 159, 167

Pwll yr Whiad 15

Quaritch, Bernard 85

Railways, Chemnitz 109
  Dowlais 111, 119-20
  Genoa and Turin 110
  Grand Junction 67
  Great Indian Peninsular 134
  Great Western 47, 110
  Hungarian State 108-109
  Lower Silesian 95
  London and Birmingham 133
  London and South Western 117
  St. Petersburg-Pauloffsky, aka Tsarskoye-Selo 98, 145
  Manchester and Liverpool 24, 67, 135
  Taff Vale 47-8, 59, 67, 80, 89-91, 94, 111, 115, 119-20, 160
  Thuringian 108-109

Rammell, William 139

Ranelagh Club 116

Ranken, Charles 70

Ranken, Maria (John Guest's 1st wife) 12, 19-22

Rassam, Hormuzd 103

'Red Book of Hergest' see *Llyfr Coch o Hergest*

Recreation Ground at Dowlais 105, 139, 144, 147, 149

Rees, William of Llandovery 76, 78

Rhondda Bridge, see Pontypridd

Rickards, Josiah 44-5

Ross, Anne, see Divett, Anne

Roy, Richard 90-91

Royal Society of Arts 69

Russell, John (Dowlais Ironworks Surgeon) 30, 39, 93

Russell, Lord John (Architect of 1832 Reform Act) 30, 112, 124

Scott, Sir Walter 25, 27, 81

'Scotch Cattle' 28

Schreiber, Charles 130, 145, 147-8, 158-9, 162-171

Schreiber, Mrs (Charles Schreiber's mother) 145, 147-8, 168

Schreiber family 169

Schools, Charlotte's interest in 106-8, 169, 171

Scrivenor, Harry 69

Seymour, Henry Danby, MP 124-5, 129

Sharp, Roberts & Co, Manchester 24

Sims, William 53

Skey, Joseph 93

Stamford 2, 4, 6-7

Steam engines 17, 24, 44-5, 53, 160

Stephenson, Robert 91-2

Stuart, Lord James (Lord Bute's brother) 91

Stuart de Rothesay, Lady 42-3, 48

Stuart de Rothesay, Lord 42-3

Stephens, Thomas 85

Sully Manor 1, 19-20, 49, 89, 129, 170

Swansea 22, 52-3, 63, 86-7

Sykes, Henrietta 11-12

Taitt, William 16

Talbot, Christopher Rice Mansel 63, 67

Tansillo, Luigi 172-3

Thomas, Evan (JJG's brother-in-law) 19-20, 49

Thomason, Sir Edward 23

Thomson, Thomas 68

Thompson, William, of Penydarren 27, 36-7, 47, 54, 97, 144, 147-8, 152-3

Treherne, Georgina 125

Trevithick, Richard 17, 53

Troedyrhiw 34, 126, 135, 154

Truran, Samuel 53, 95, 136, 138, 171

Tyrell, Sir John, MP 66

Uffington 2-9, 18, 21, 23, 25-6, 30, 39, 49, 56, 58, 70

Vaughan family of Hengwrt 83

Victoria, Queen 62, 65, 76, 114

de Villemarqué, Théodore Claude Henri 78-80, 83

Wales, Thomas Errington 134-6, 138, 145, 149-50, 171

Walkinshaw, James 122-3

Ward, Robert Plumer 10, 13

Wellington, Duke of 30

Welsh Manuscript Society 73-4

White, John Ludford (Dowlais Ironworks Surgeon) 93-5, 126-7, 145, 162

Wilkins, Charles 19

Wilkinson, Isaac and John 15

William IV, King 30, 62, 102

Williams, B. (illustrator of the *Mabinogion*) 76, 79

Williams, Edward, see Iolo Morgannwg

Williams, Taliesin 22, 30, 38, 76, 82

Willoughby of Eresby, Lady 42

Willoughby of Eresby, Lord 117

Windsor, Lady 87

Wolrige, John 136-7, 160

Wood, Nicholas 135-6, 138, 160-61

Wood, William 121-2

Worsley, Lancashire (home of Lord and Lady Ellesmere) 104-105

Wyndham-Quin, Edwin Richard Windham, See Adare

Ynyscedwyn Ironworks 101